PHOTOGRAPHING
CORNWALL

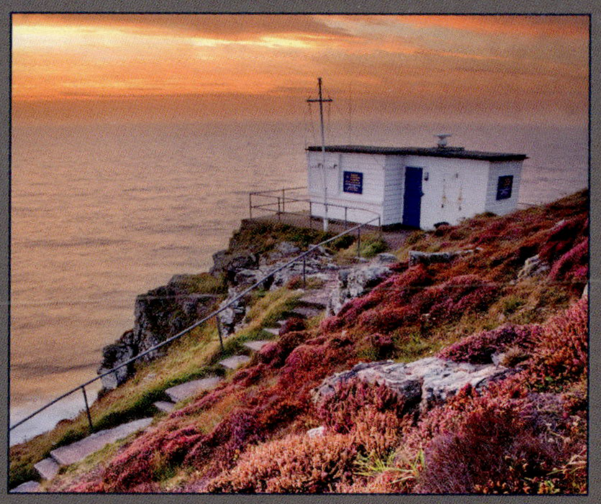

DAVID CHAPMAN

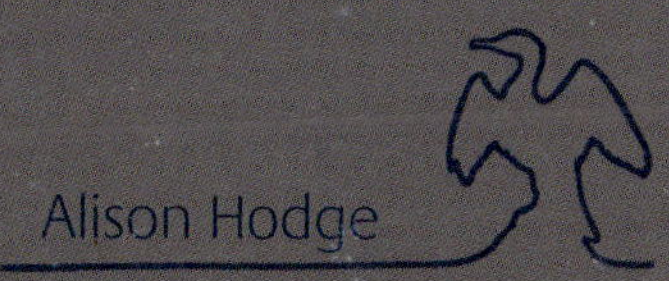

Published in 2011 by
Alison Hodge
2 Clarence Place, Penzance, Cornwall TR18 2QA
info@alison-hodge.co.uk www.alison-hodge.co.uk

ISBN 13 978 0 906720 77 6

British Library Cataloguing-in-Publication Data
A catalogue record for this book is available from the British Library.

Book design and origination by
BDP – Book Development & Production, Penzance, Cornwall
Cover design by Christopher Laughton

Printed in China

Title page: The Lookout, Cape Cornwall

CONTENTS

Oyster fishing, Carrick Roads ▶

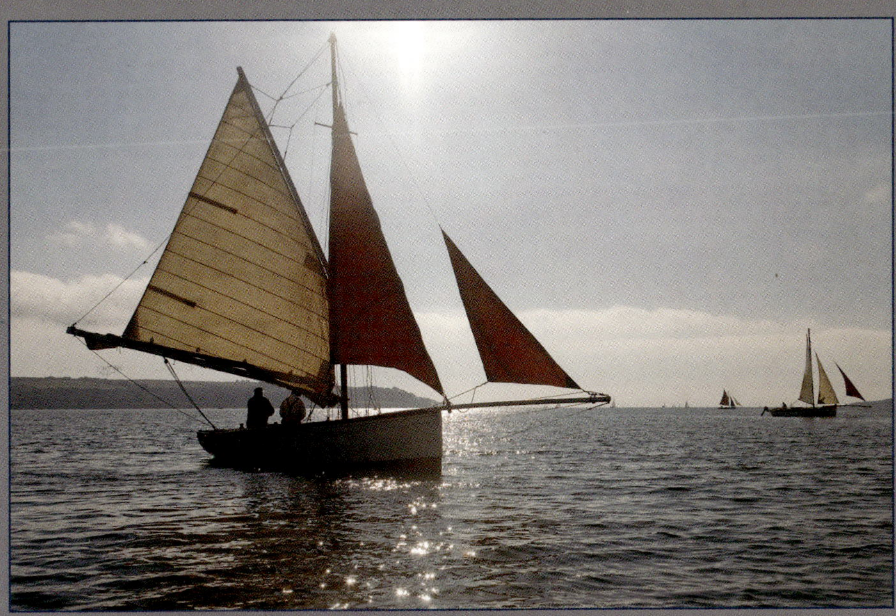

INTRODUCTION

For me, Cornwall is the most beautiful and varied county in Britain. When I think of Cornwall, I think primarily of the wonderful coastline which comprises some of the best beaches in the world: an amazing array of cliffs, stacks and arches; the clear water of the often dramatic Atlantic Ocean and, by way of contrast, the gentle waters of the natural harbours formed in the flooded valleys and creeks of the south coast. But there is much more to Cornwall than its coastline. We have moorland which rises to a peak at Brown Willy, but which also extends to the far west of Penwith, where heather-clad hills look down over an ancient farmed landscape and beyond to the cliffs. Scattered everywhere are the remains of a once-industrial landscape: engine houses are an icon of Cornwall. Our hand might have helped to shape the county we see today, but nature always has the upper hand! Every spring I take pleasure from the swathes of flowers of thrift growing on the coast; I delight in the bluebells that grow not just in woodland but also on cliffs. In summer I always seek out the arable flowers of farm fields and, later, I walk on the heaths and moors, alive with flowering heather.

The images in *Photographing Cornwall* aim to capture the varied spirit, atmosphere and beauty of the county. As well as transporting you around Cornwall, to some of its most stunning locations, I have provided information about each image. In the Notes on the Photographs (pages 100–111), I have tried to explain the factors that inspired me to take the photograph, and given technical details about it. So I hope this book will appeal not just to those who love looking at attractive photographs of Cornwall, but also to those with a keen interest in photography or art.

David Chapman, 2011

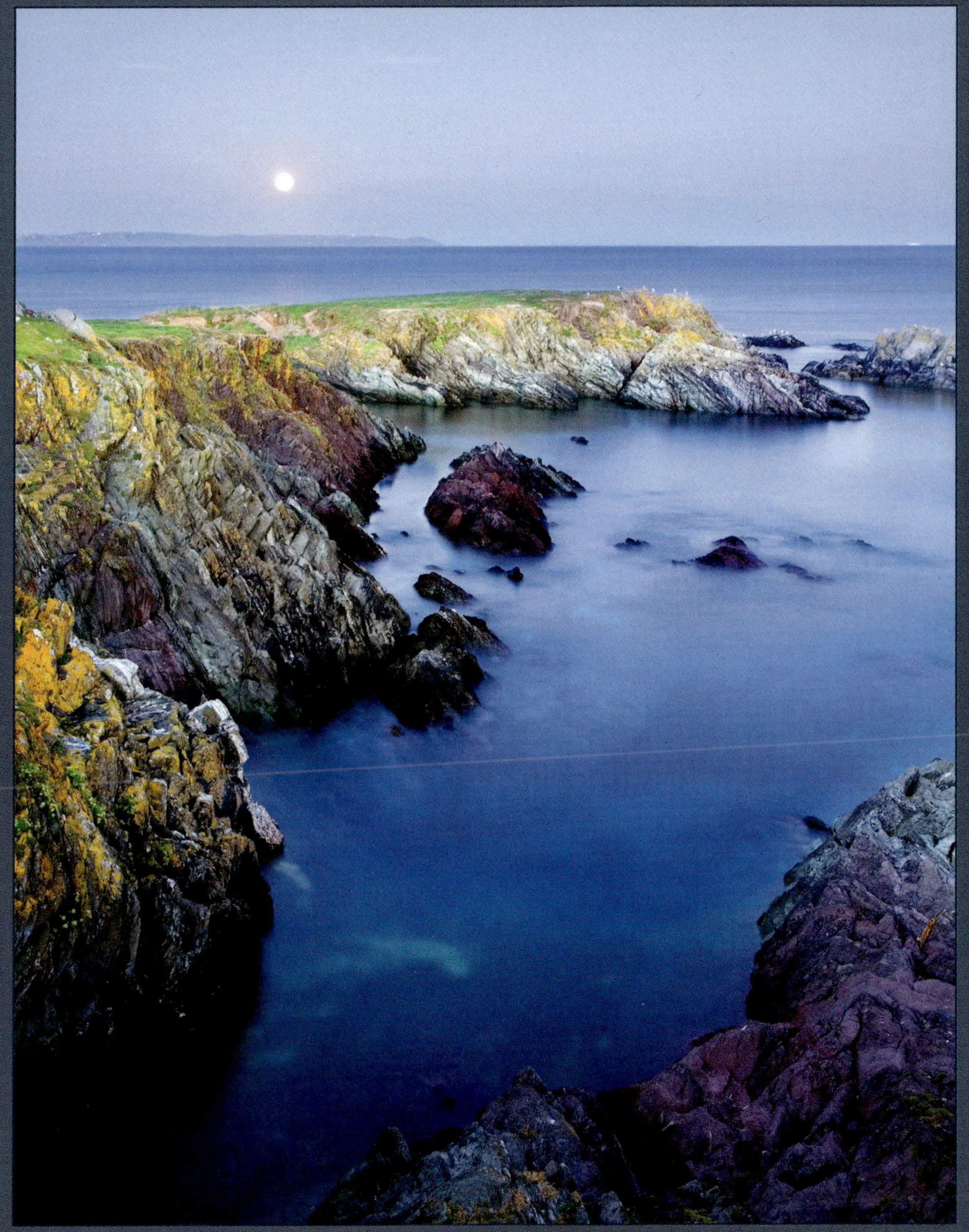

Looe Island ▶

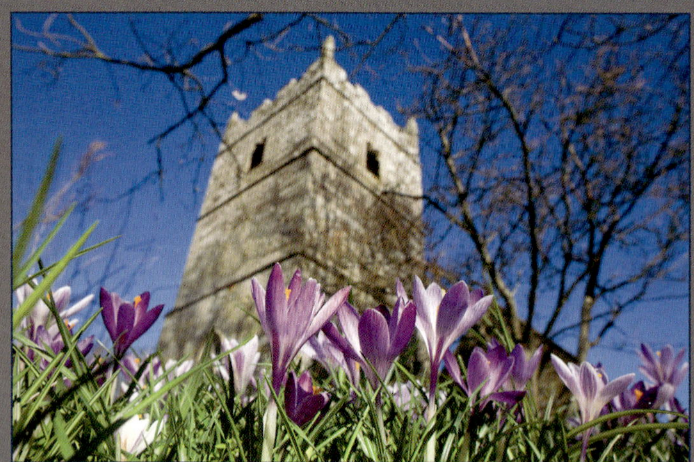

▲ Crocuses, churchyard, St Teath
Bluebells, St Loy ▶

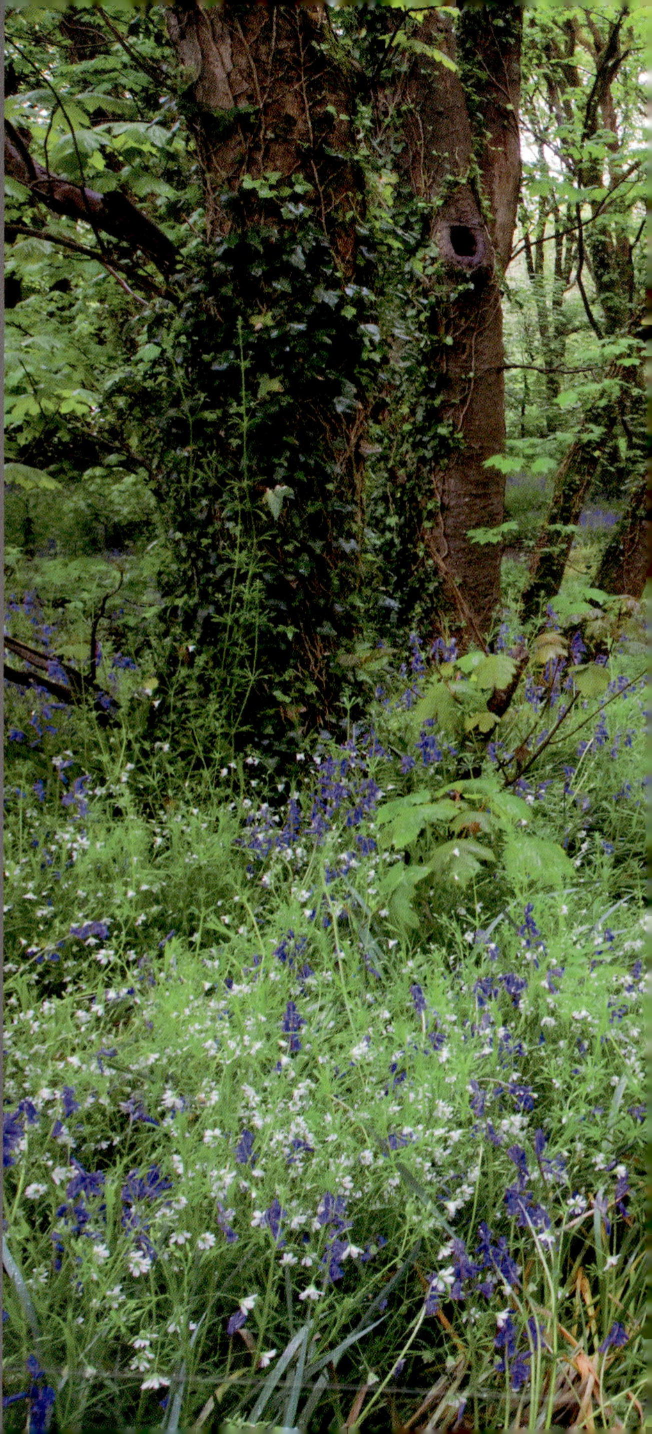

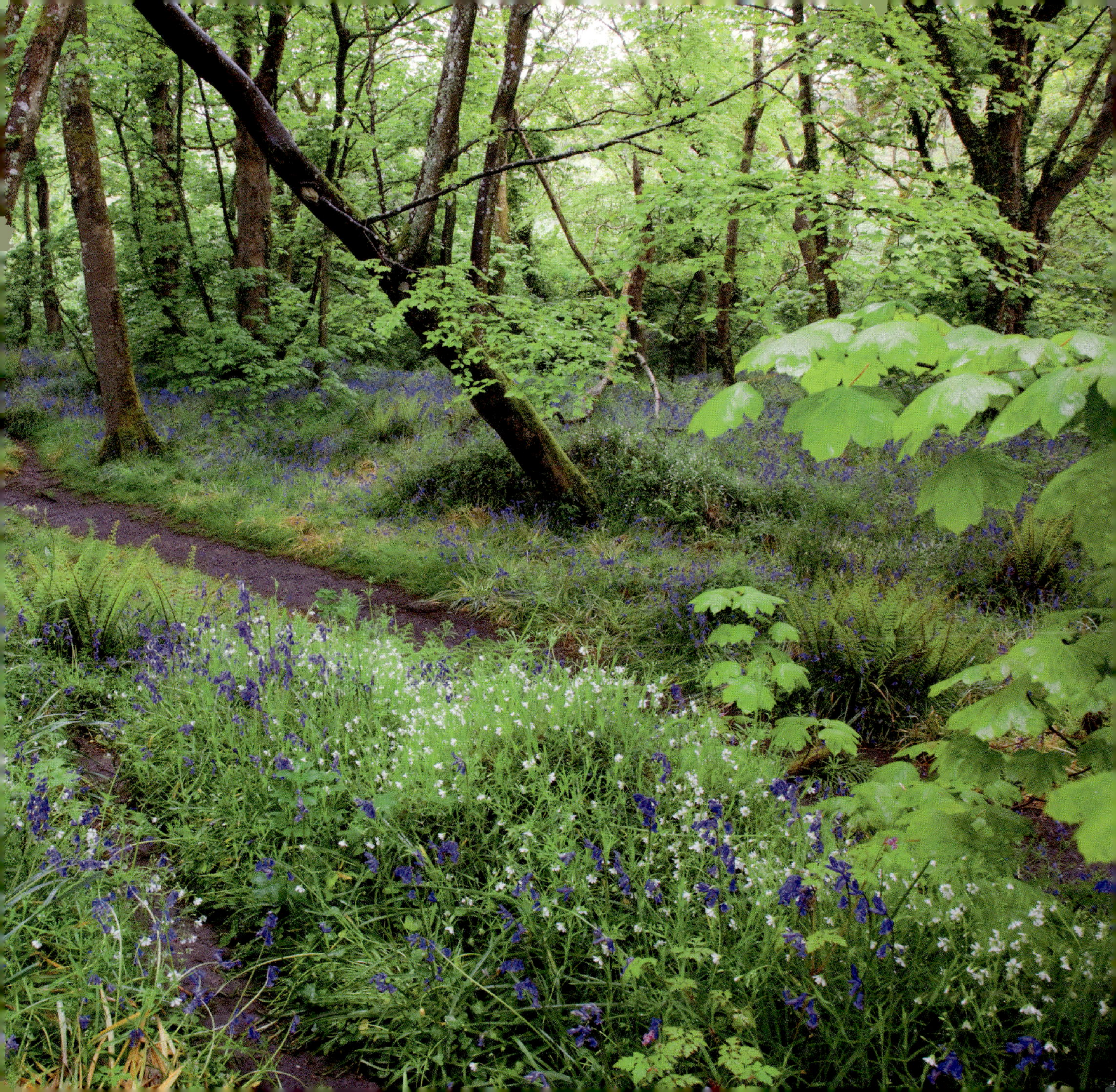

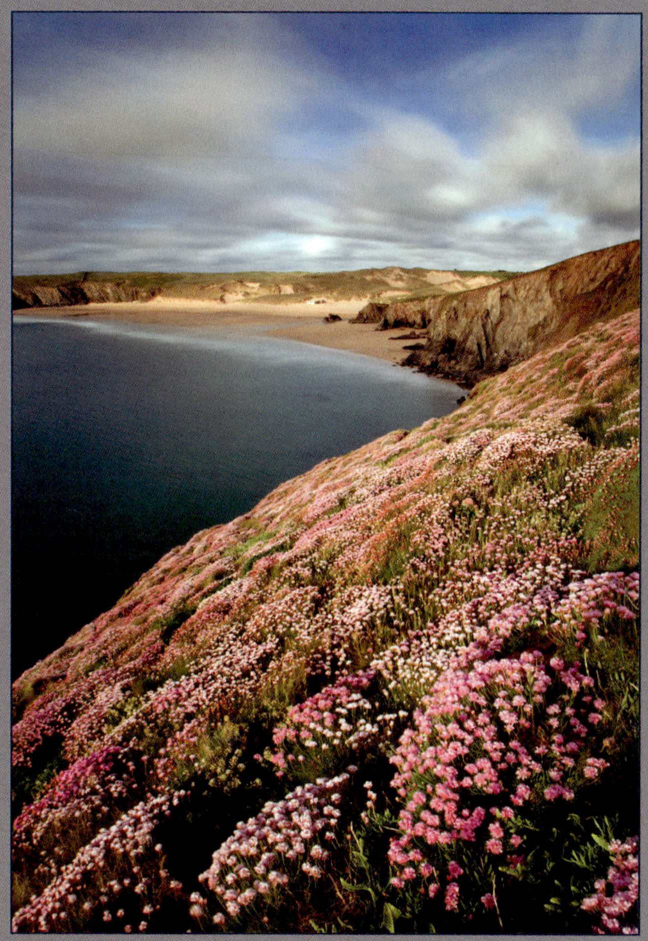

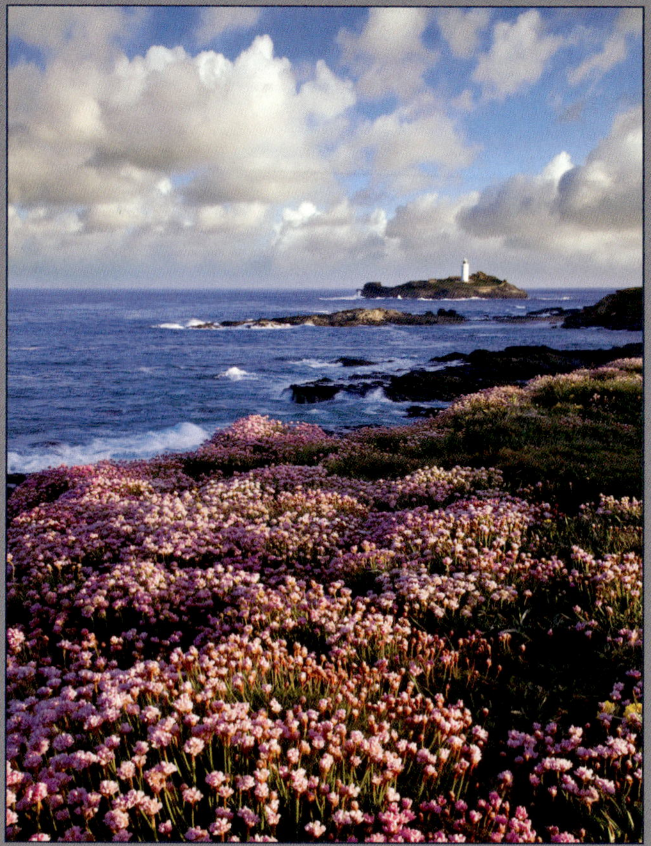

▲ Thrift, Godrevy
◄ Thrift, Holywell

Viper's bugloss, Boscregan Farm ▶
Daffodils by moonlight, Gulval ▶ ▶

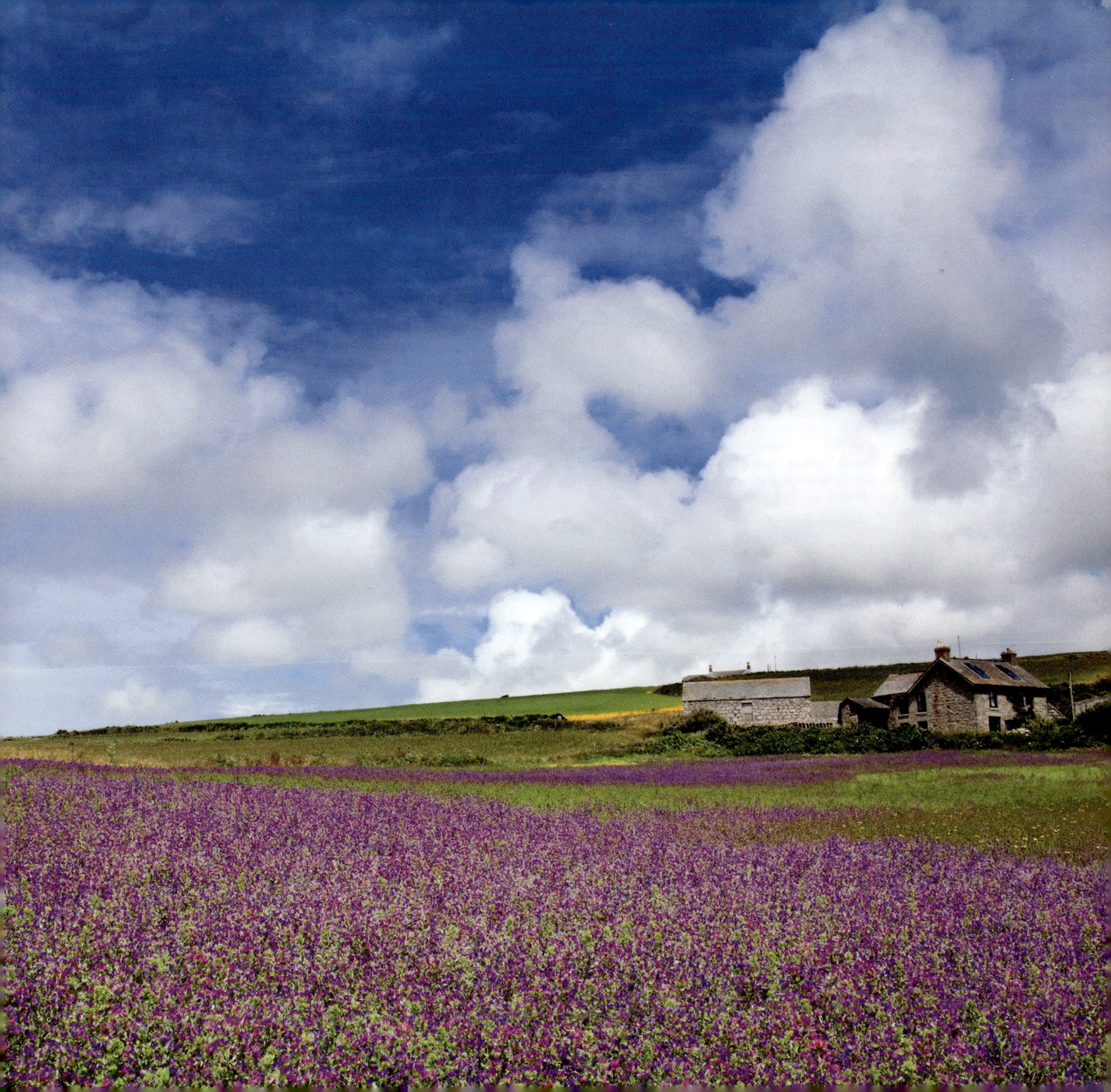

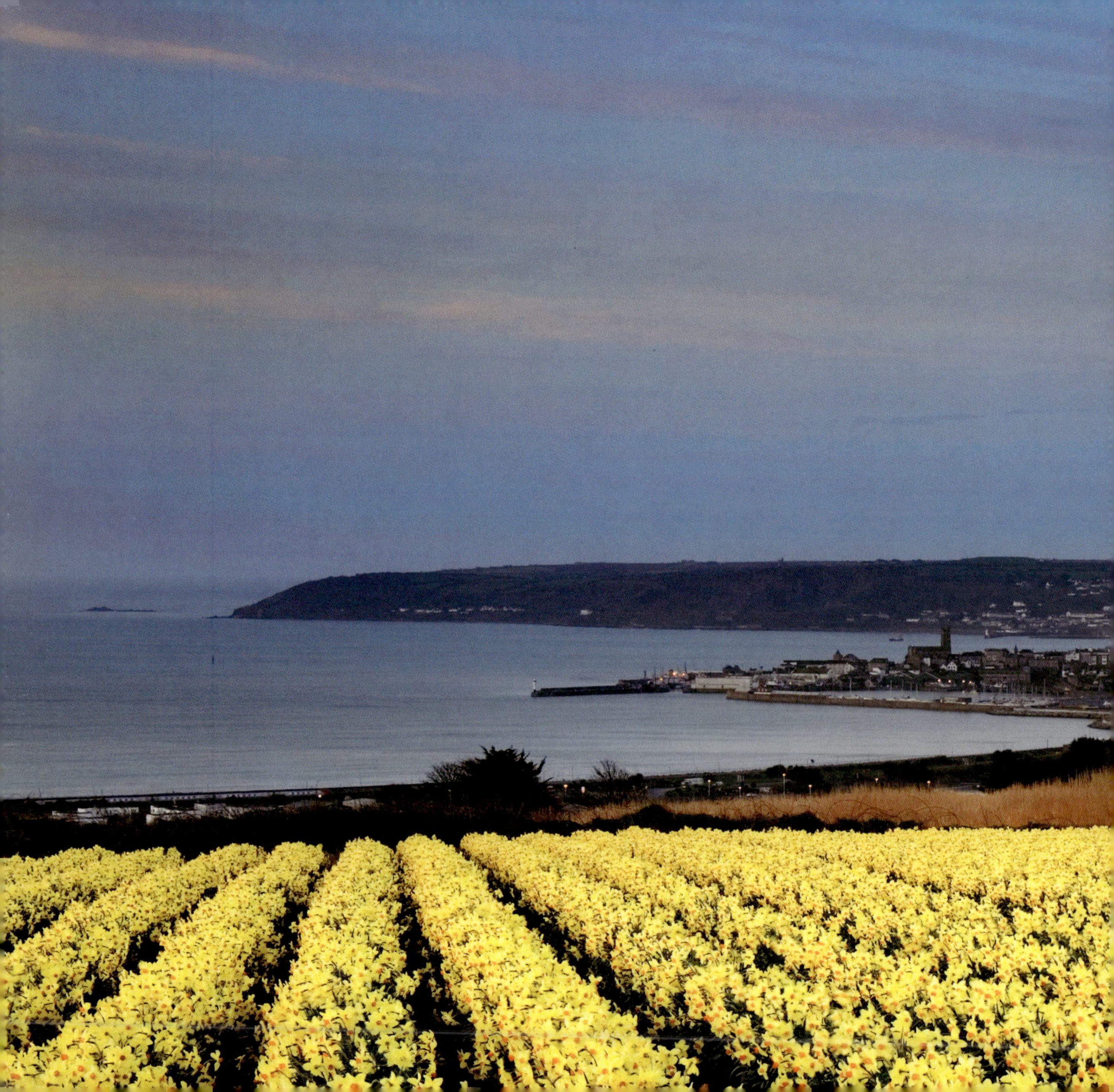

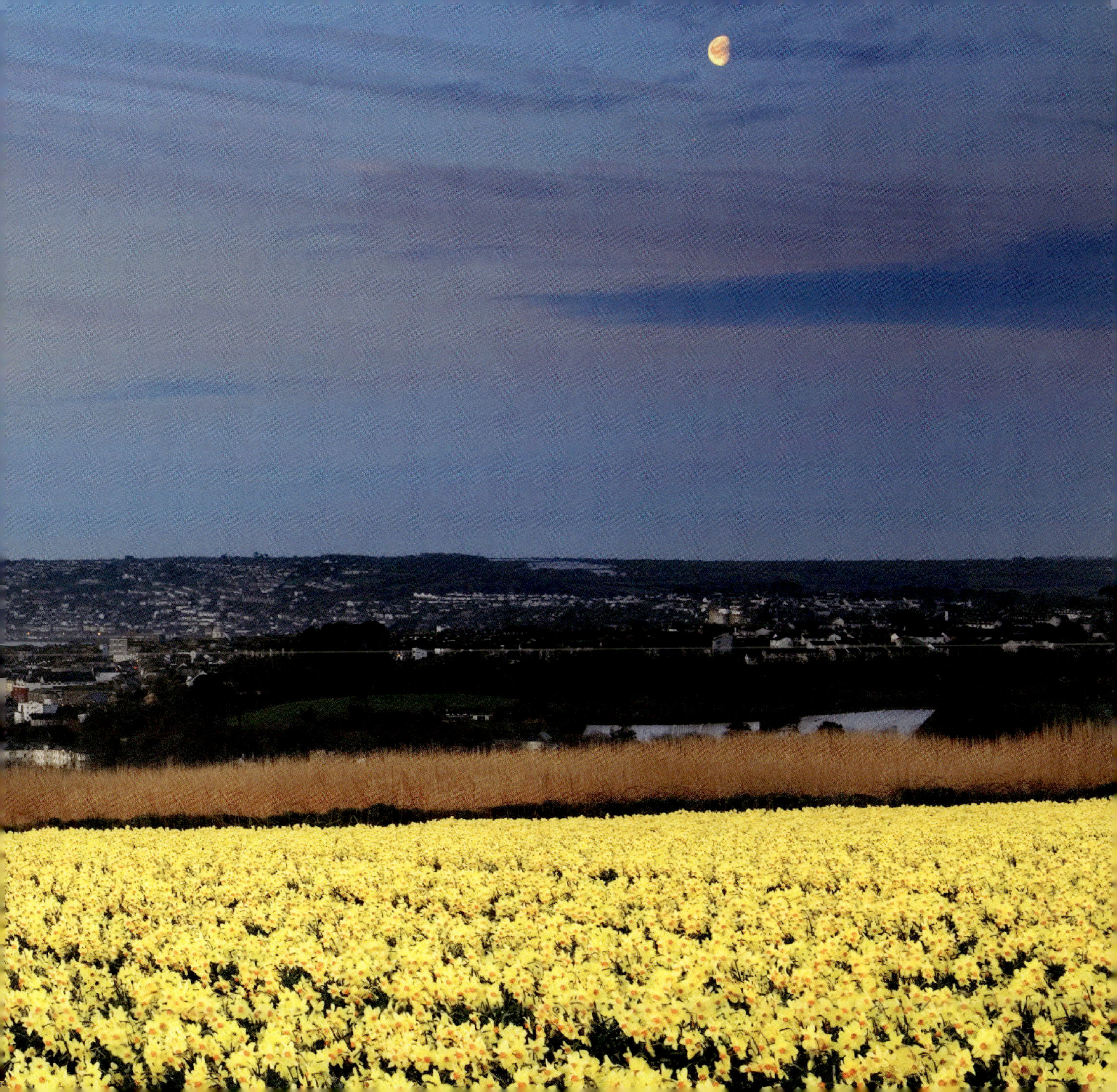

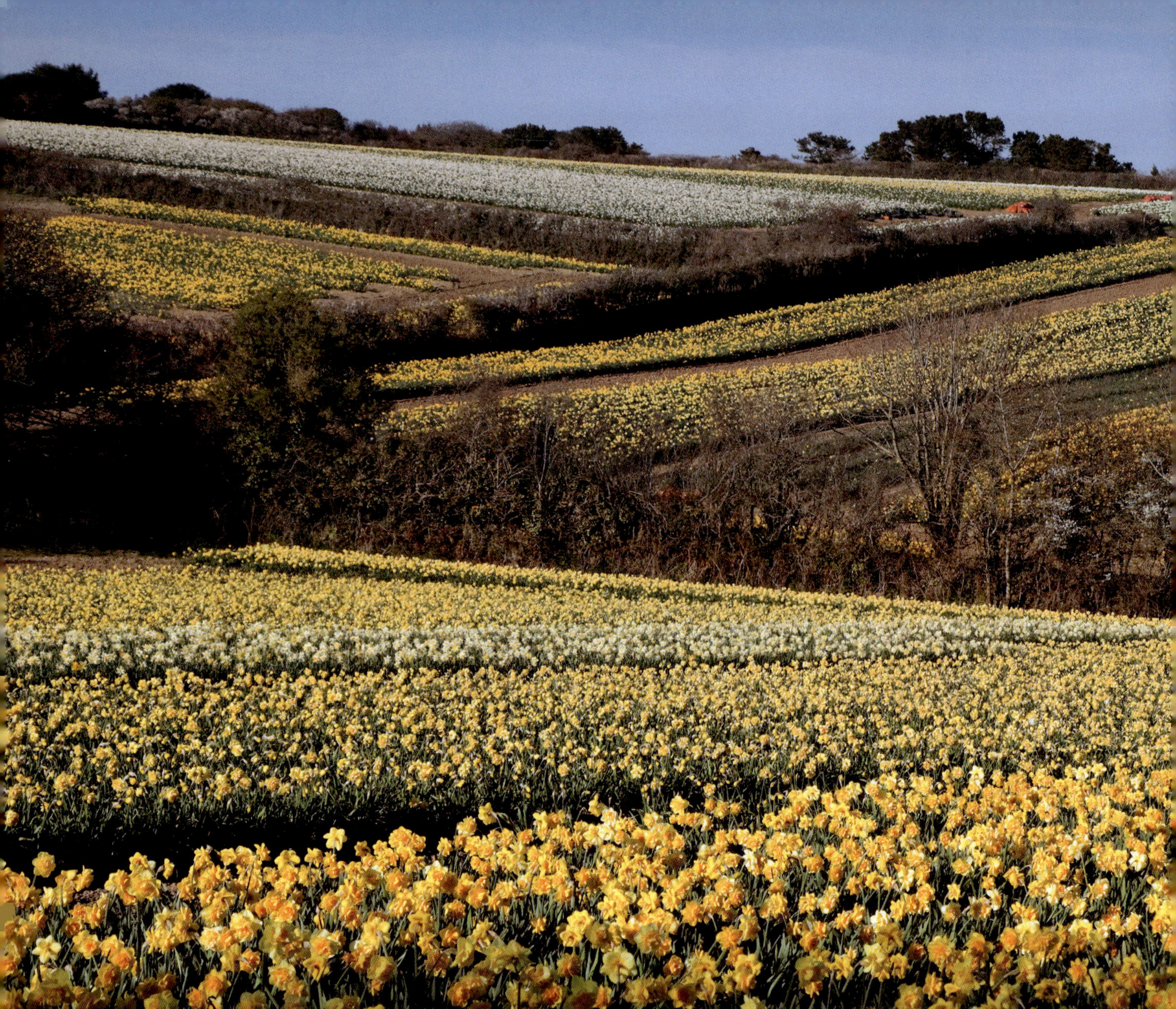

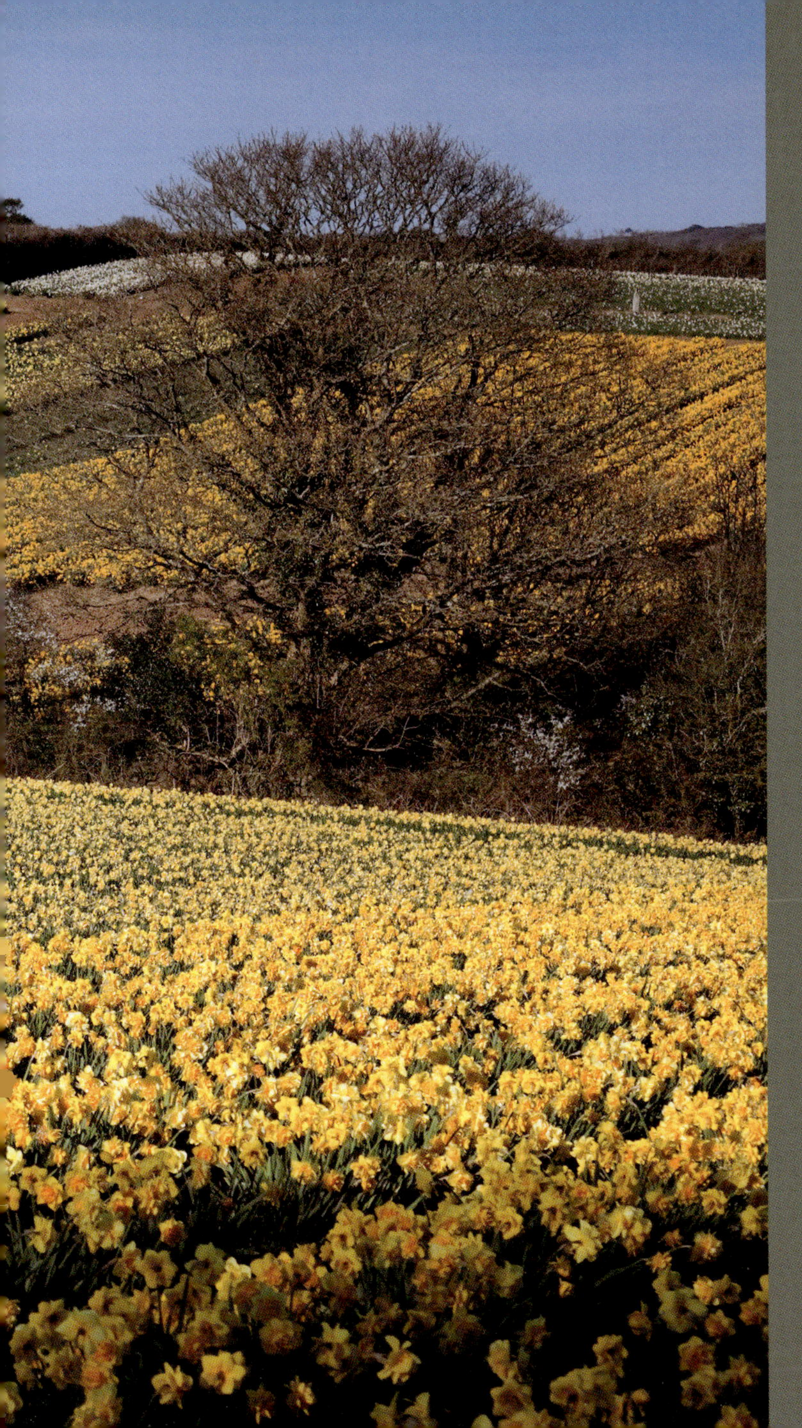

Silhouettes, Siblyback reservoir ▶
Grazing, Lanhydrock ▶ ▶

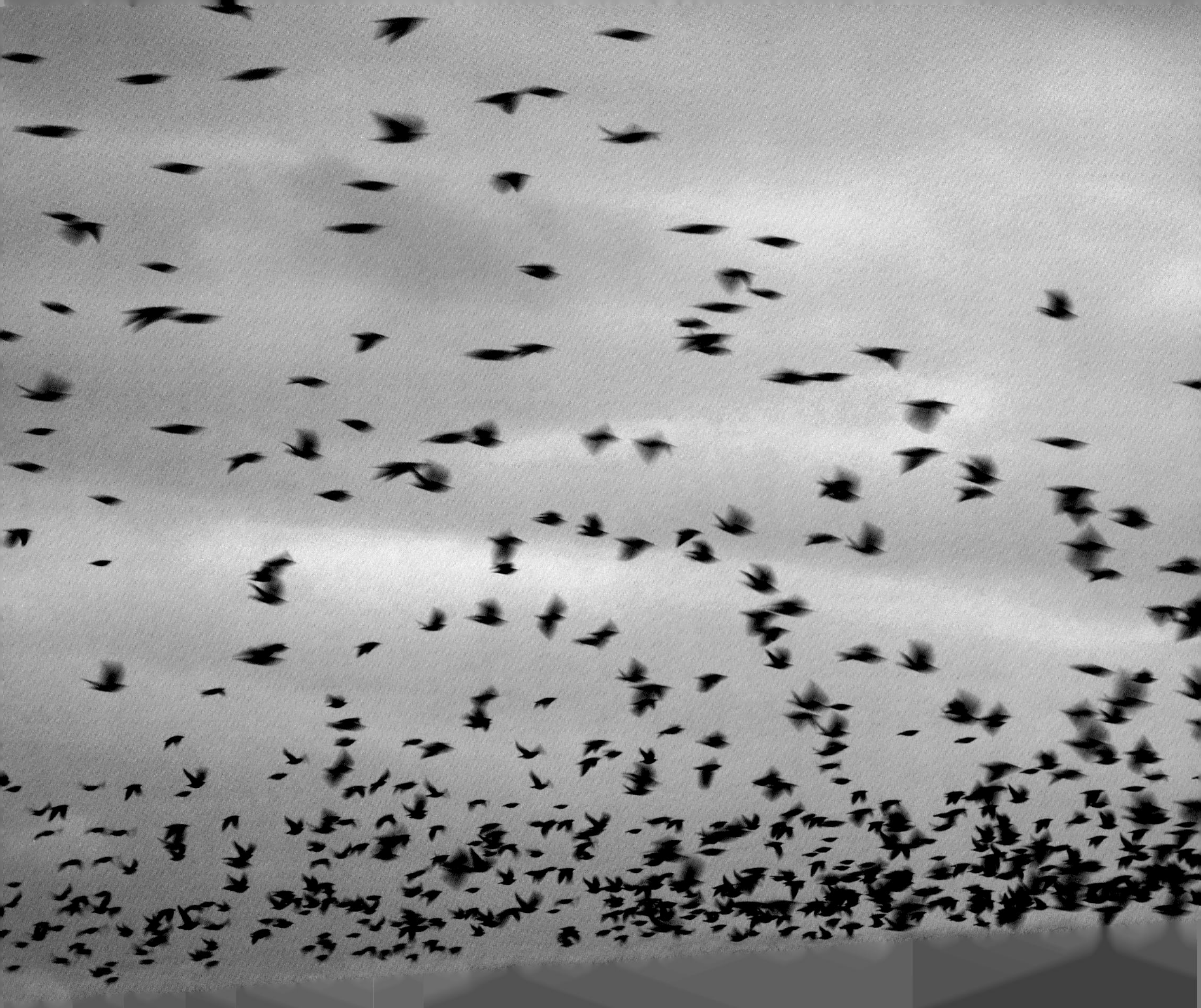

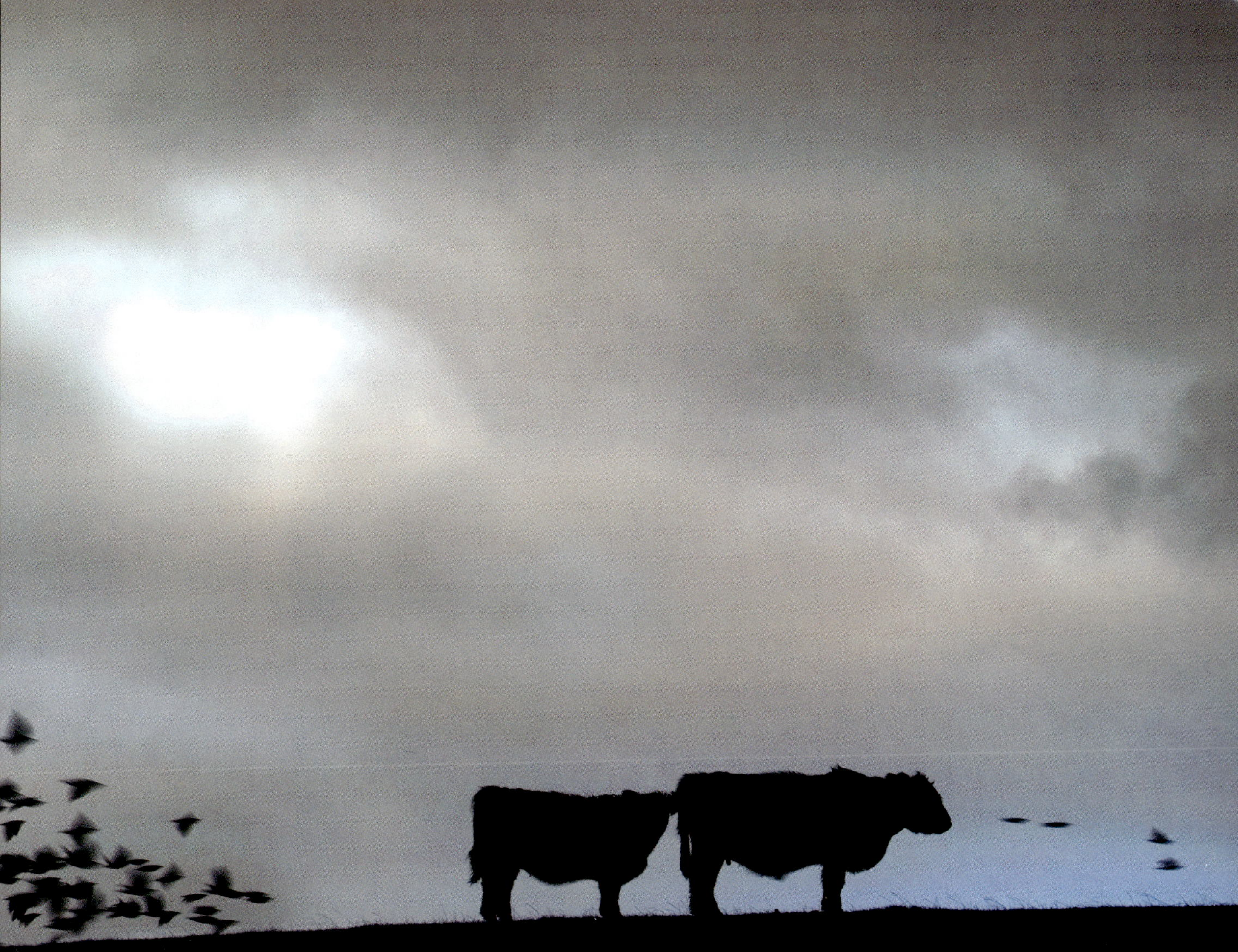

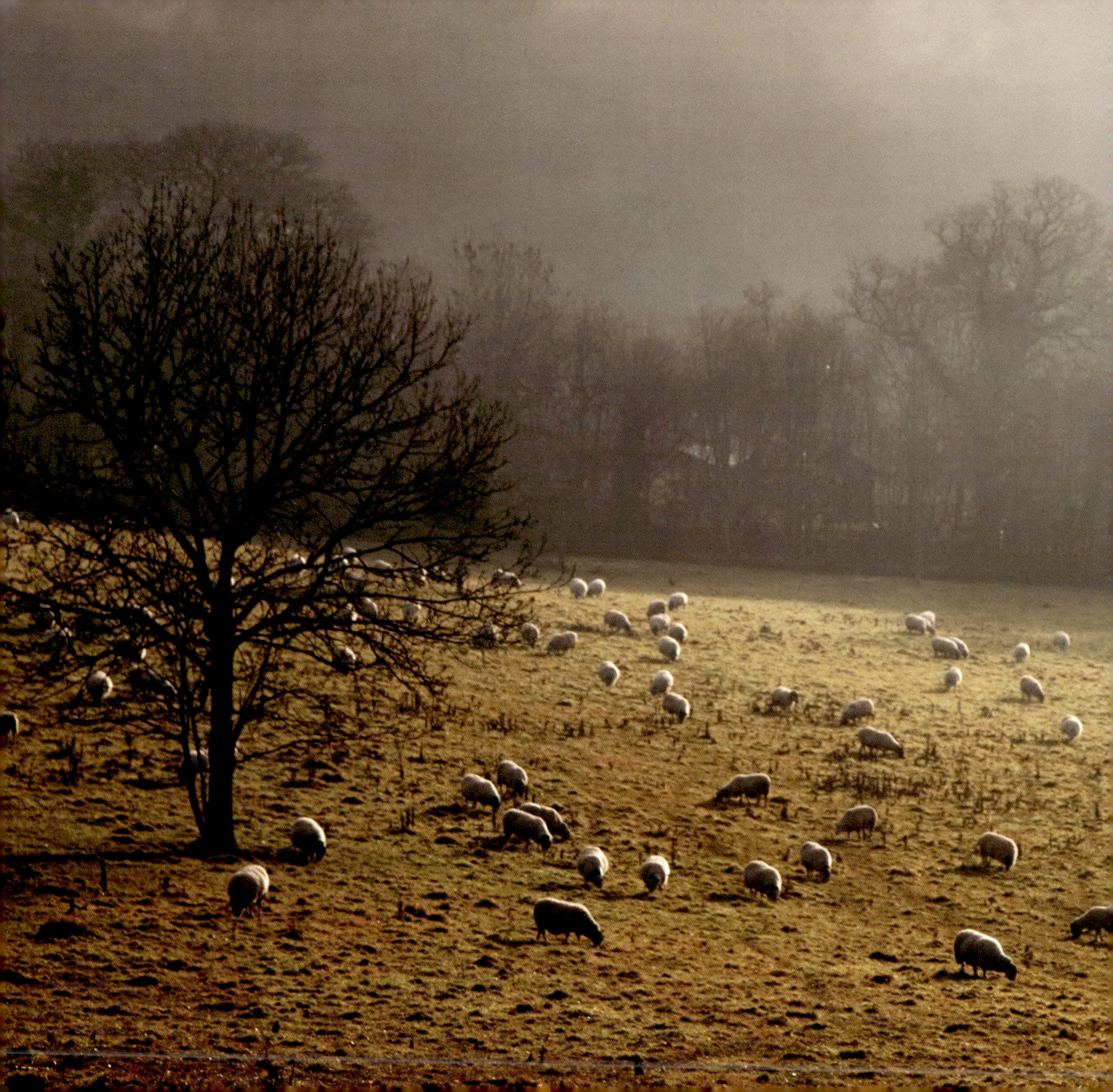

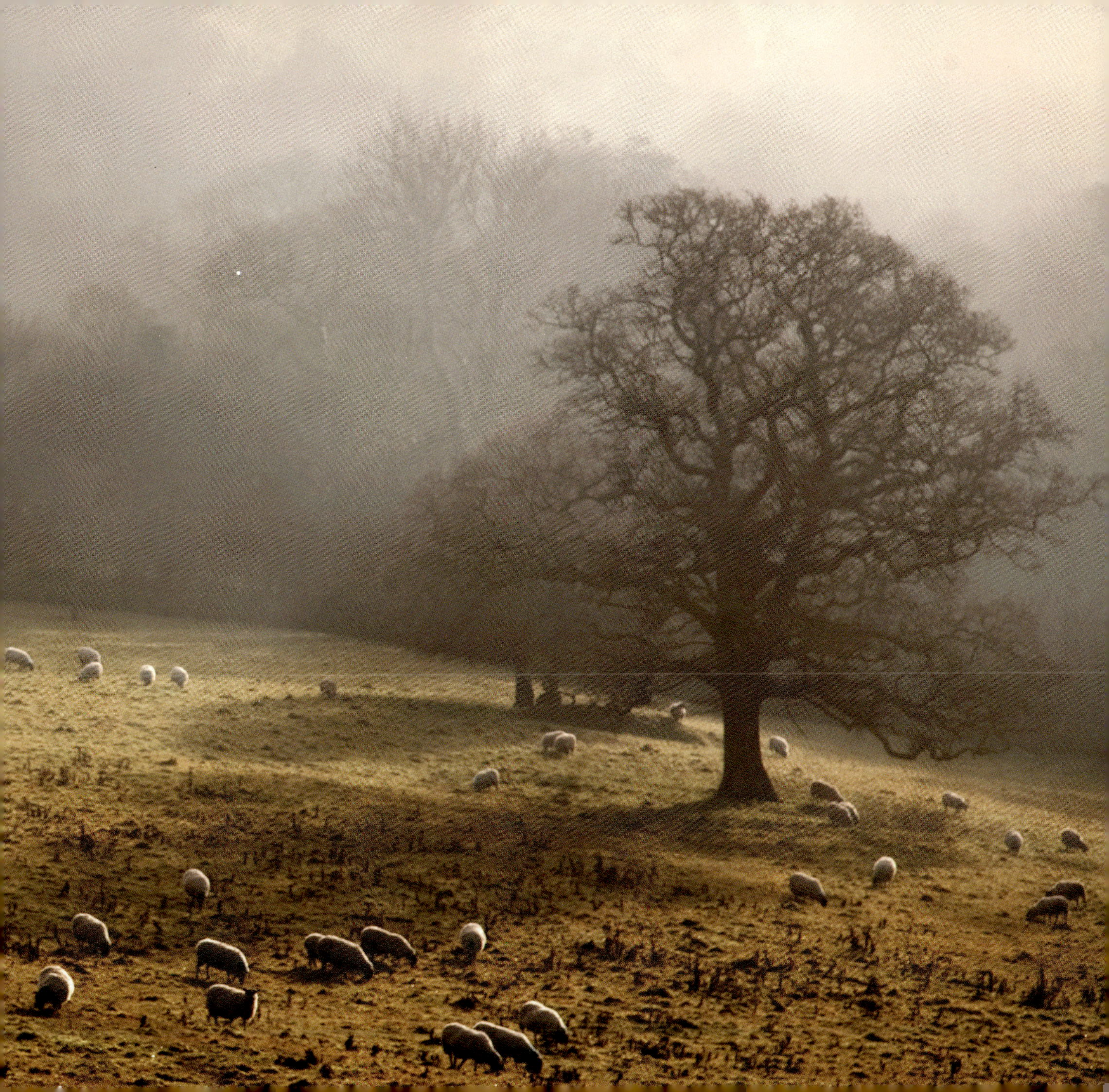

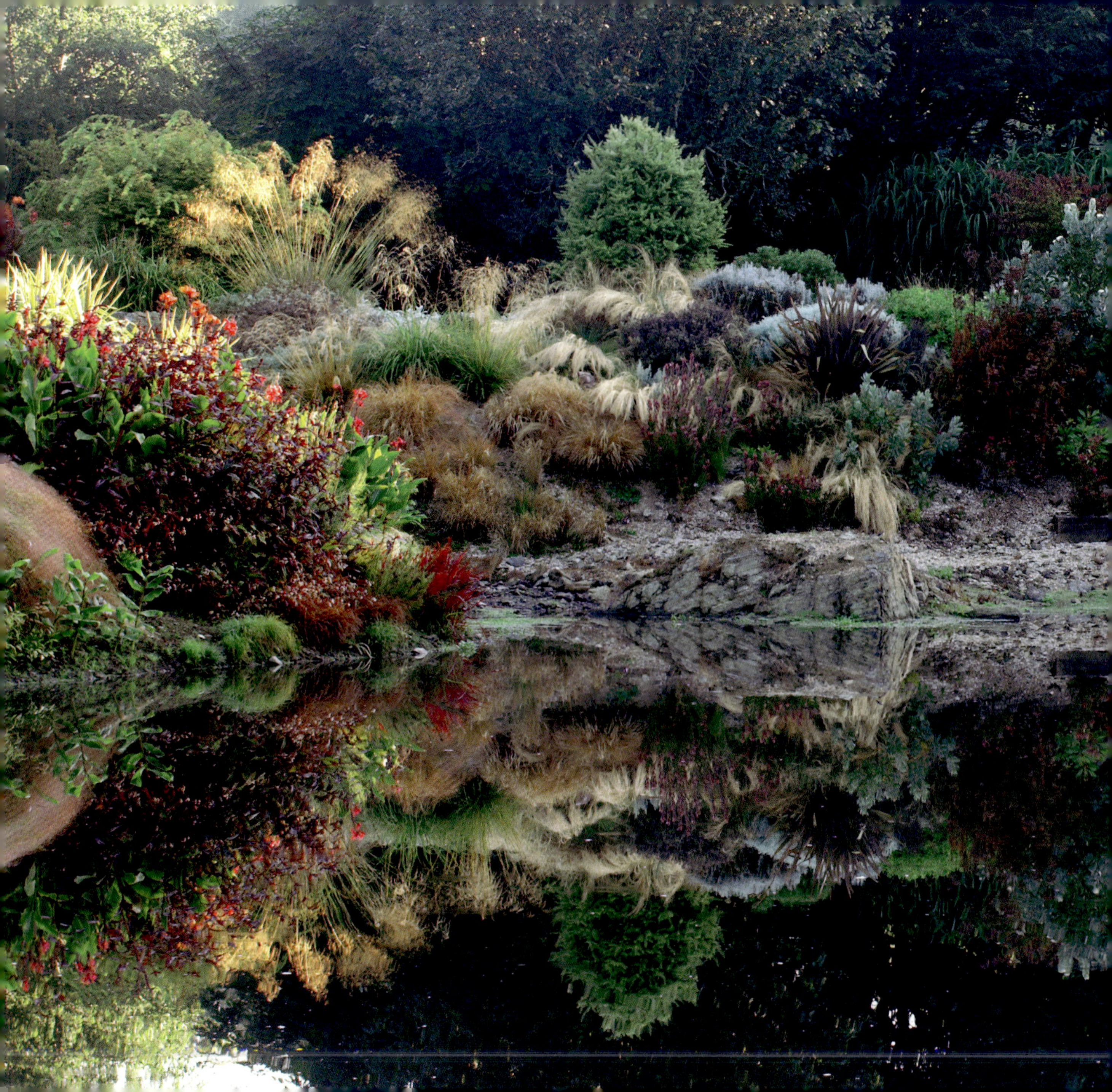

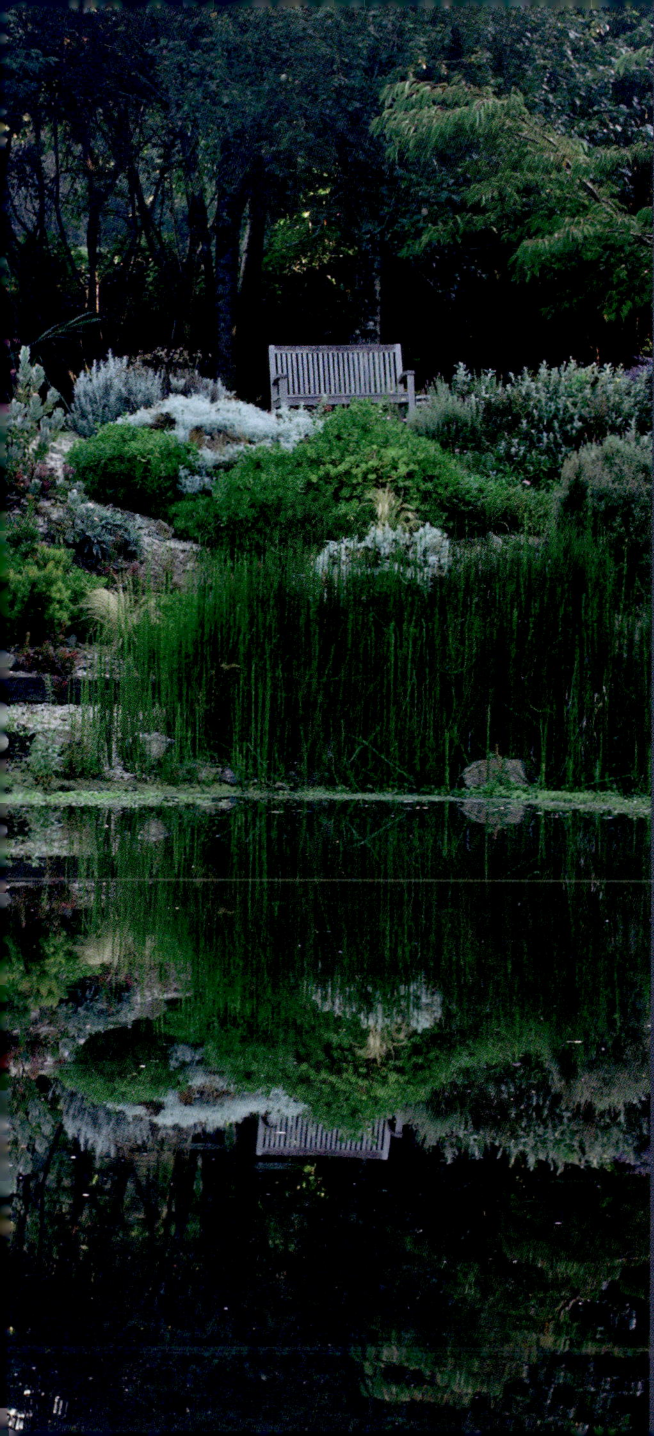

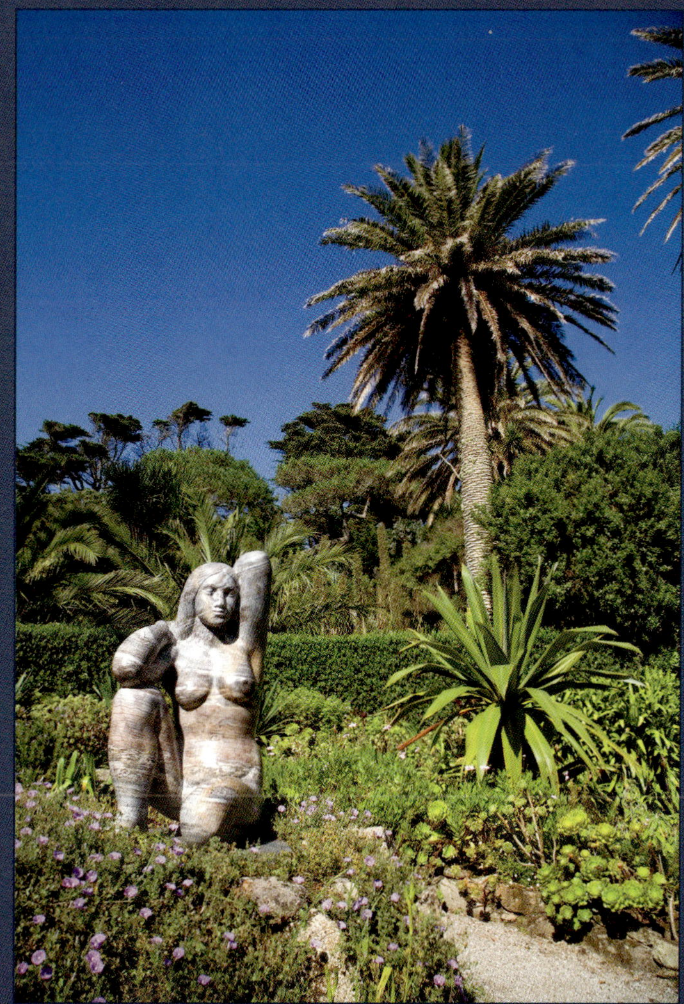

▲ Gaia, Abbey Garden, Tresco
◀ Bonython Estate Gardens

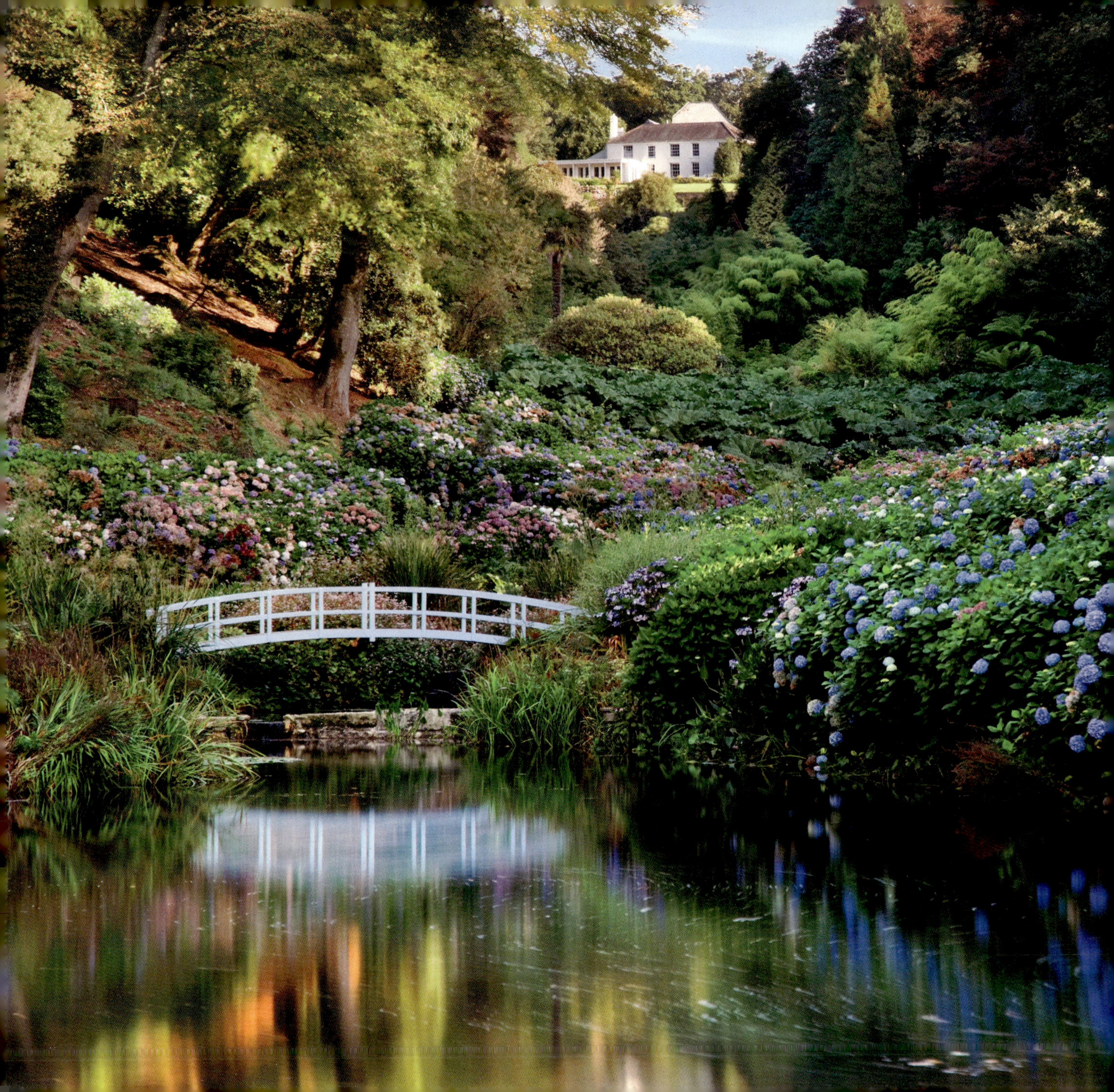

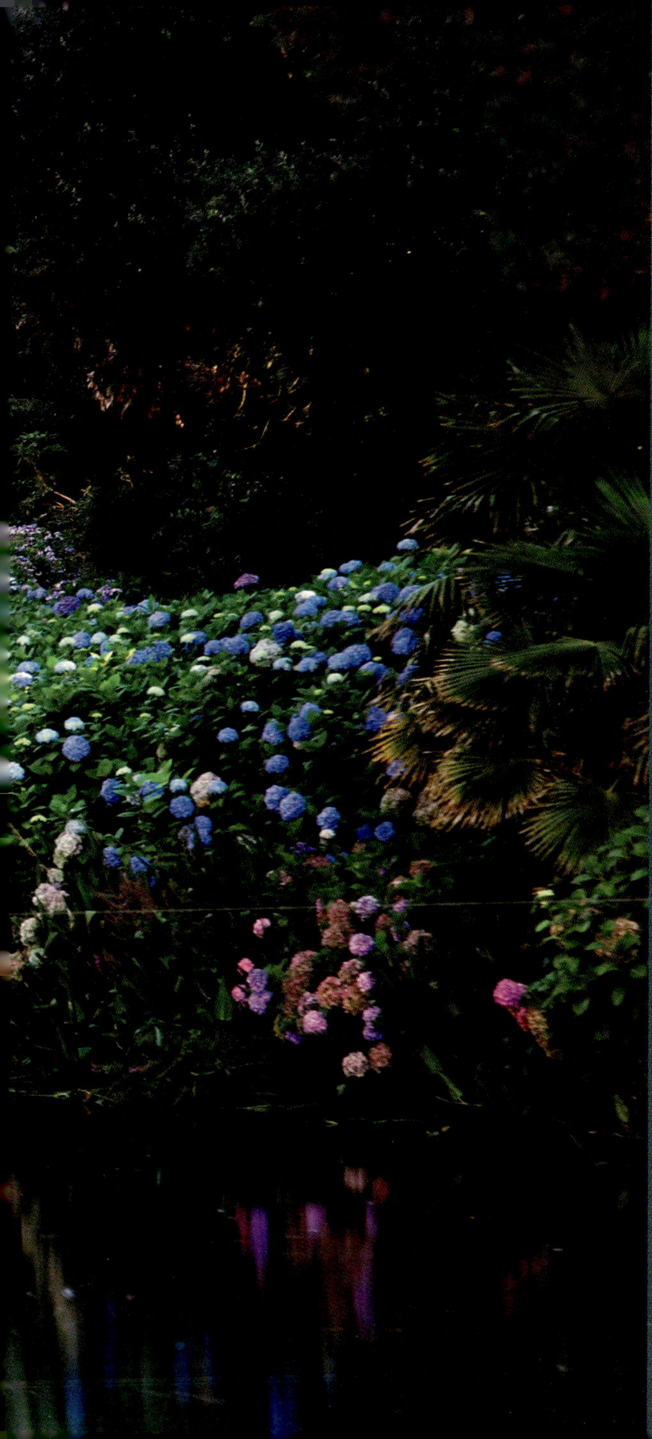

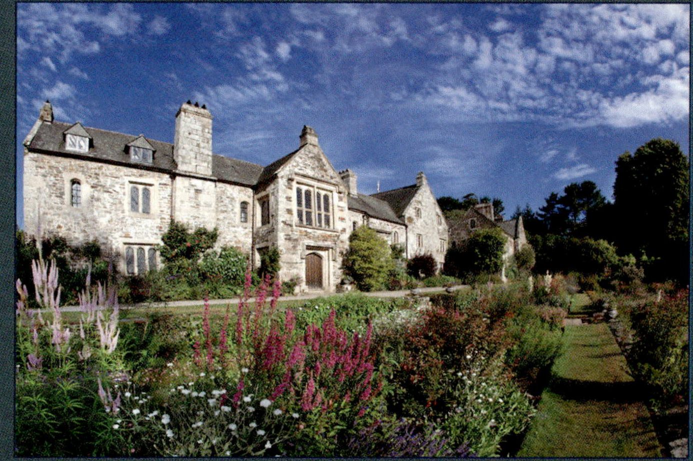

▲ *Cotehele house and terraced garden*
◀ *Trebah Garden*

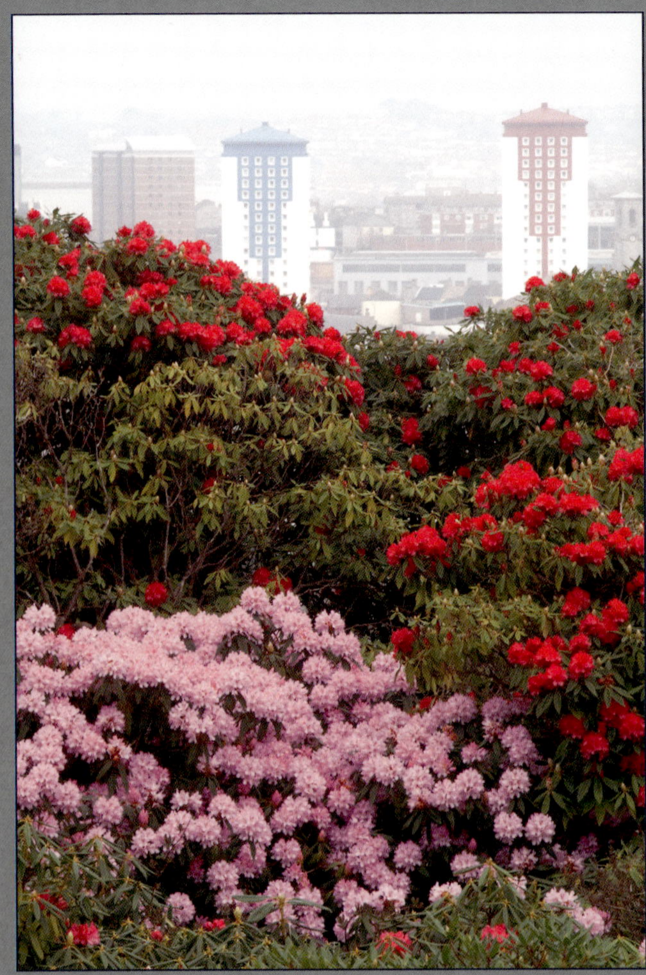

▲ *View from Mount Edgcumbe to Plymouth*

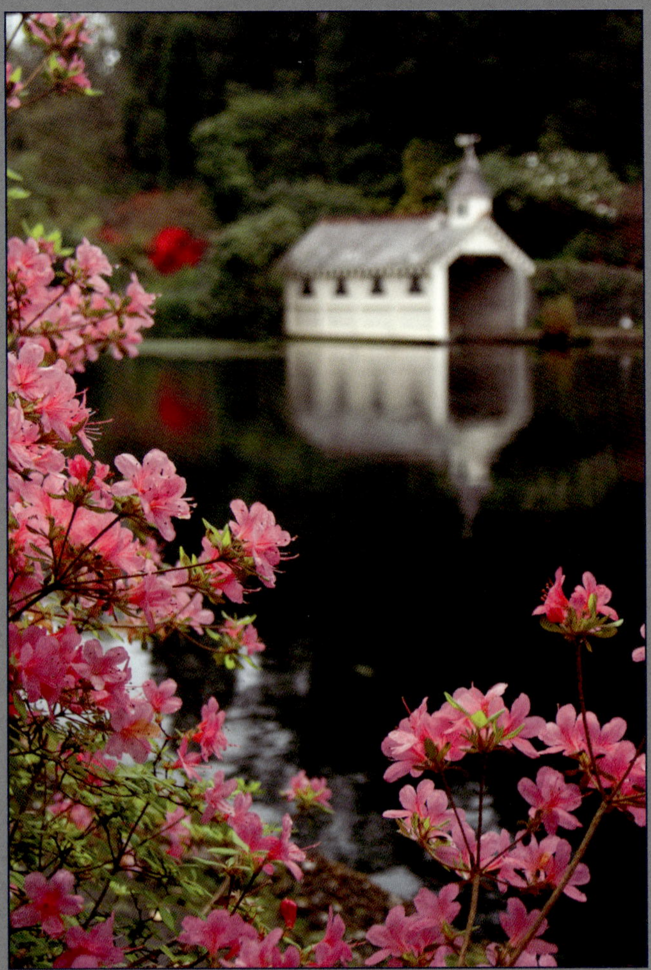

▲ *Boathouse, Trevarno Gardens*

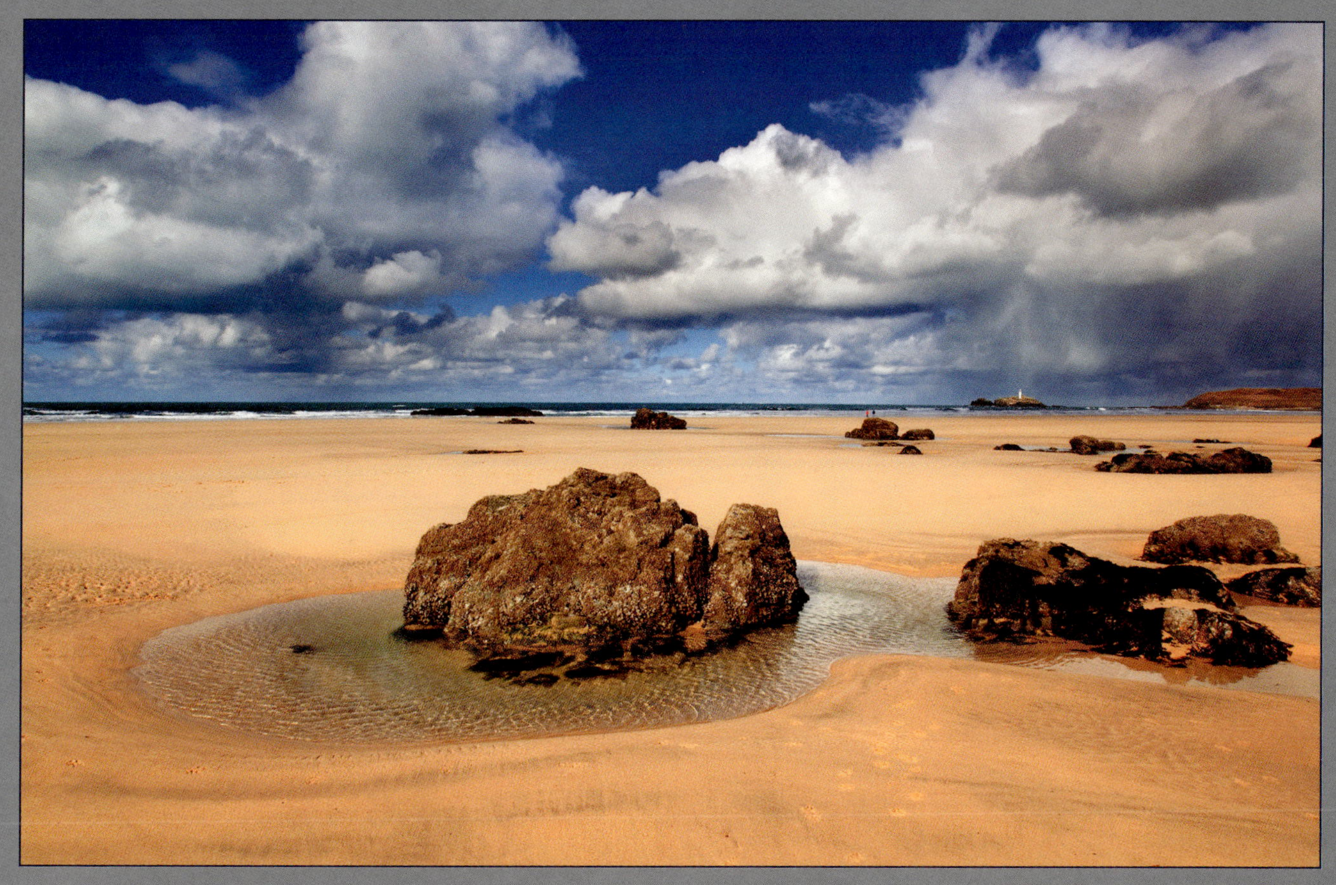

▲ *Gwithian*

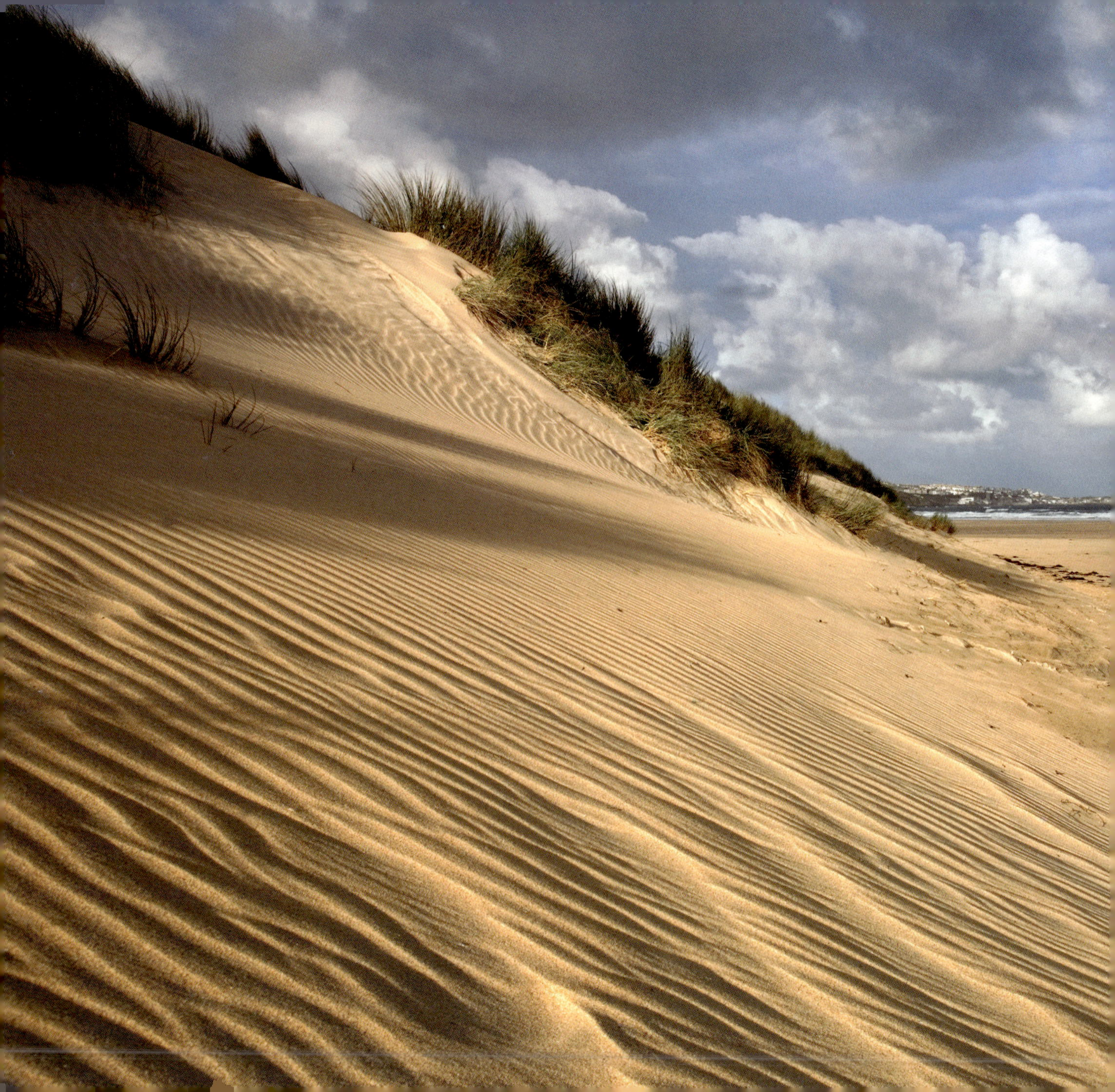

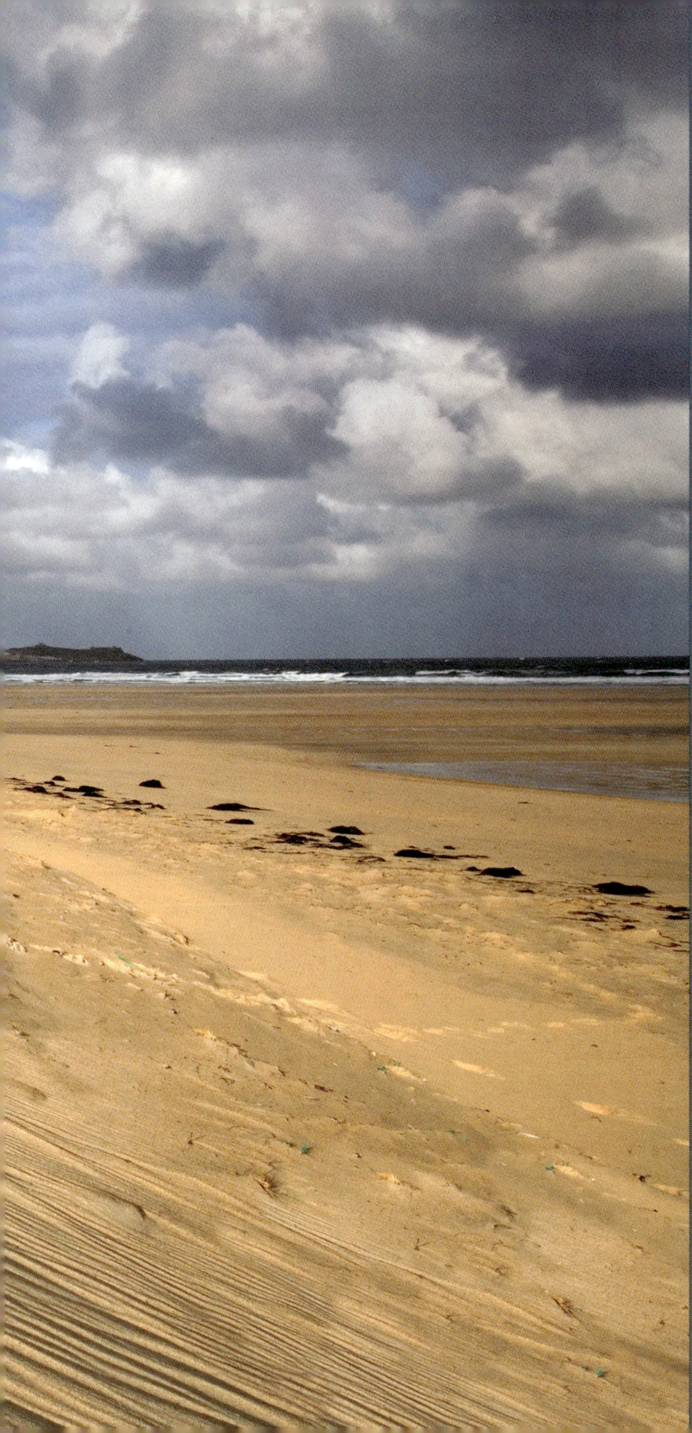

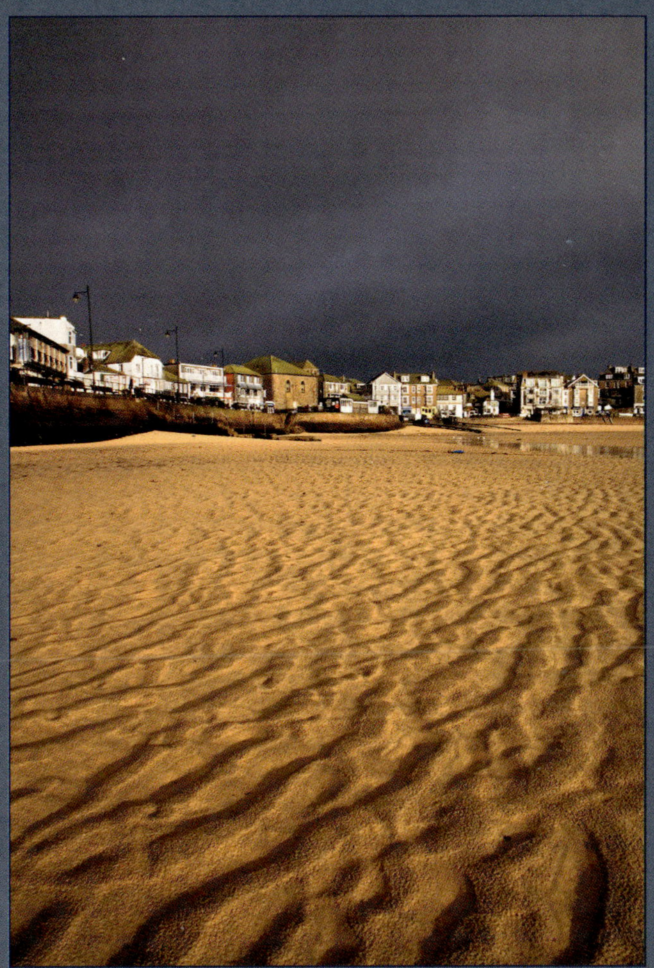

▲ St Ives
◄ Porth Kidney

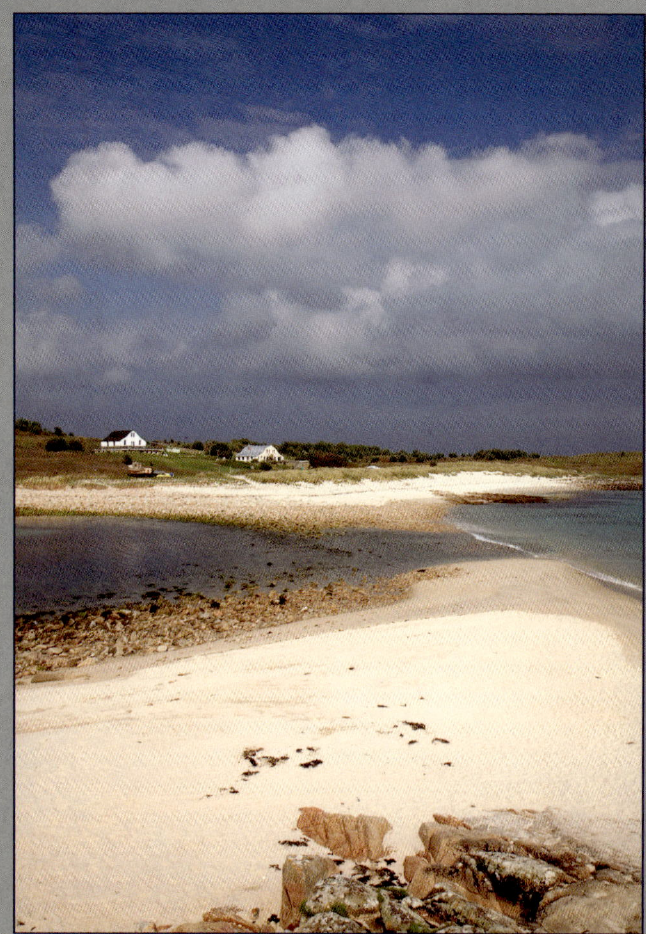

▲ *Gugh Bar, St Agnes, Isles of Scilly*

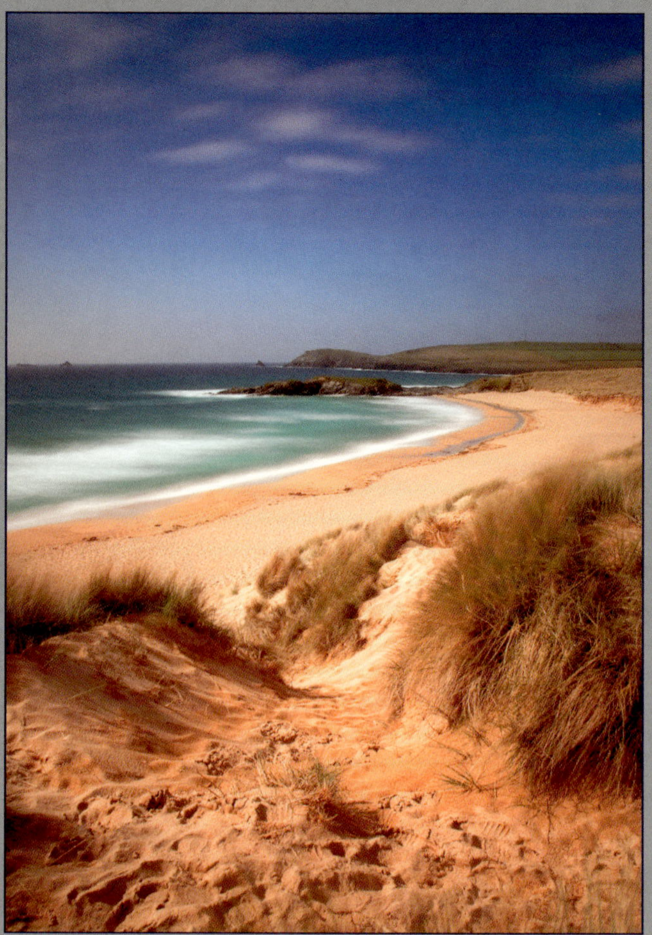

▲ *Constantine Bay*

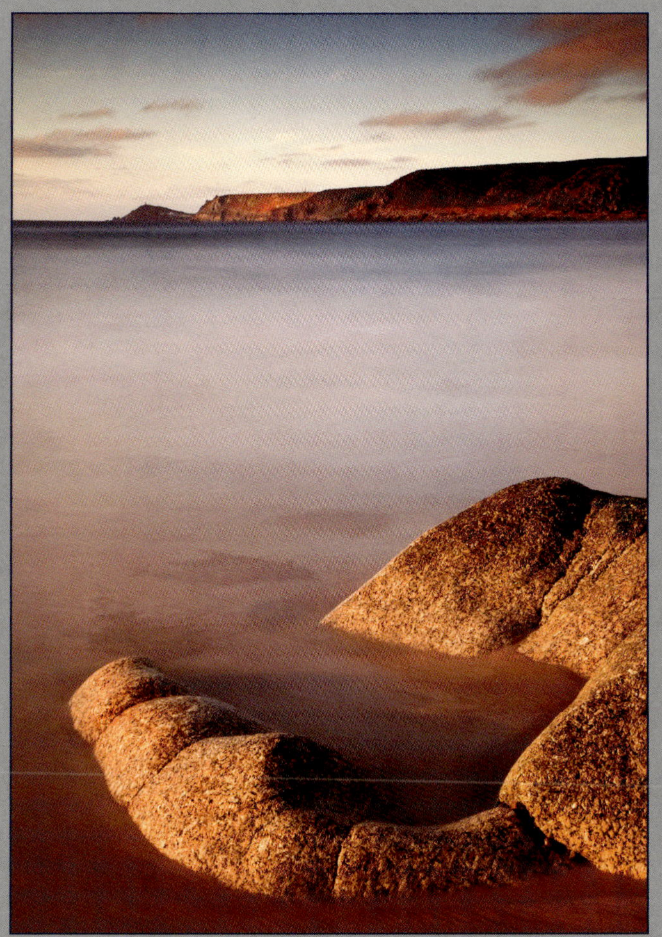

▲ Sennen

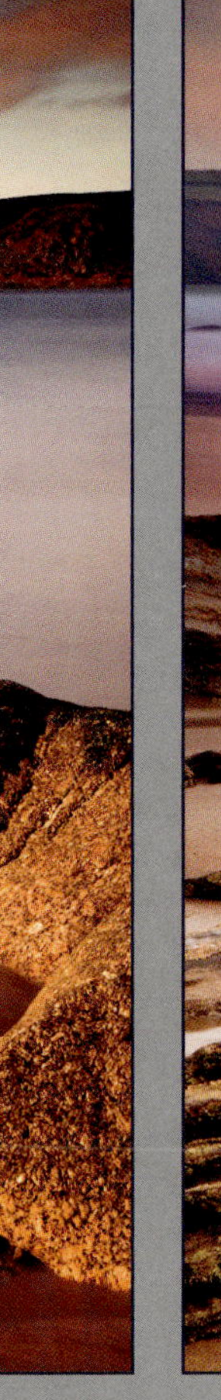

▲ *From Freathy Cliff to Rame Head*

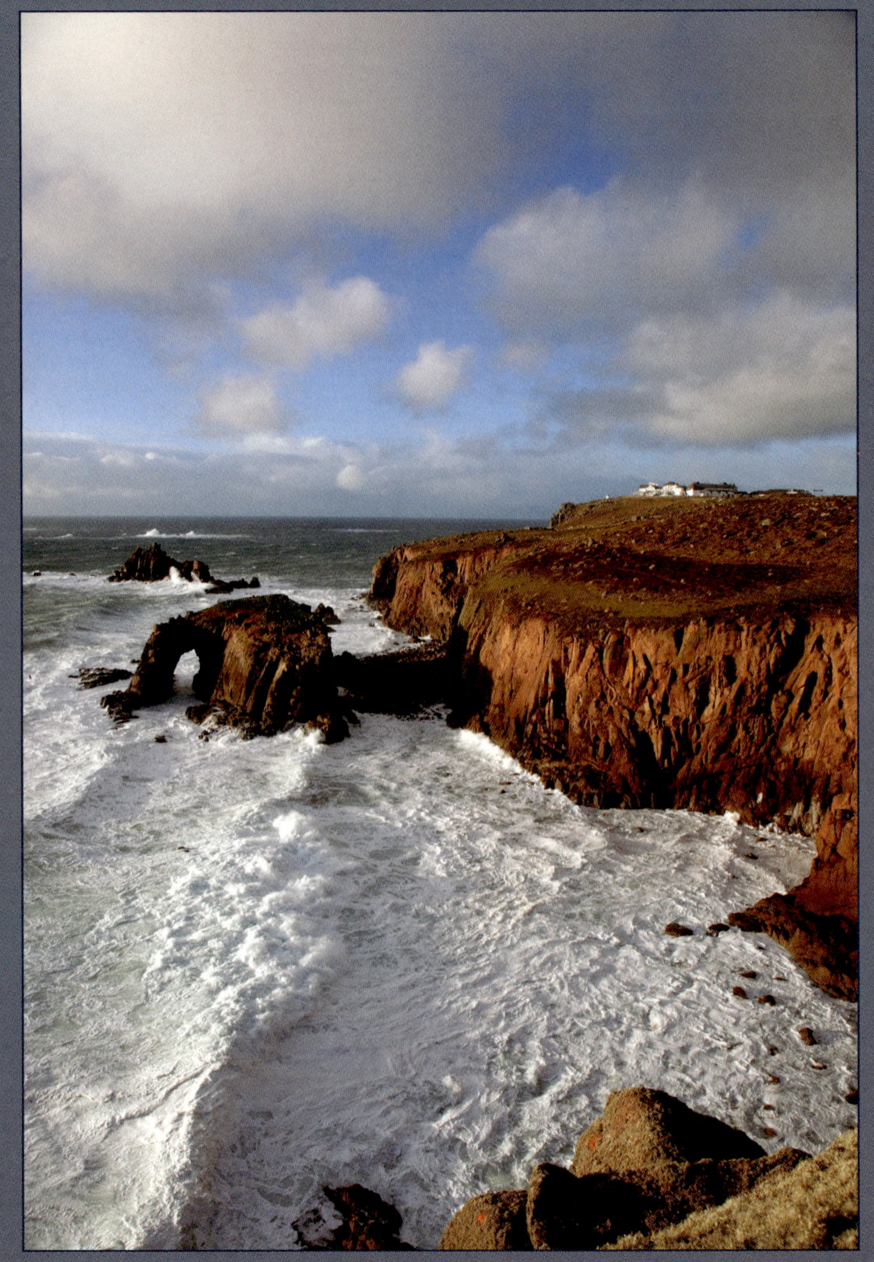

◄ *Land's End*

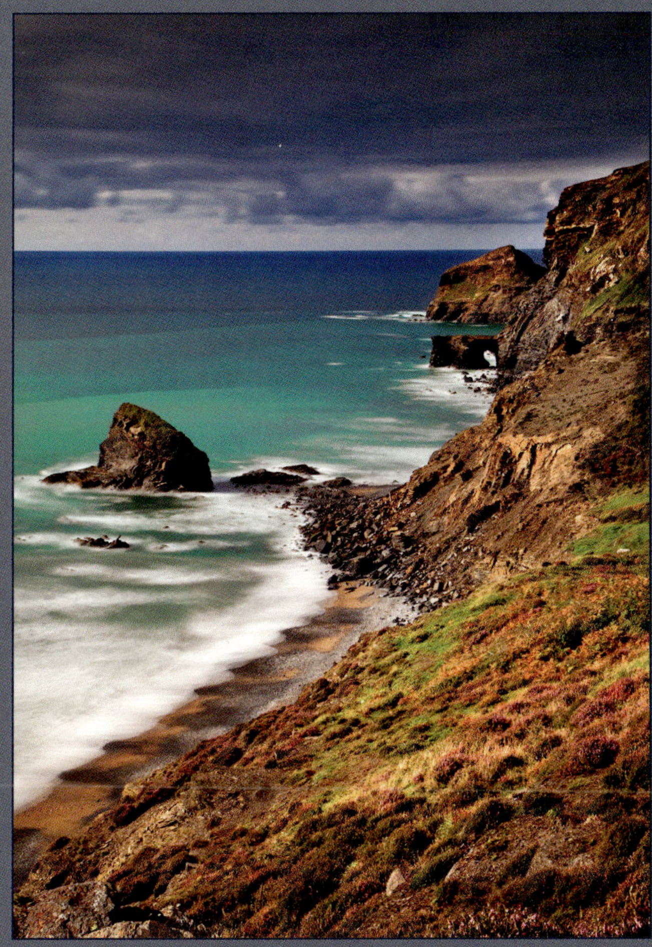

▲ *The Strangles*

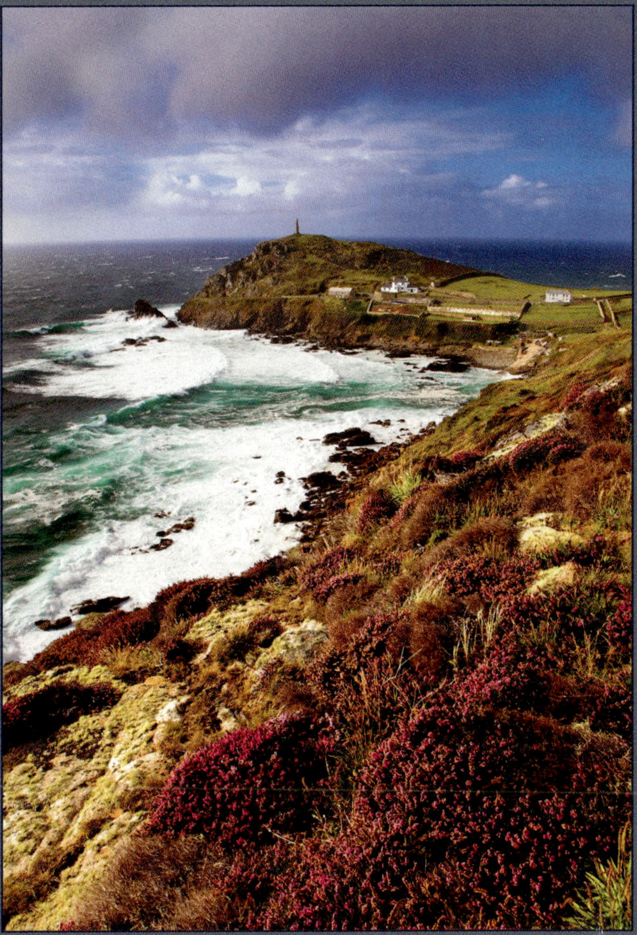

▲ *Cape Cornwall*

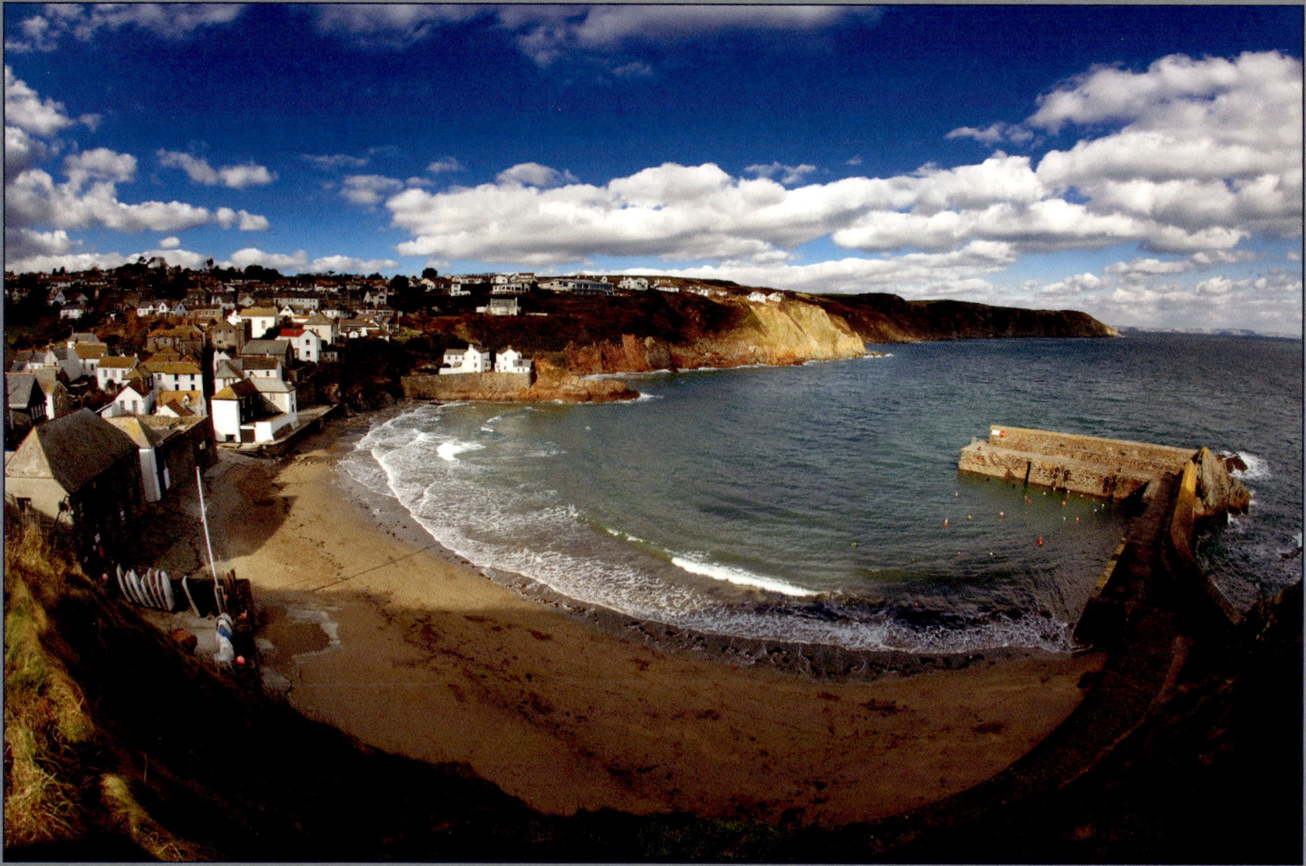

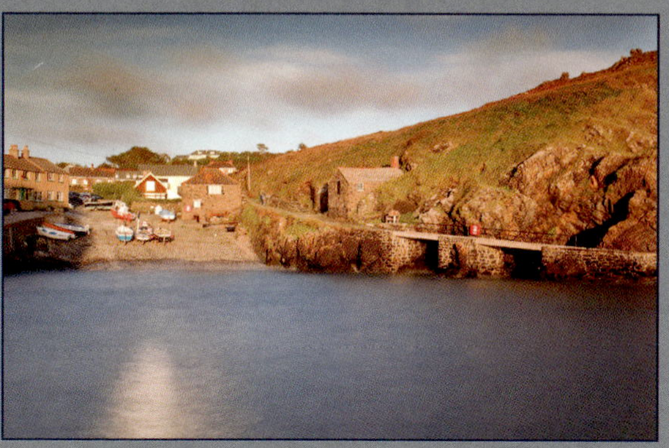

▲ Gorran Haven
◄ Mullion Cove

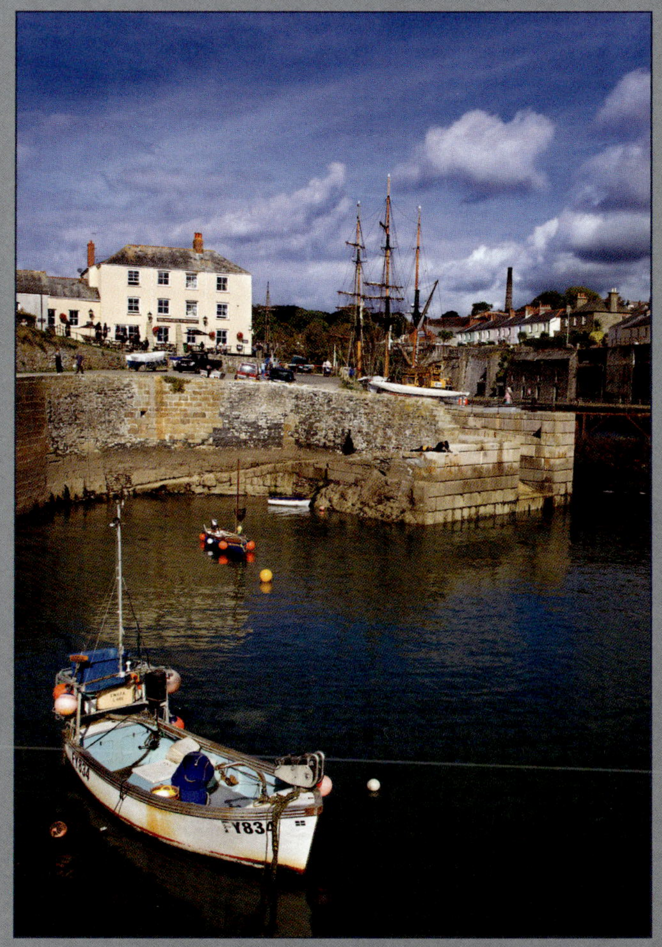

▲ *Charlestown*

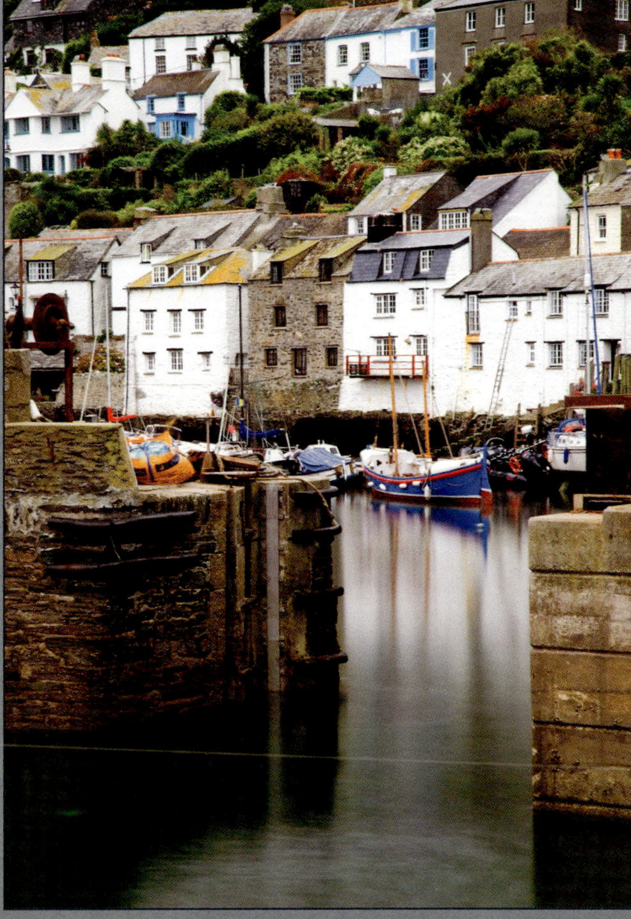

▲ *Polperro*

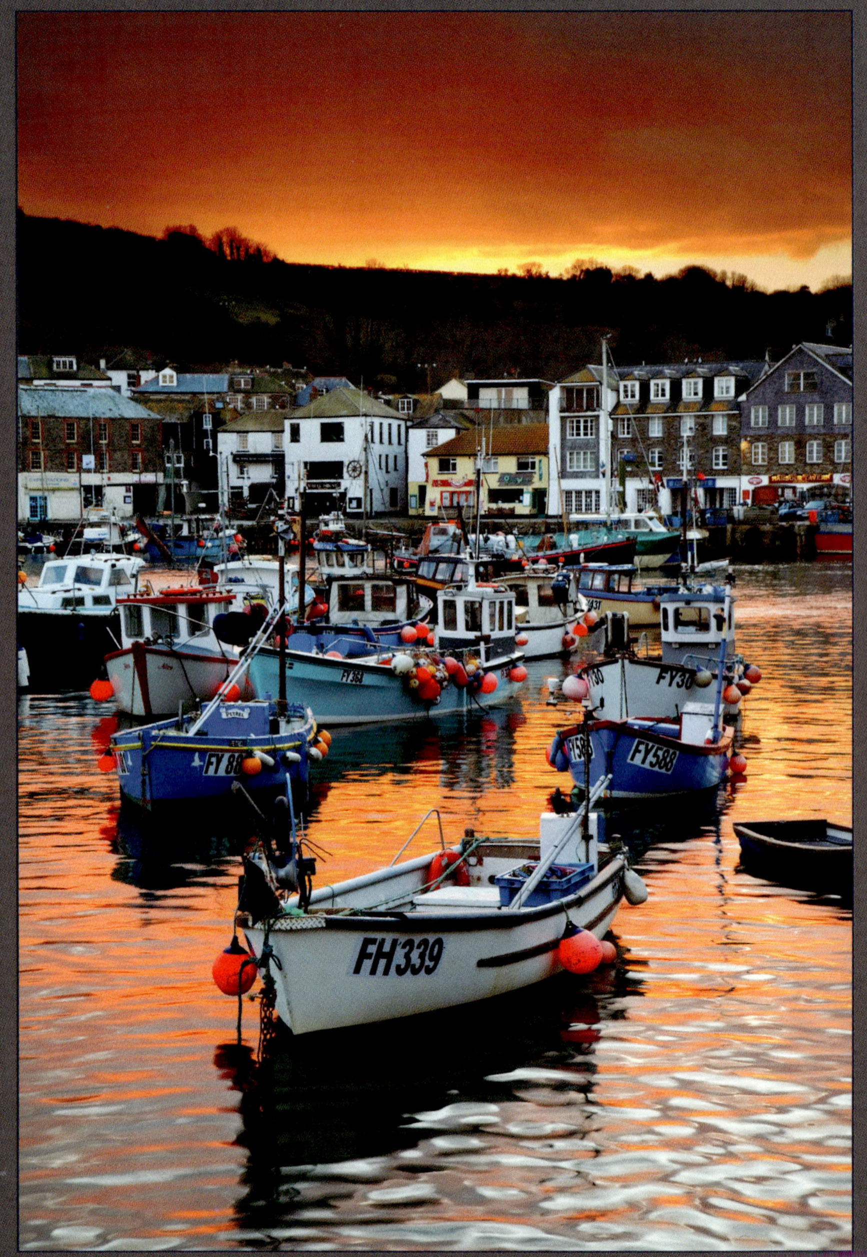

◄ *Mevagissey*

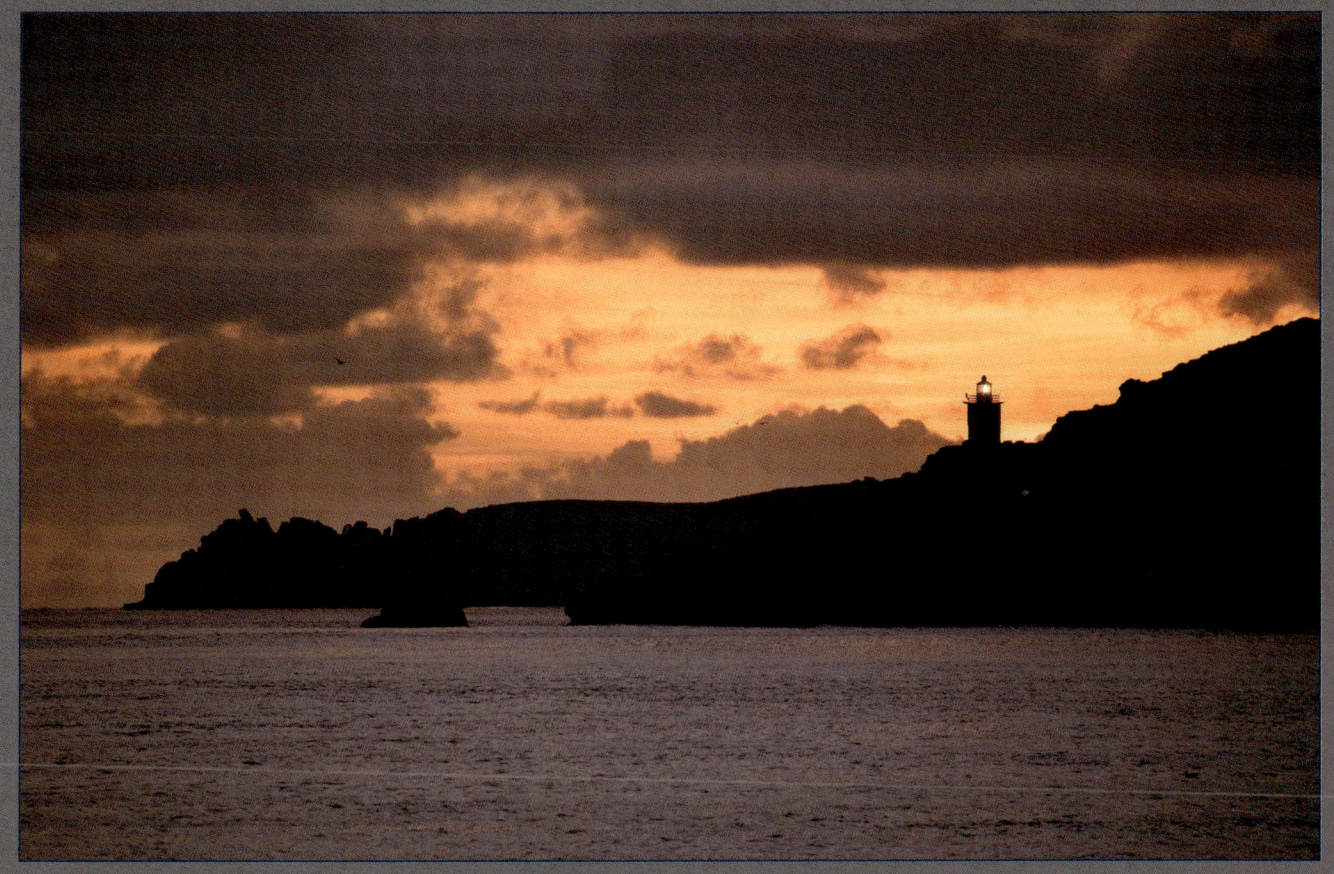

▲ *Tater-du*

Bishop Rock ▶

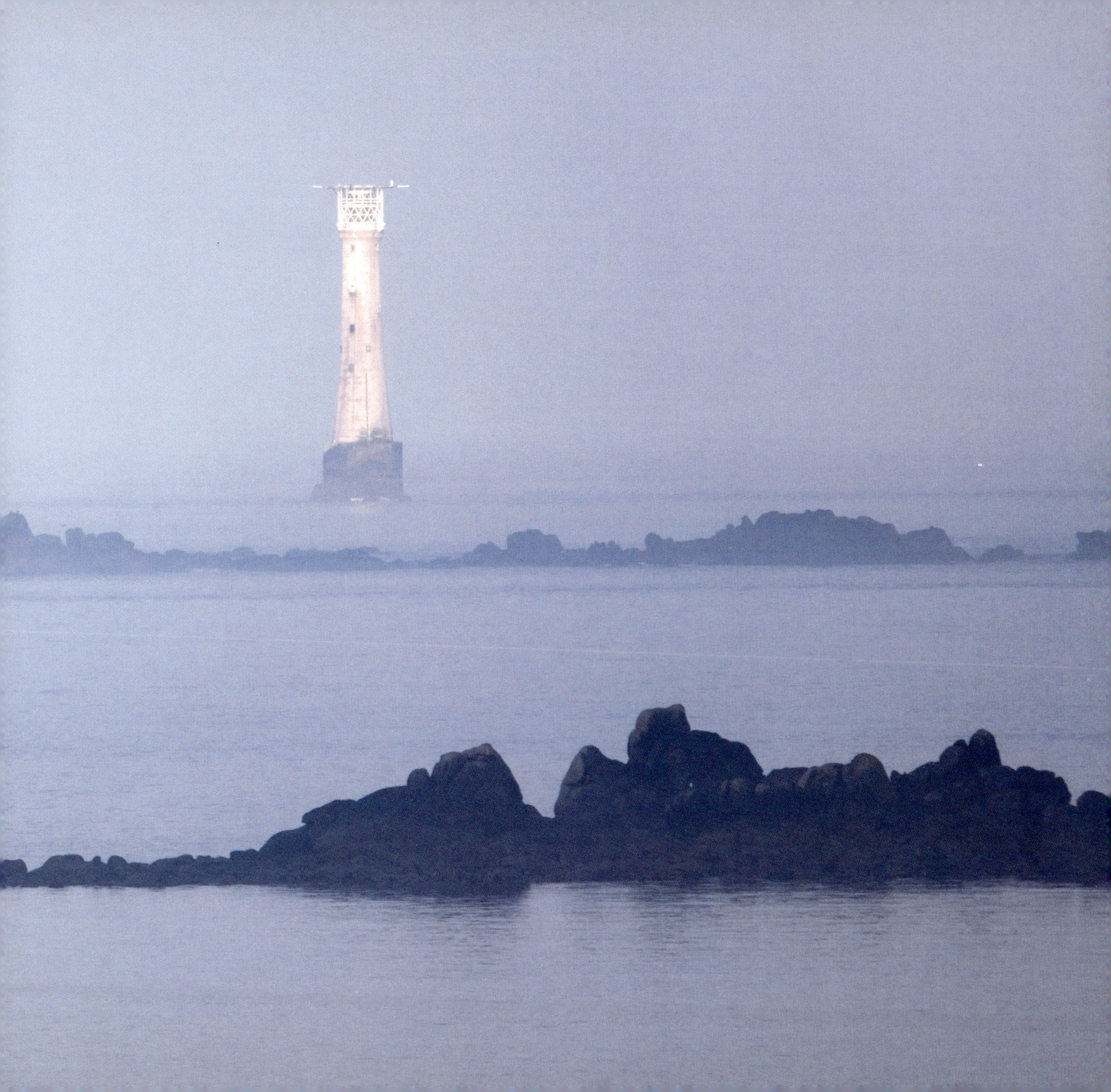

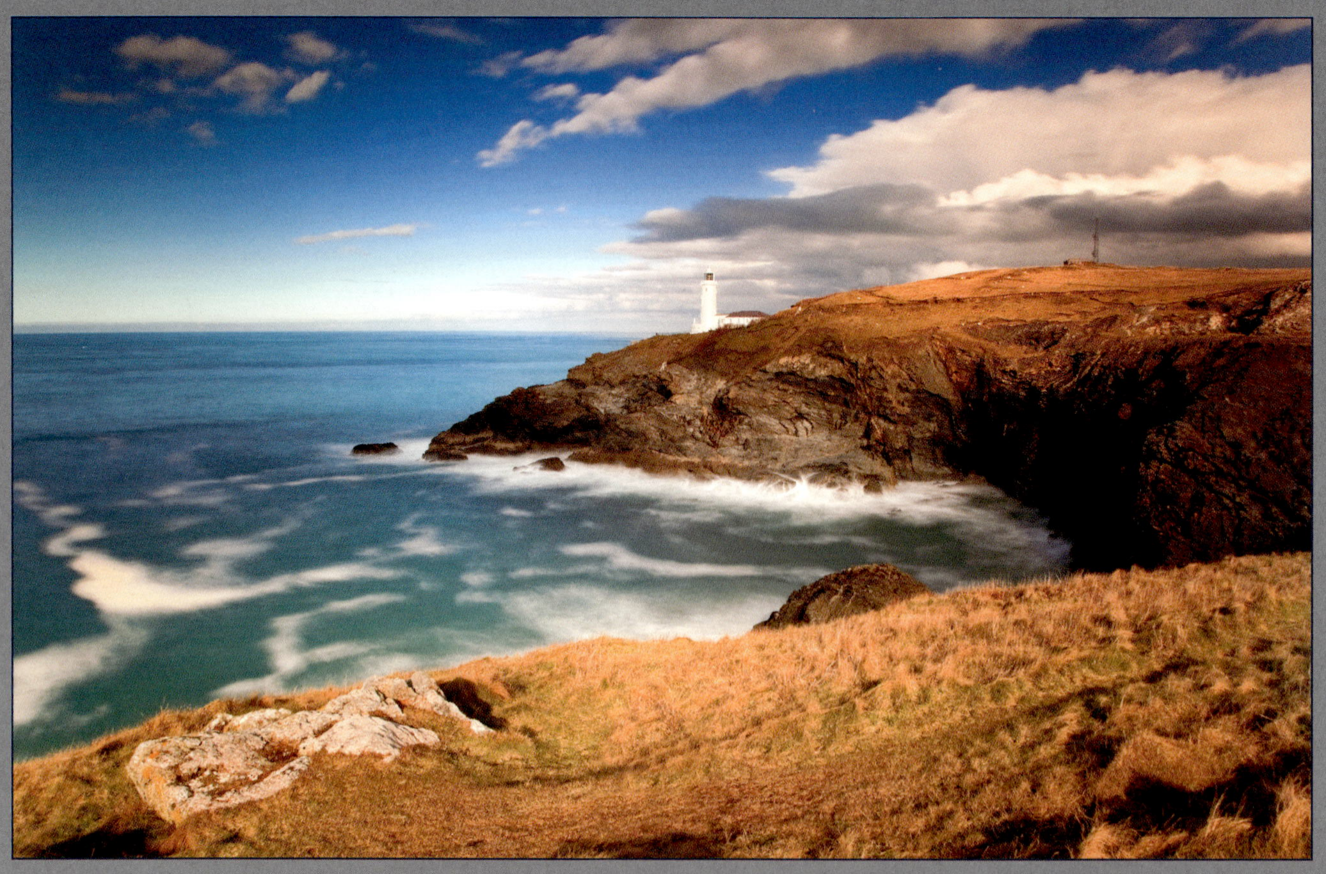

▲ Trevose Head

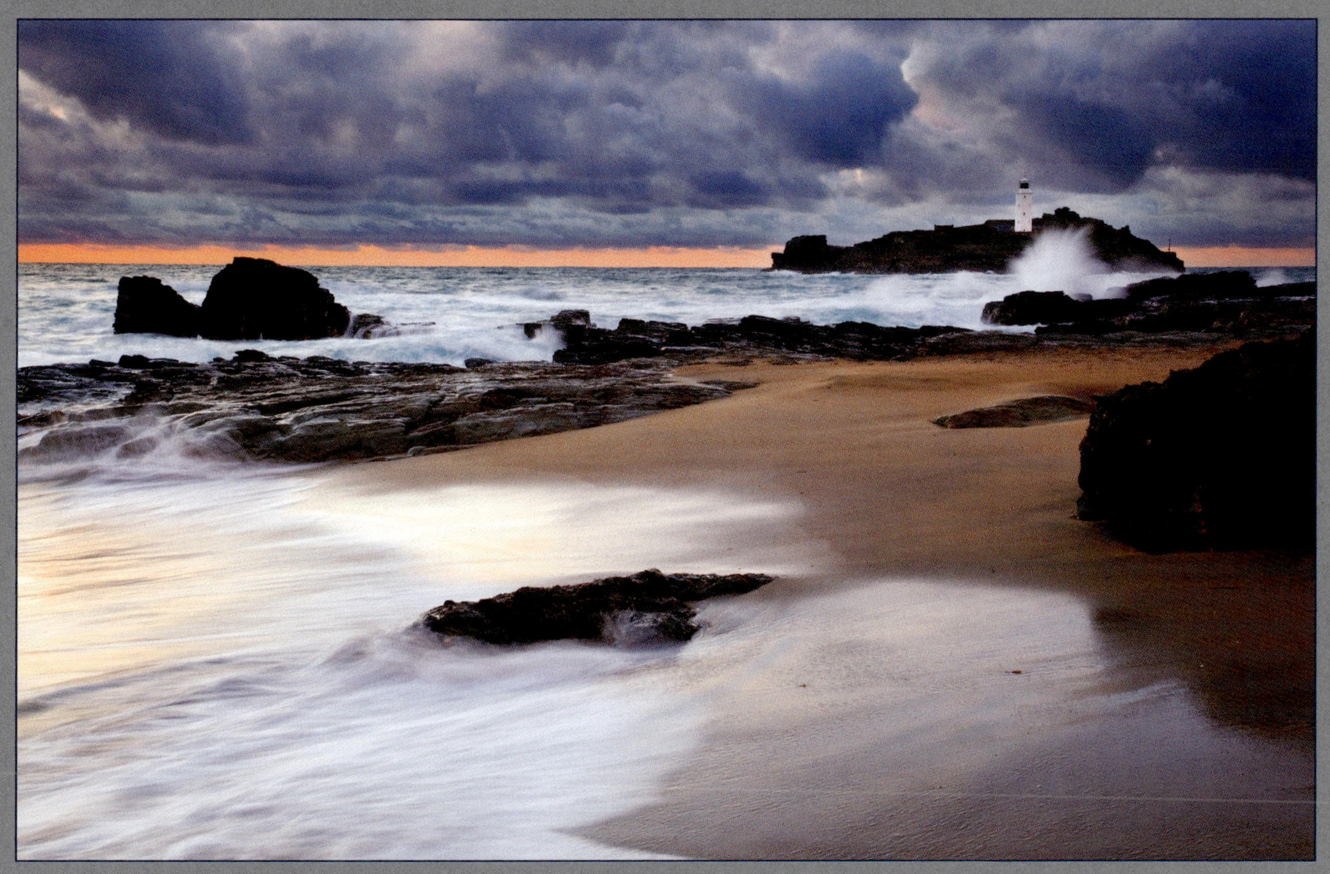

▲ *Godrevy*

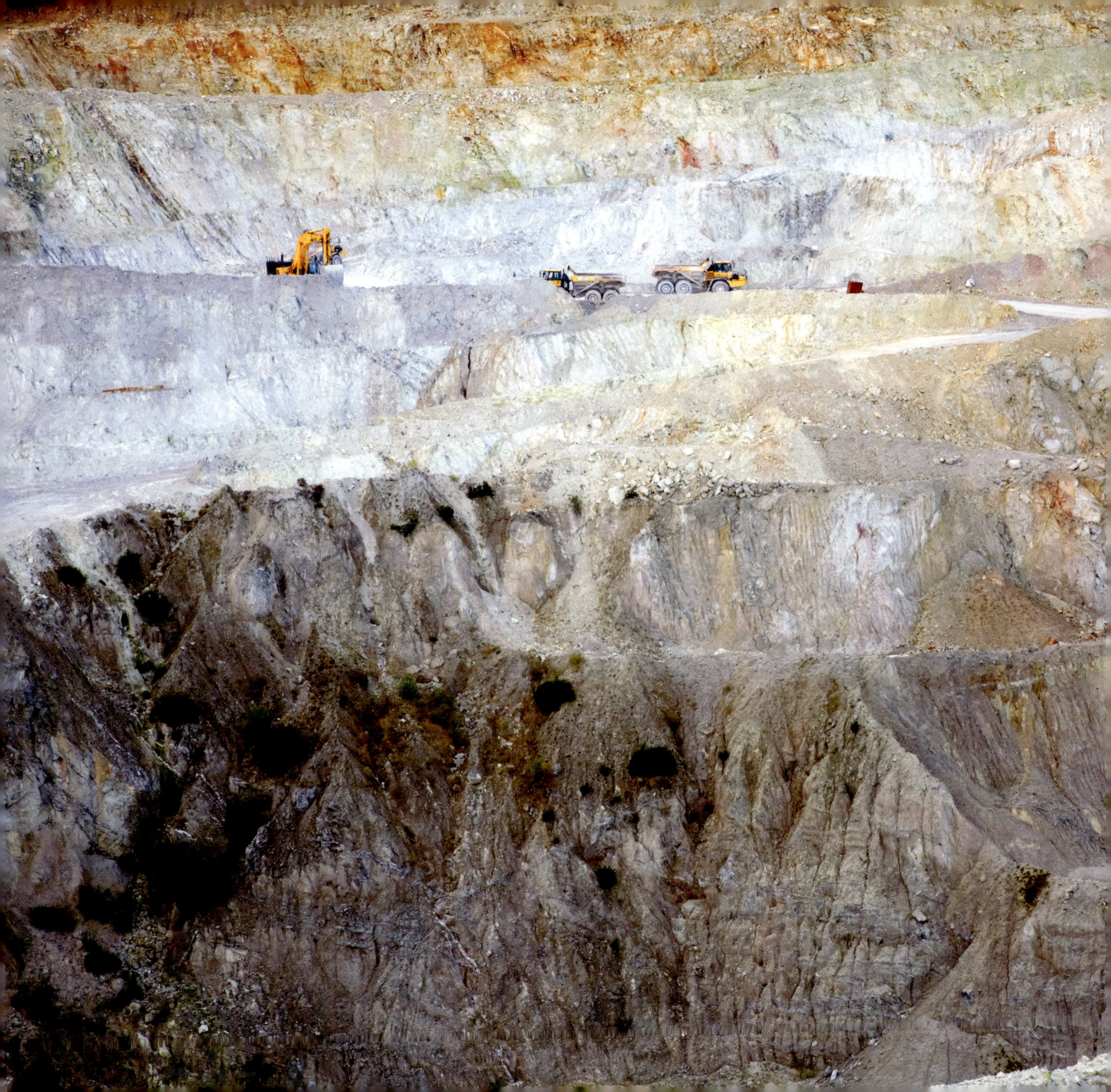

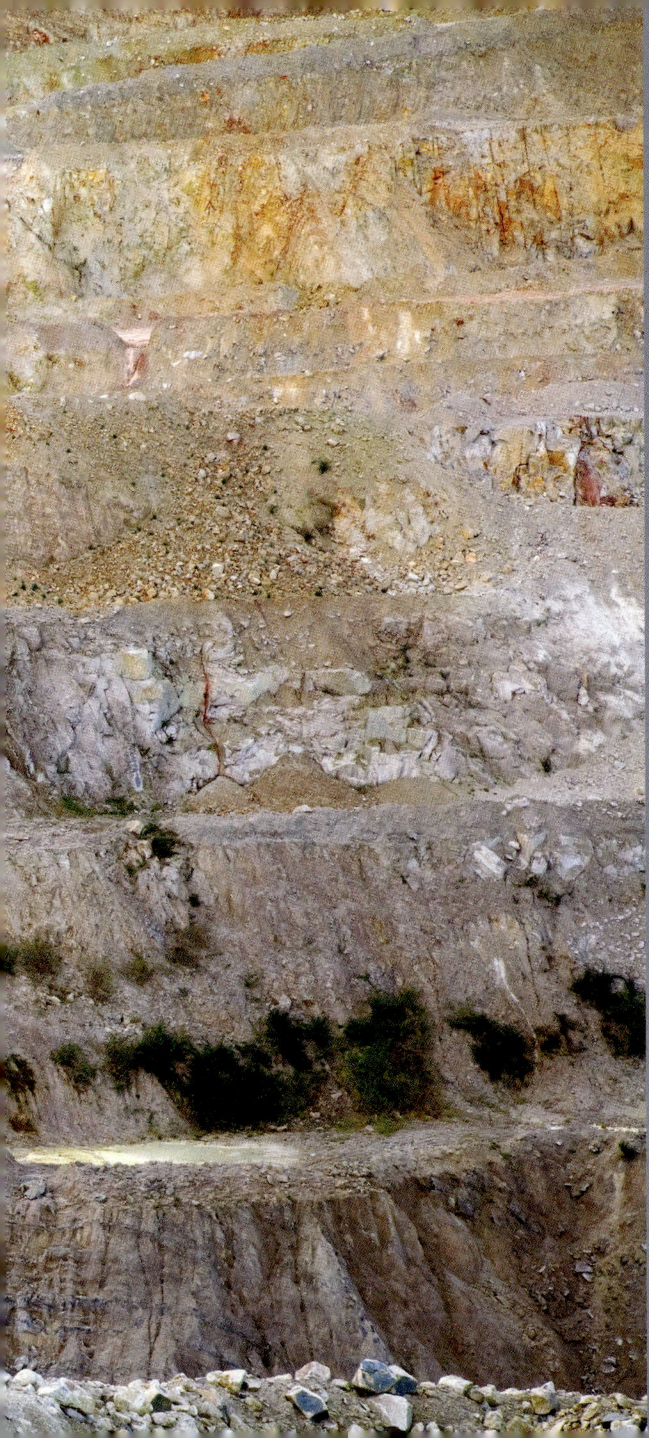

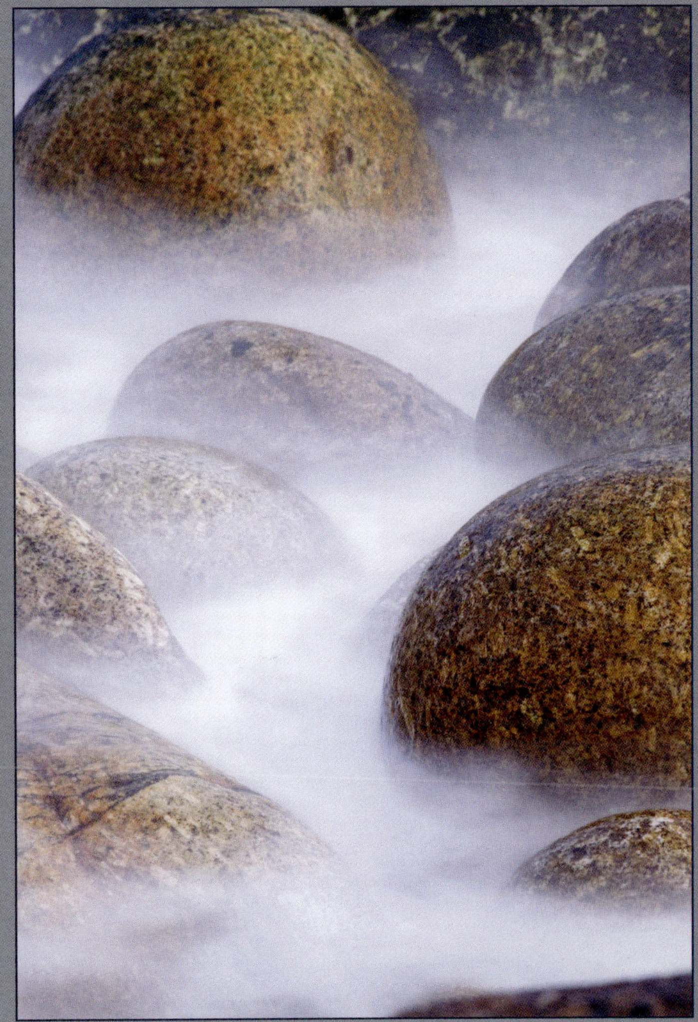

▲ Boulders, Porth Nanven
◄ China clay pit, Wheal Martyn

Colourful shales, Finnygook Beach ▶

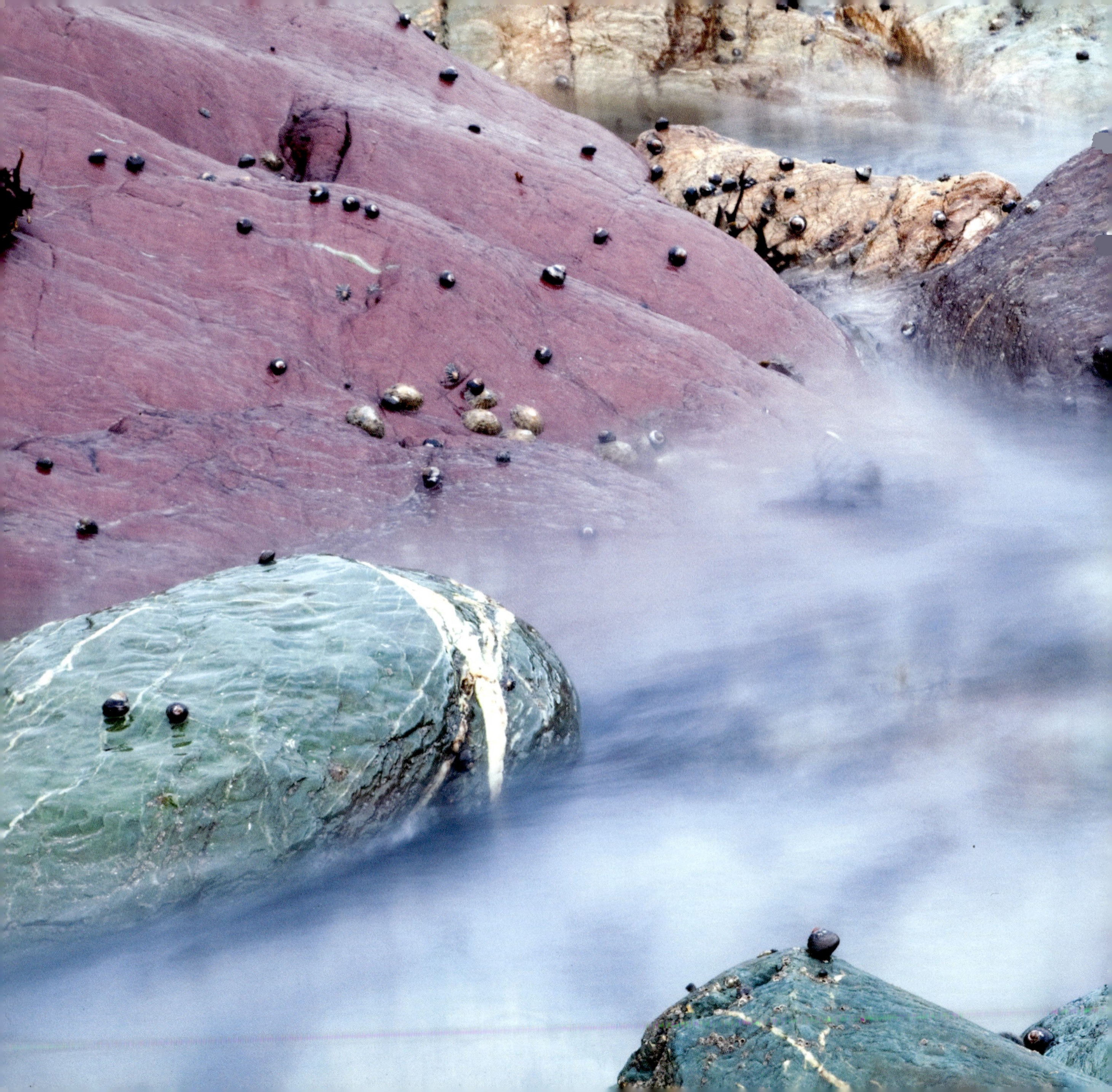

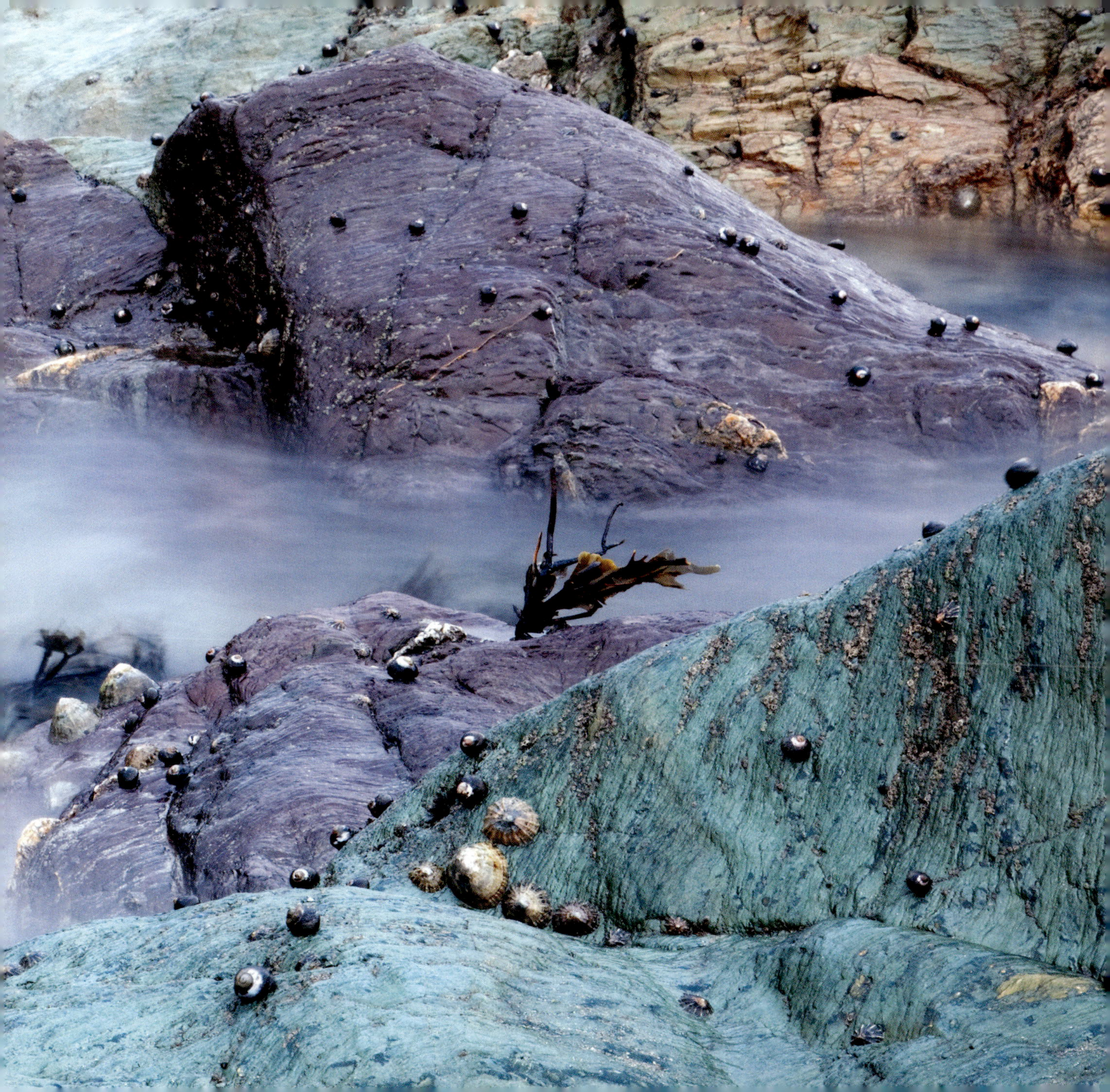

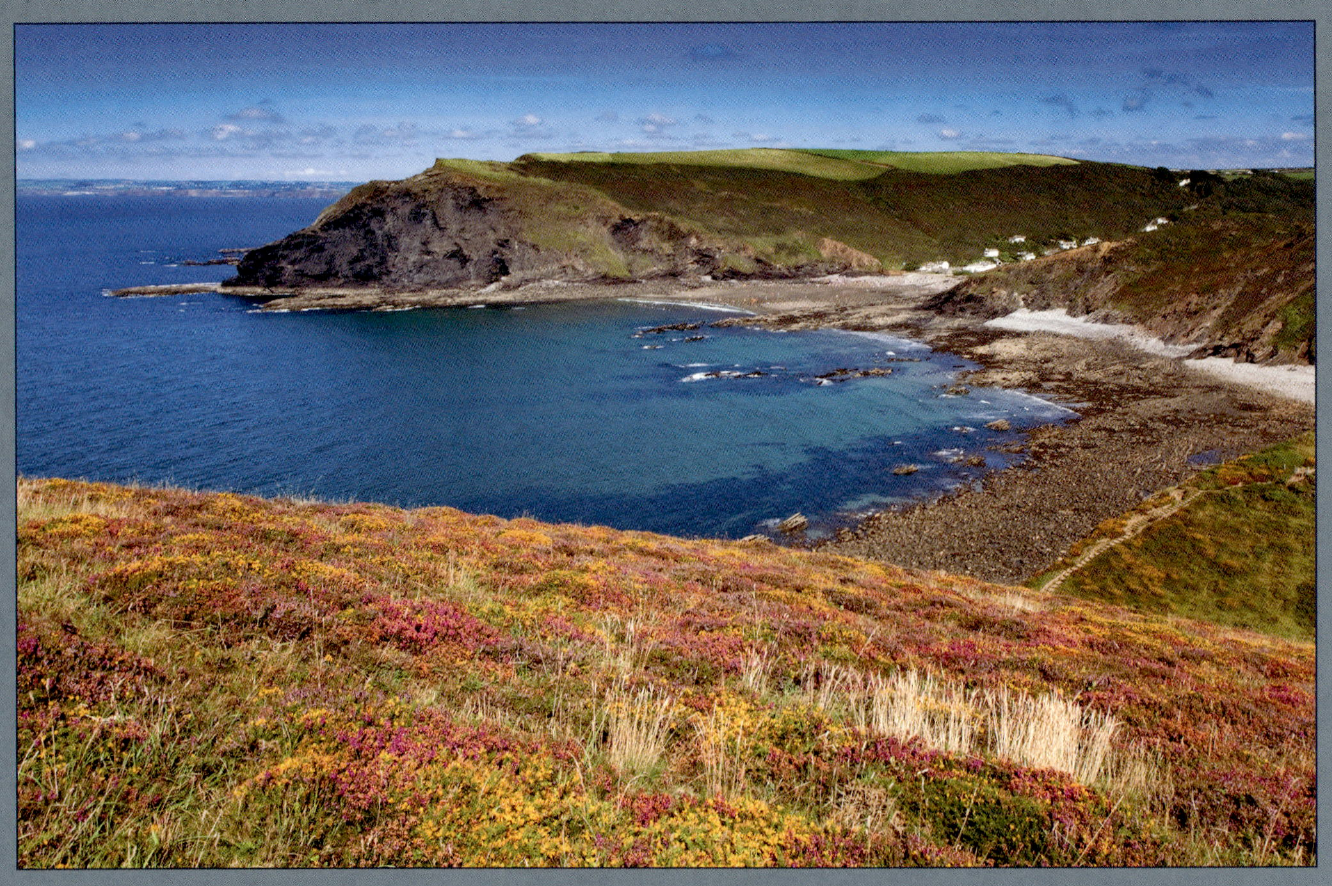

▲ *Crackington Haven*

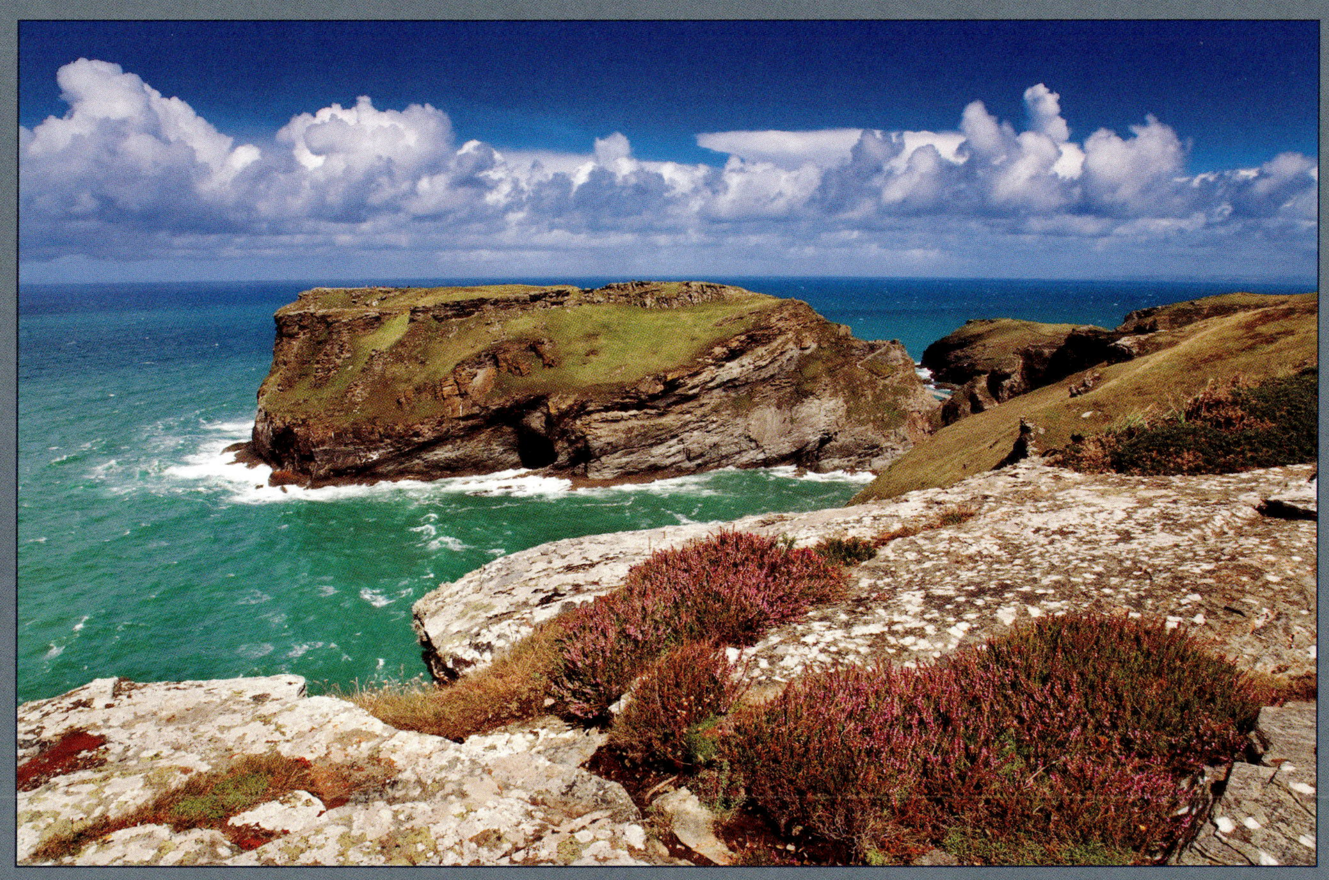

▲ *Tintagel*

Poppy field, West Pentire ▶

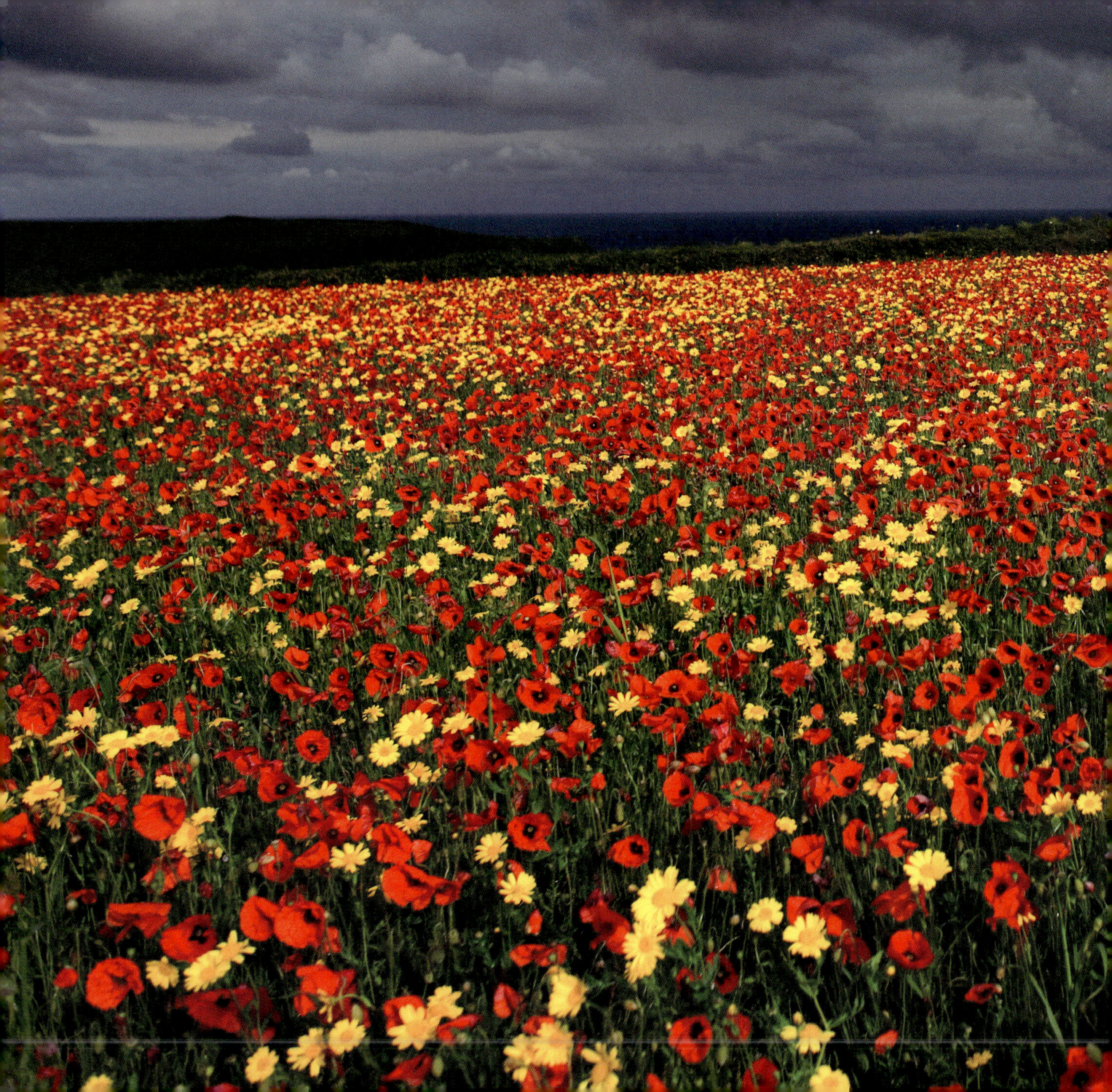

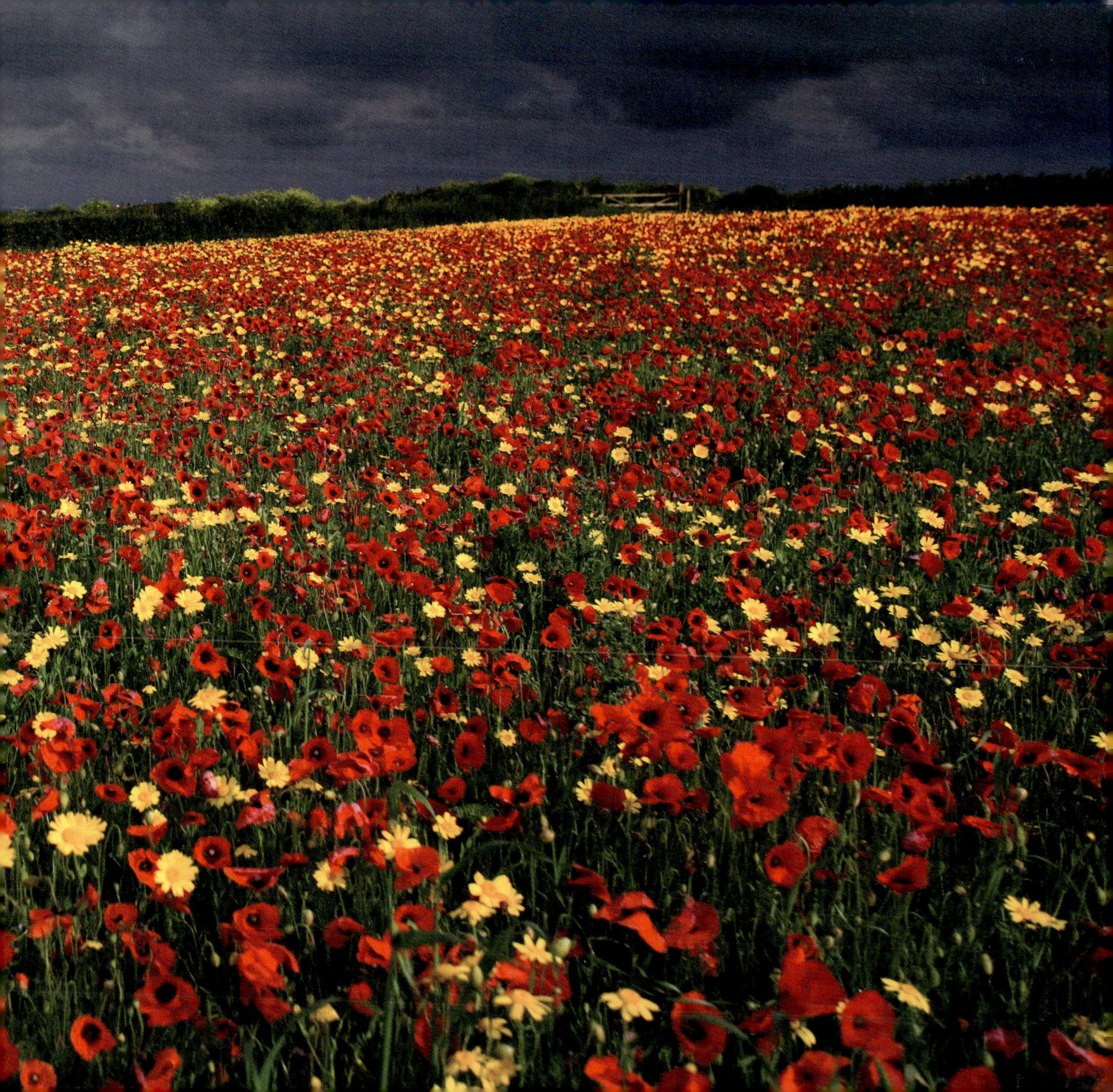

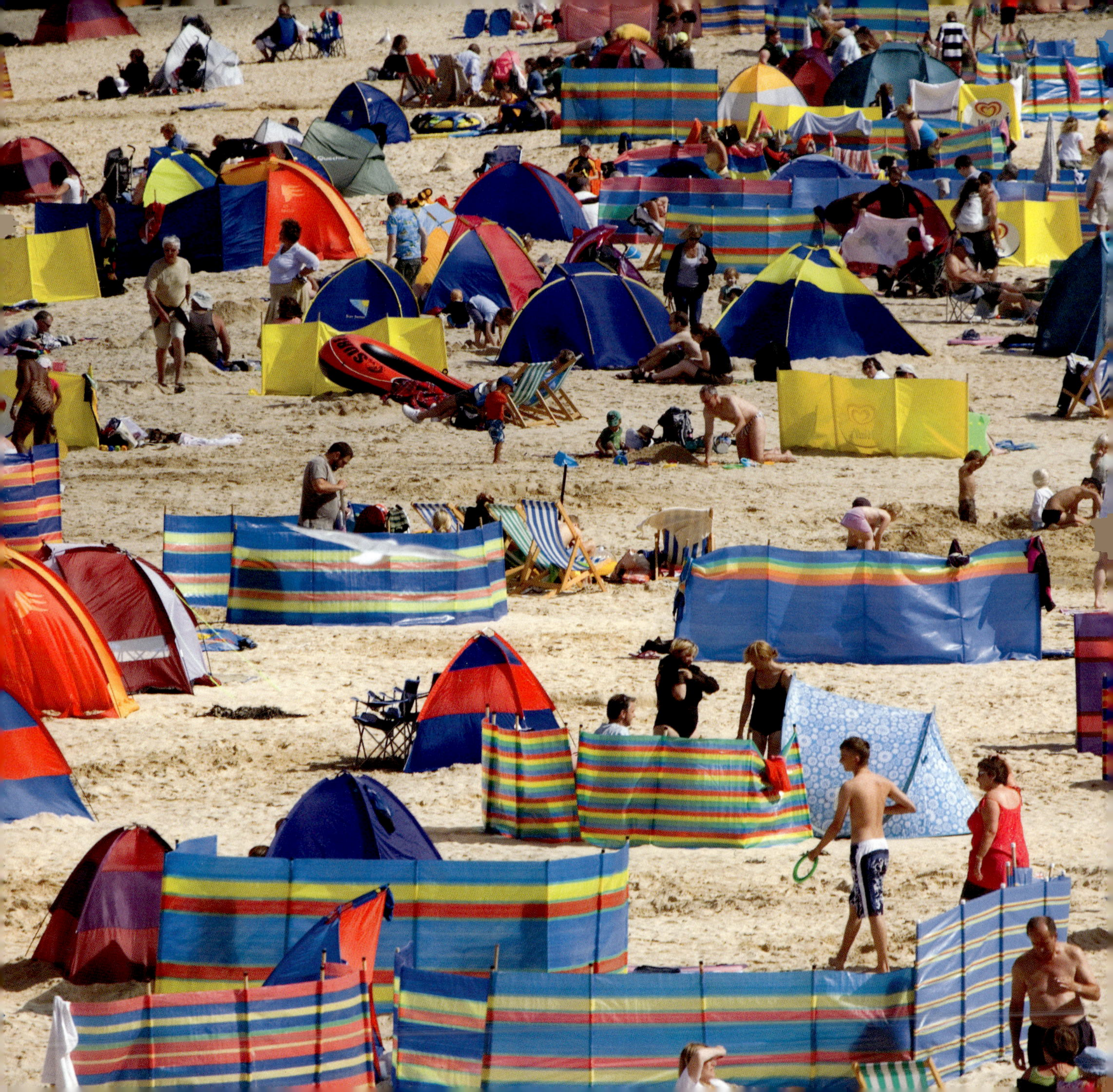

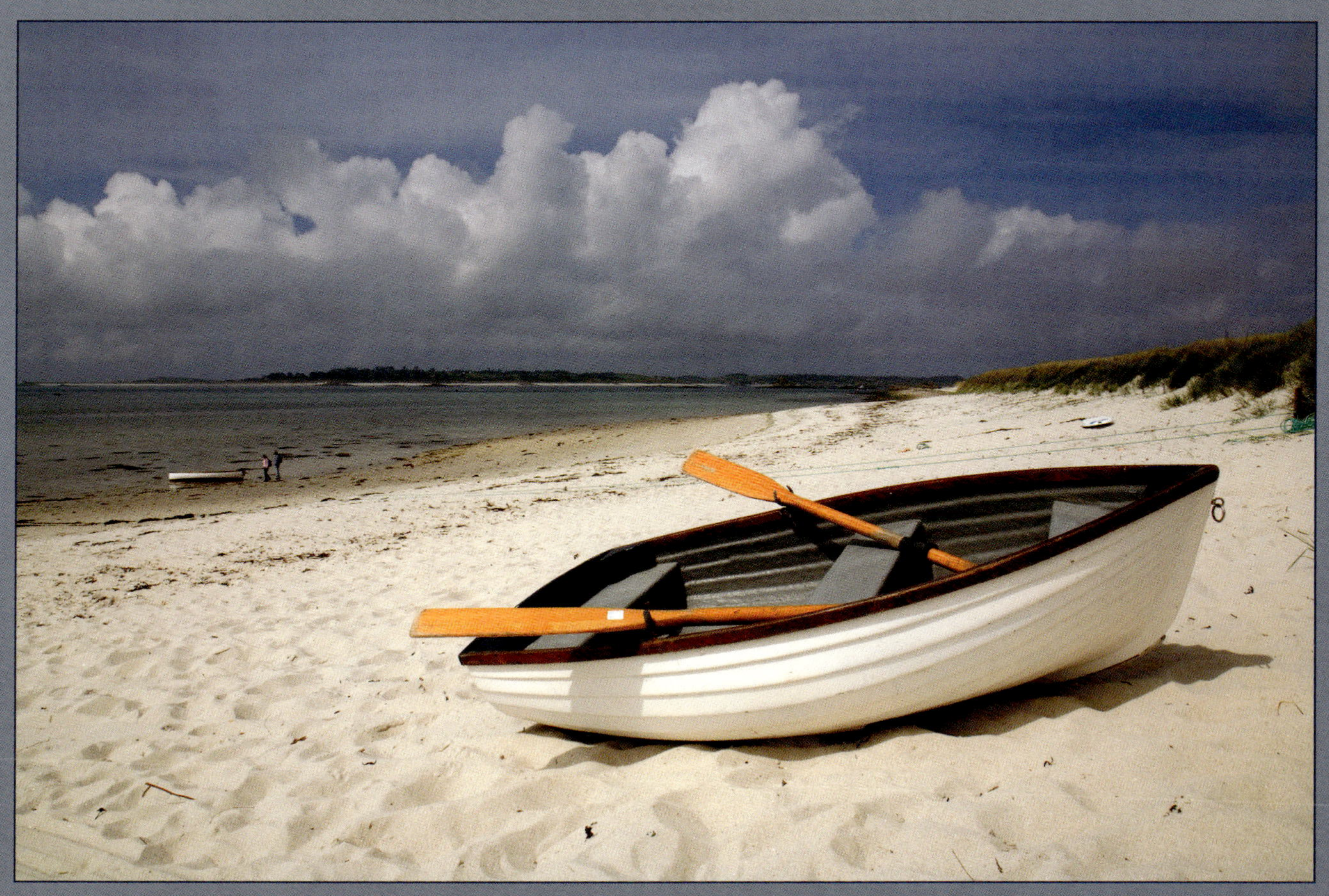

▲ *St Martin's, Isles of Scilly*
◀ *Porthminster Beach, St Ives*

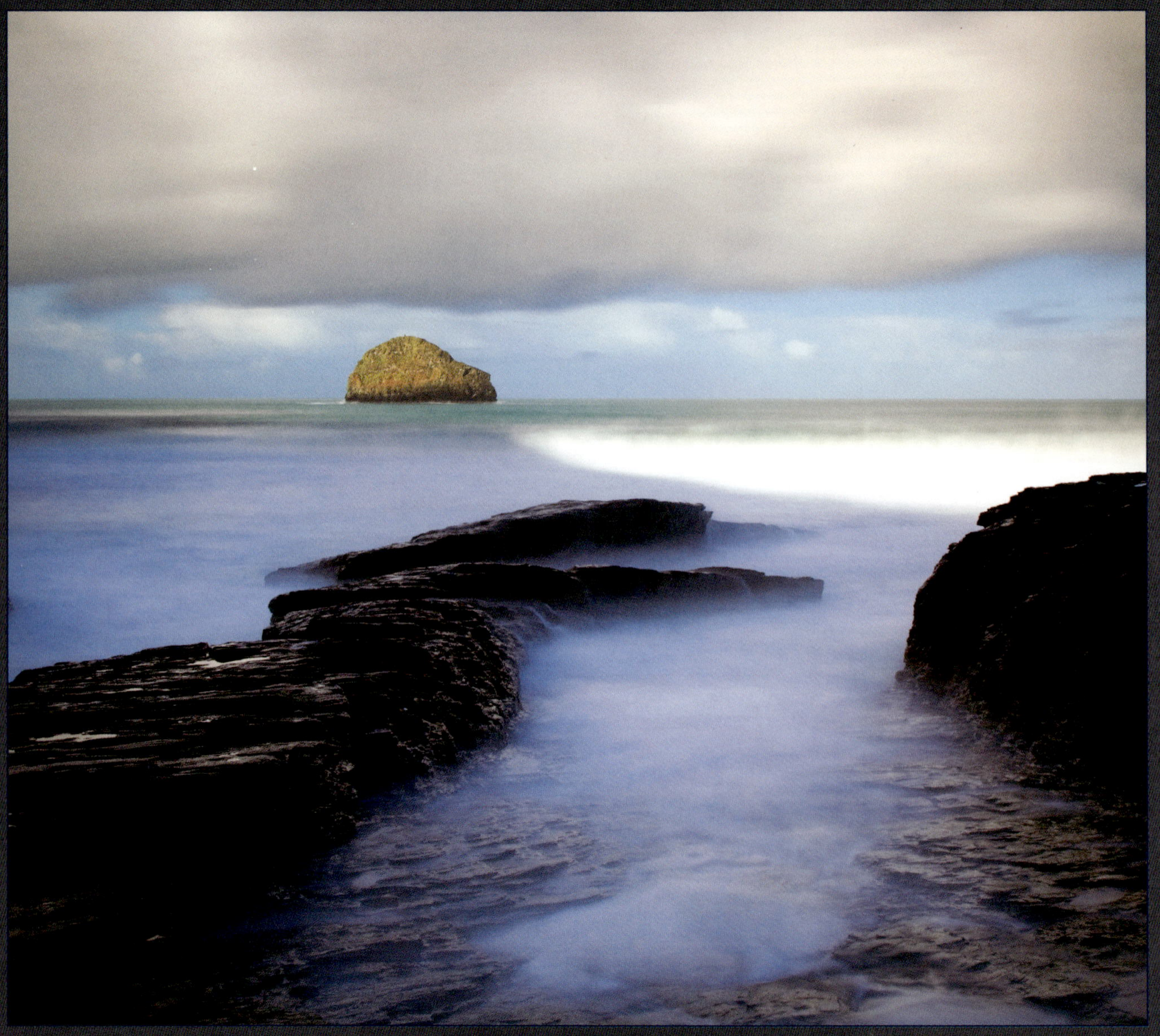

▲ *Gull Rock from Trebarwith Strand*

The Carters from Holywell Bay ▶

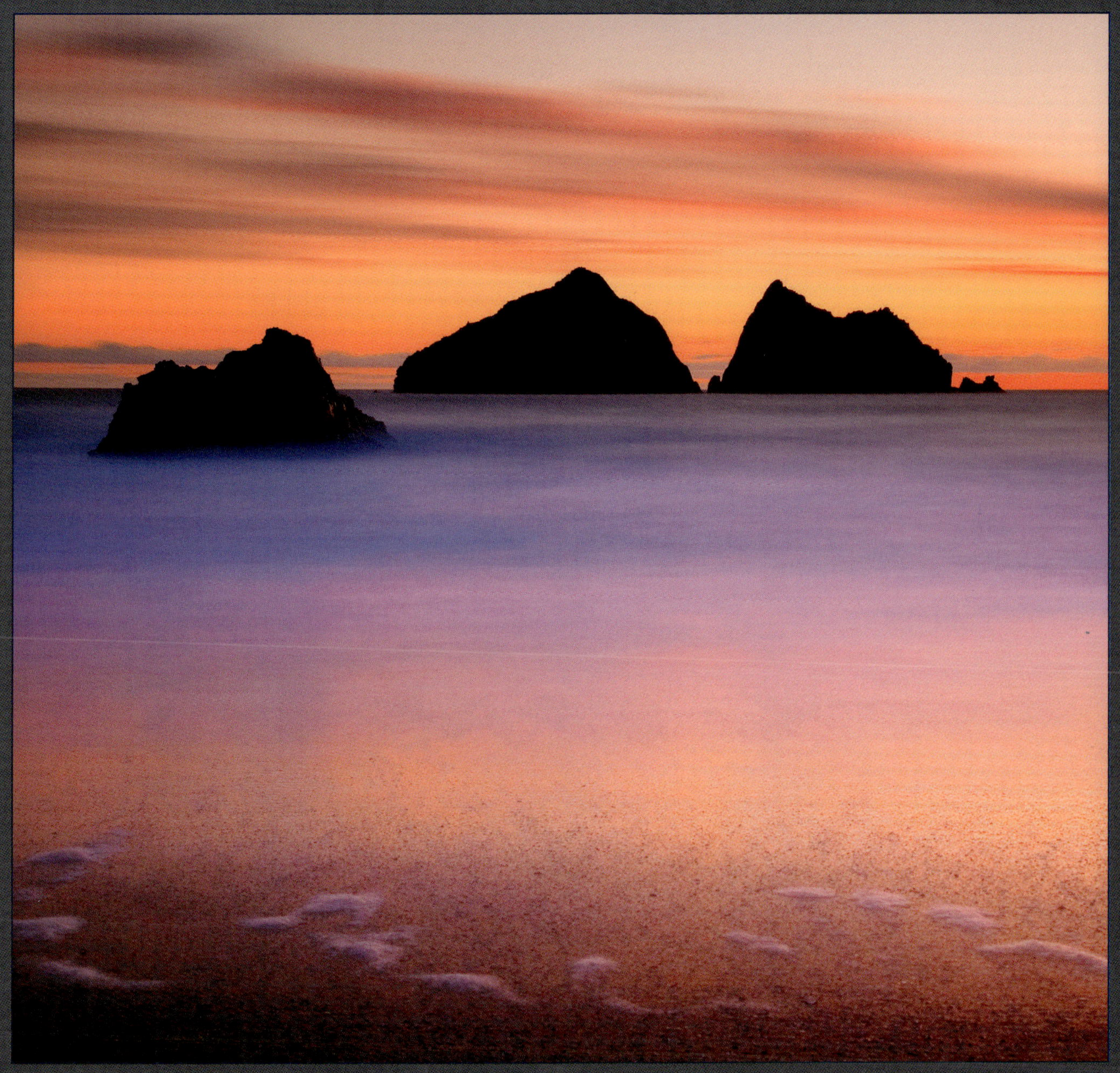

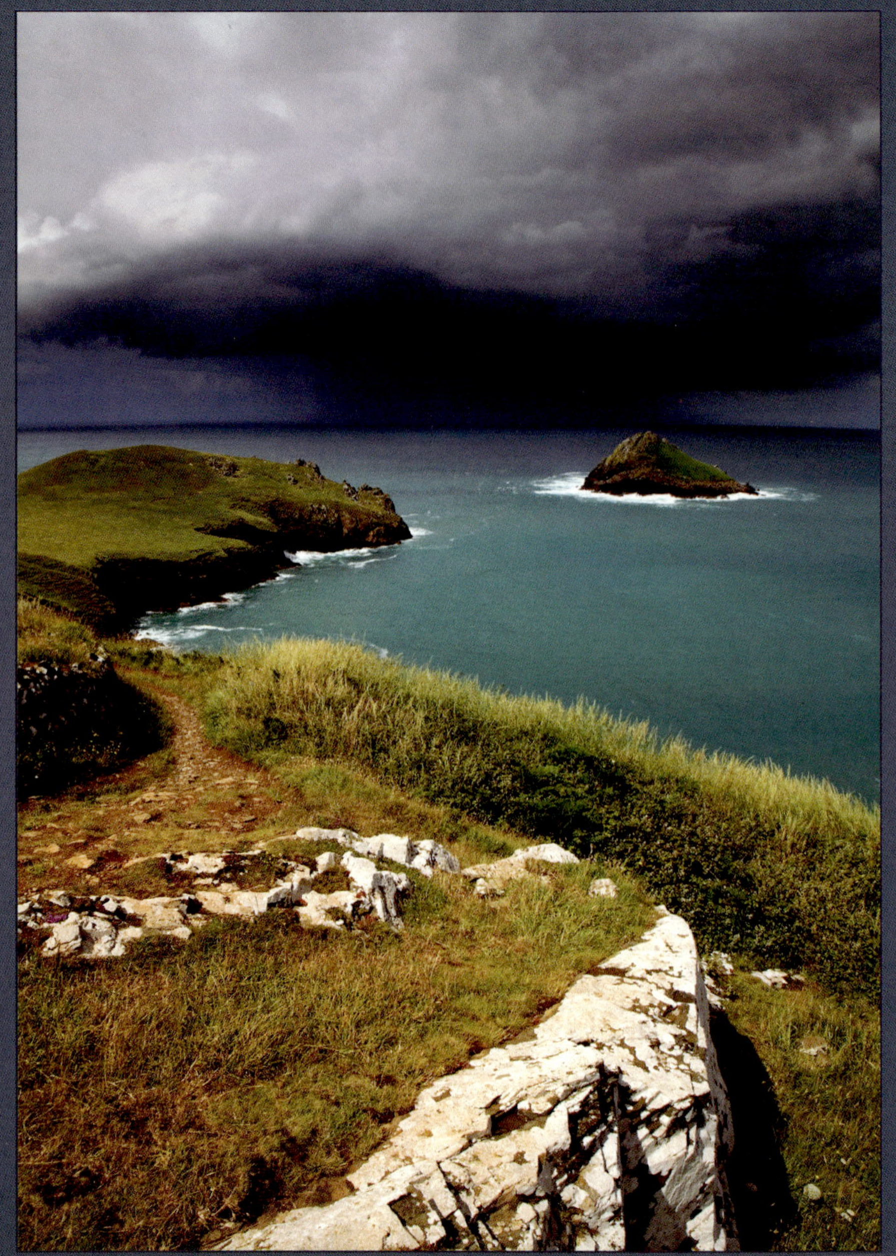

◄ *The Mouls,*
near Polzeath

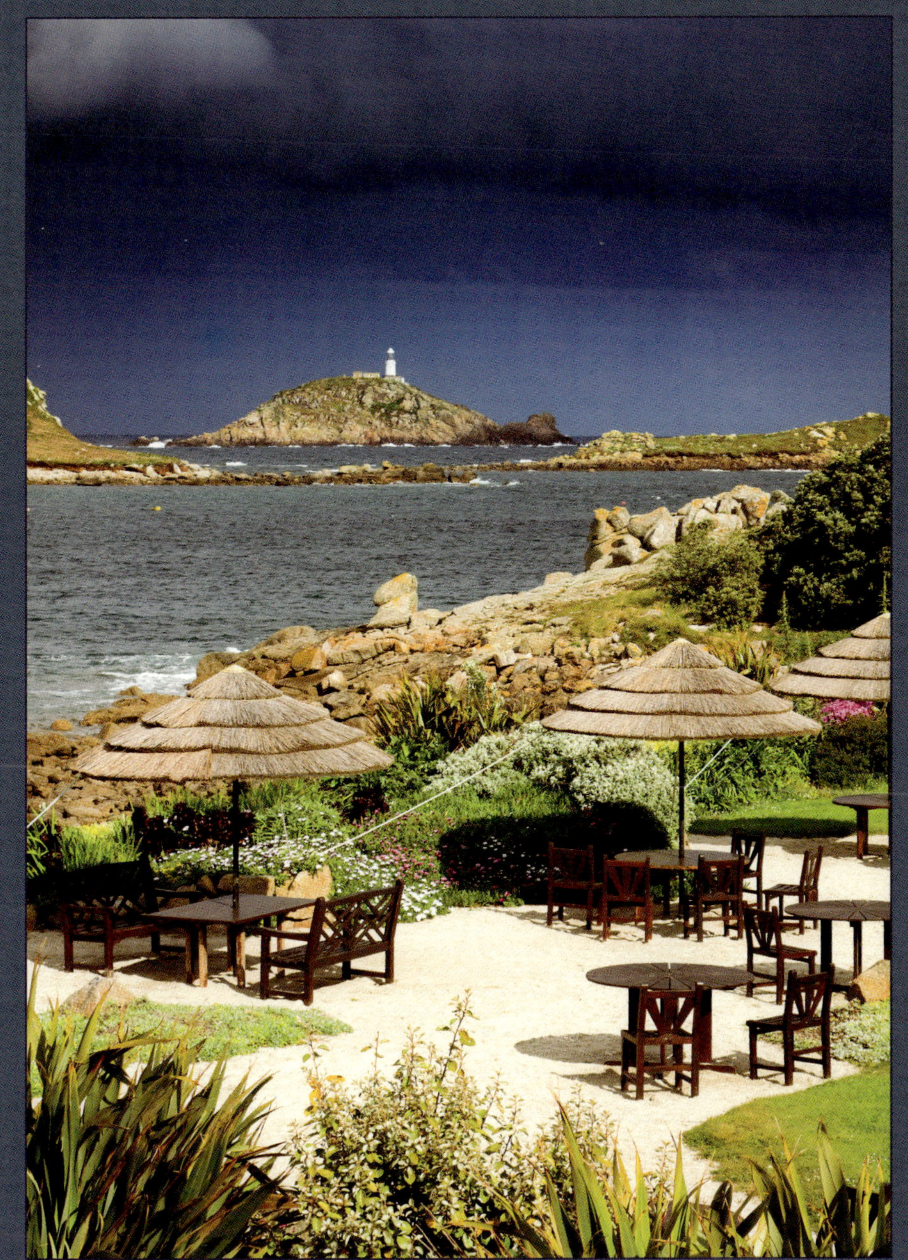

*Round Island,
from St Martin's,
Isles of Scilly* ▶

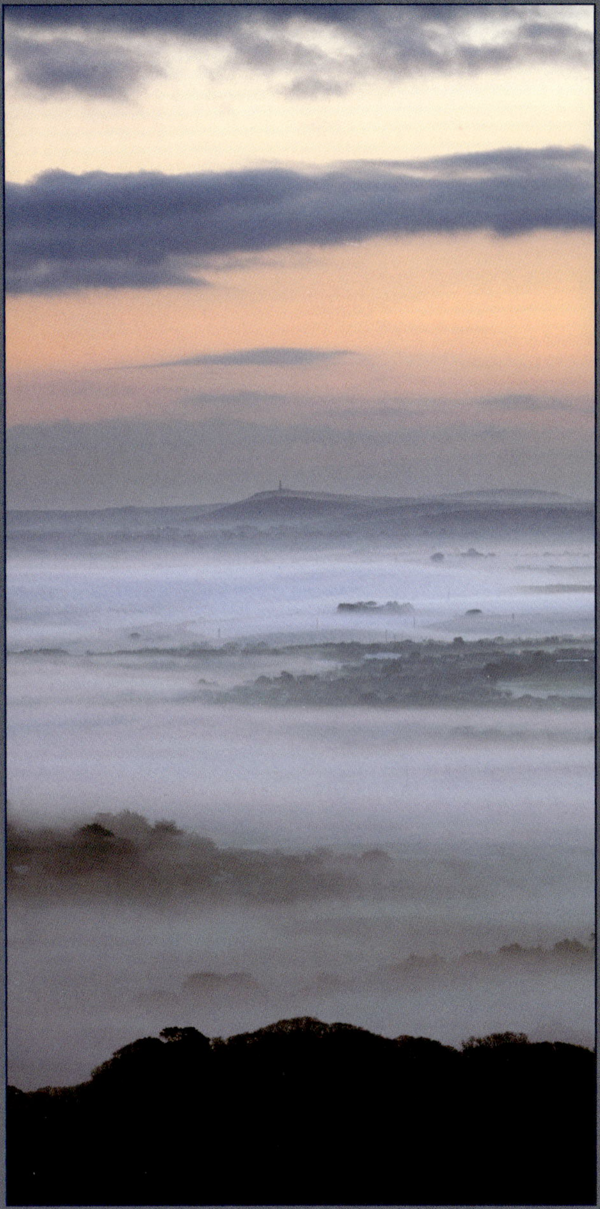

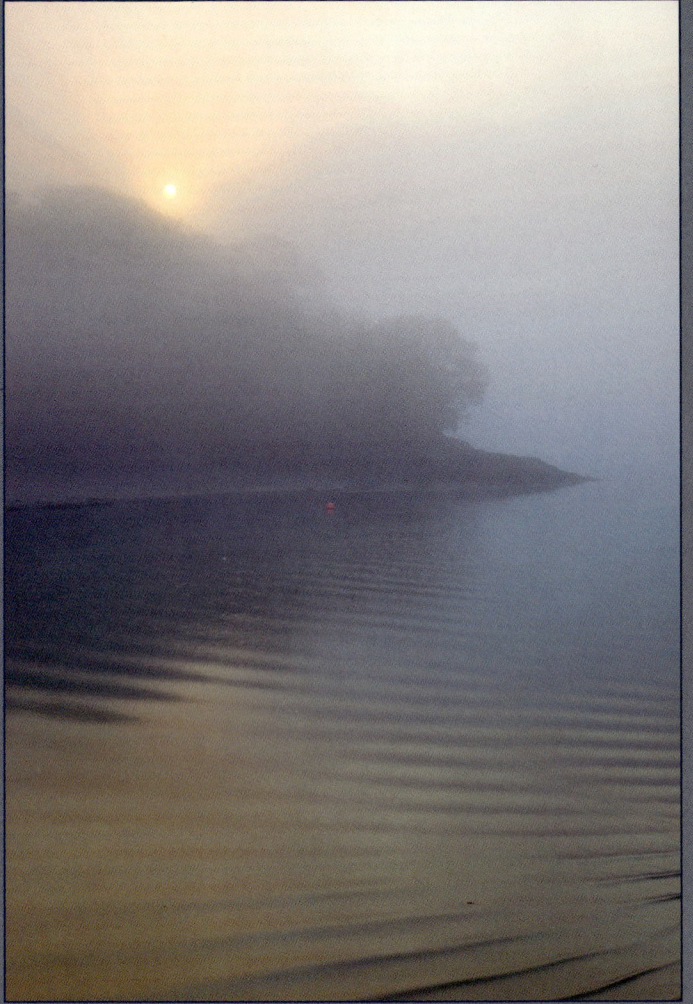

▲ Roundwood Quay, near Trelissick
◄ From Trencrom to Carn Brea

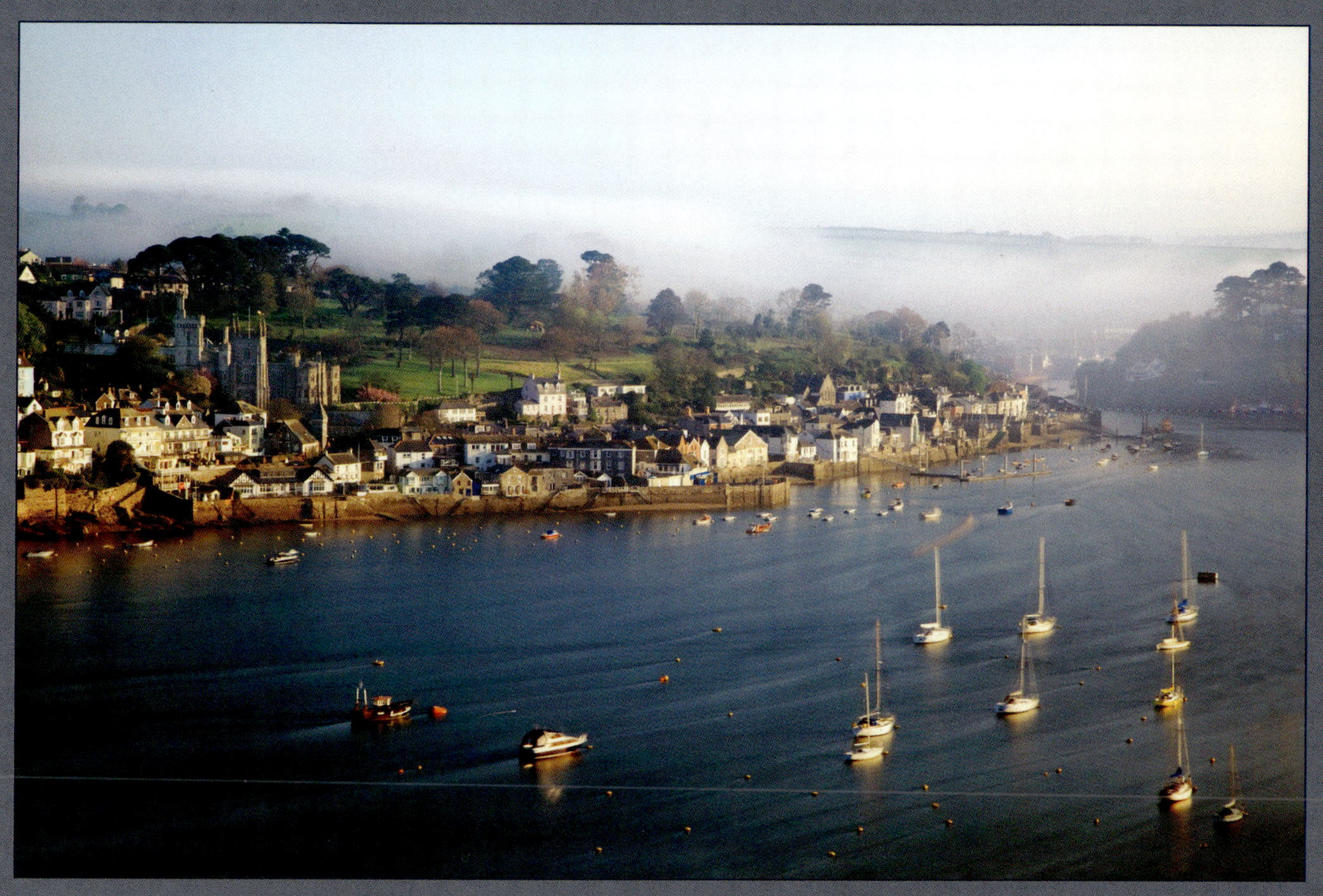

▲ *Fowey from Polruan*

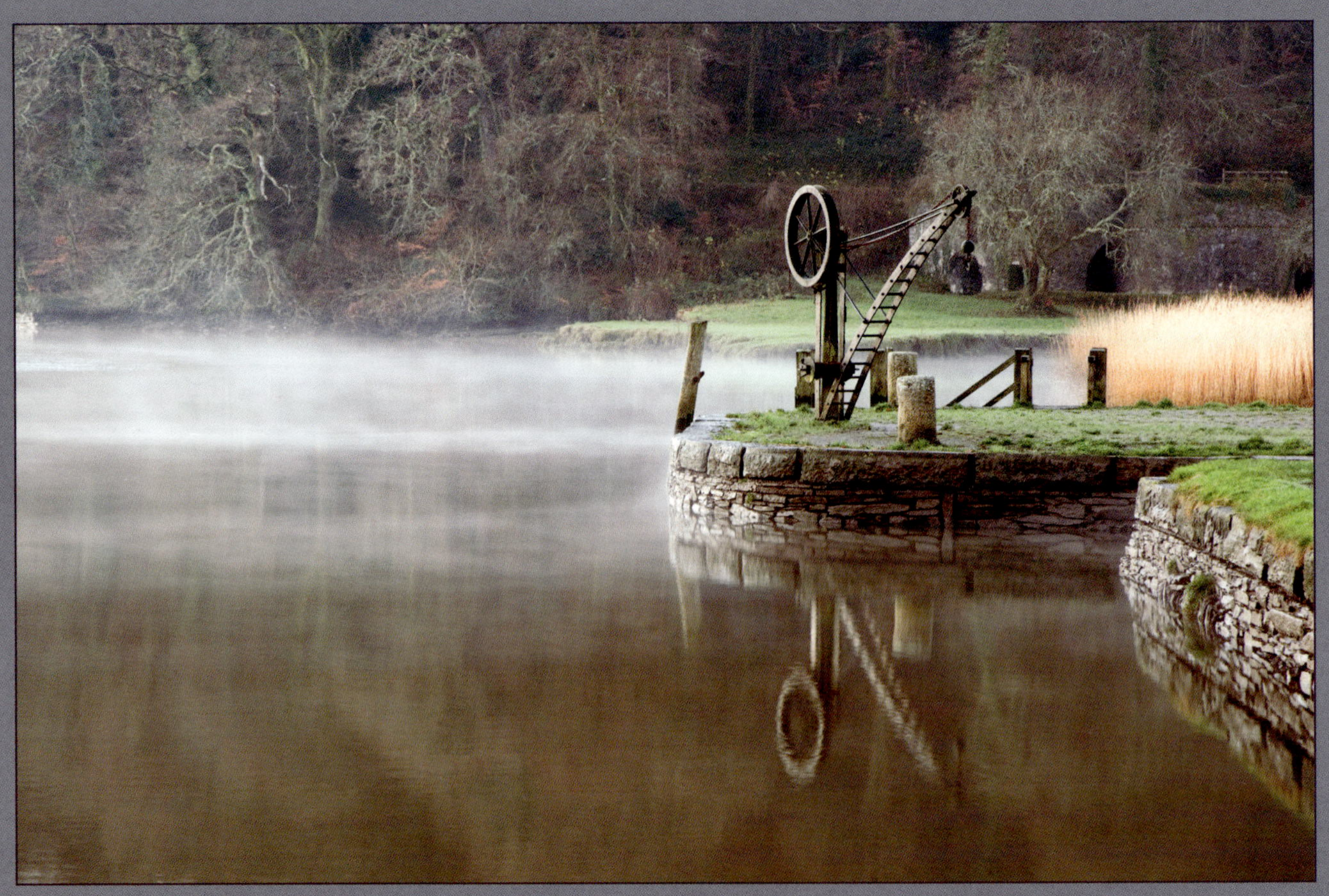

▲ Cotehele Quay

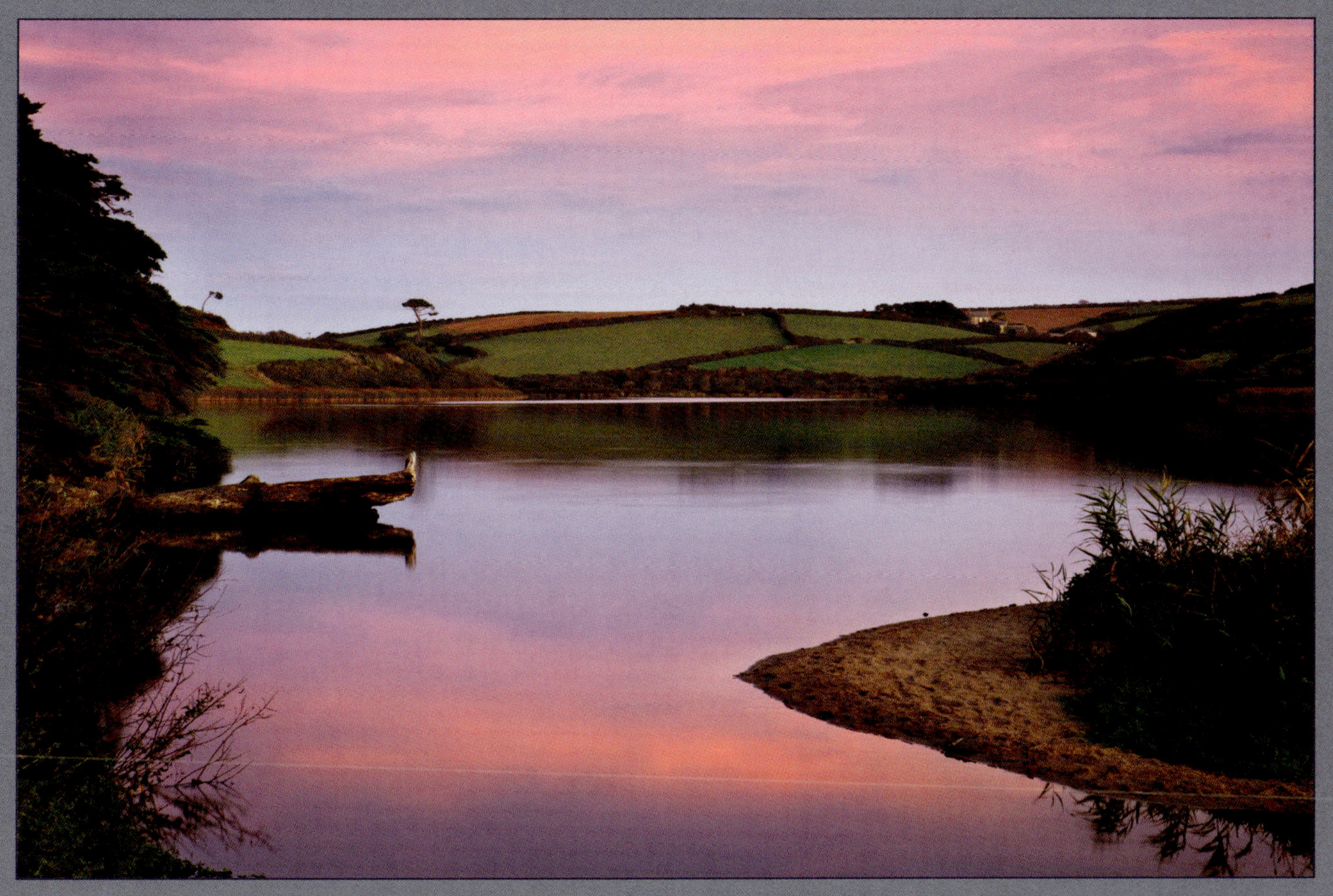

▲ *Loe Pool*

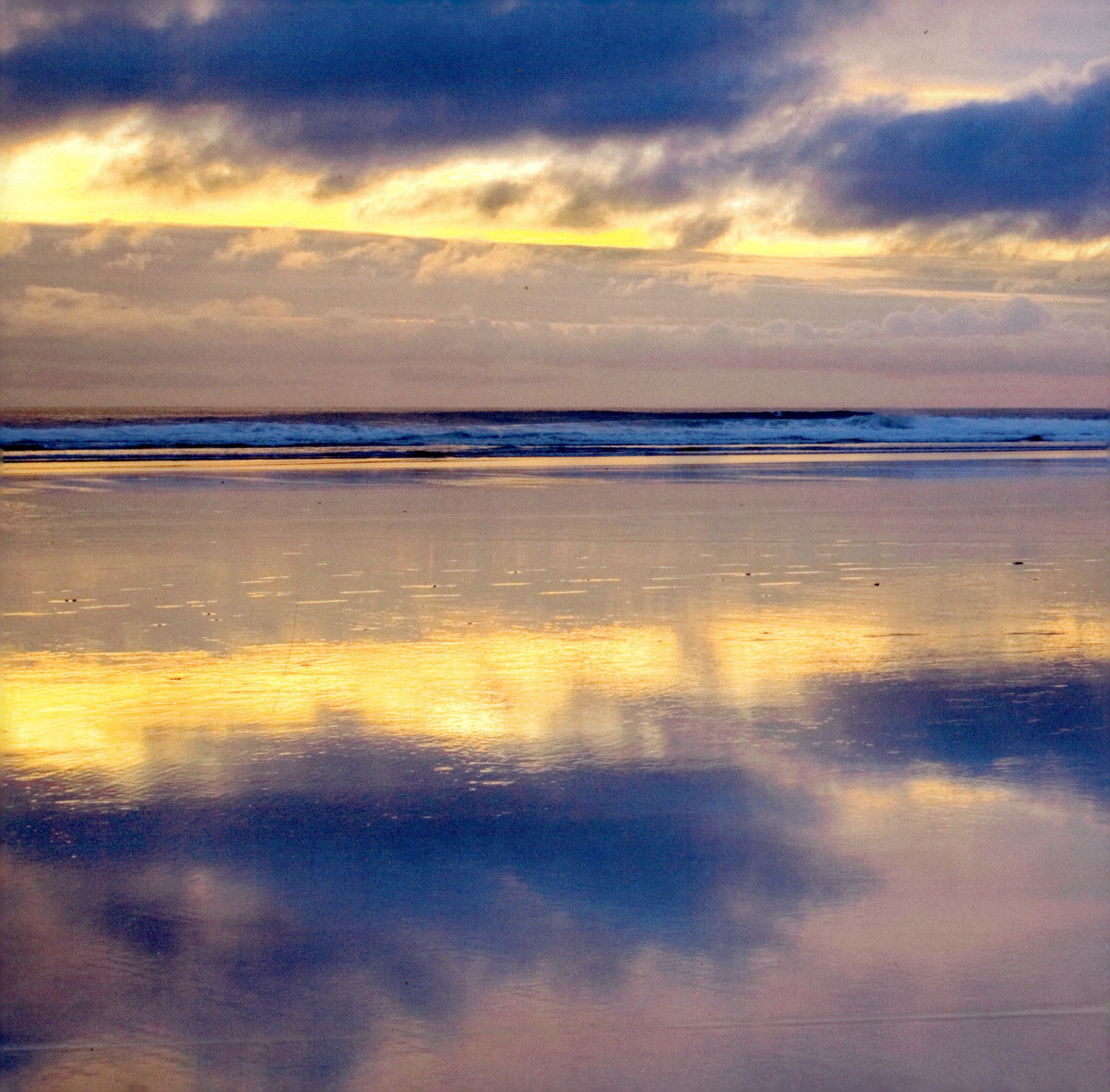

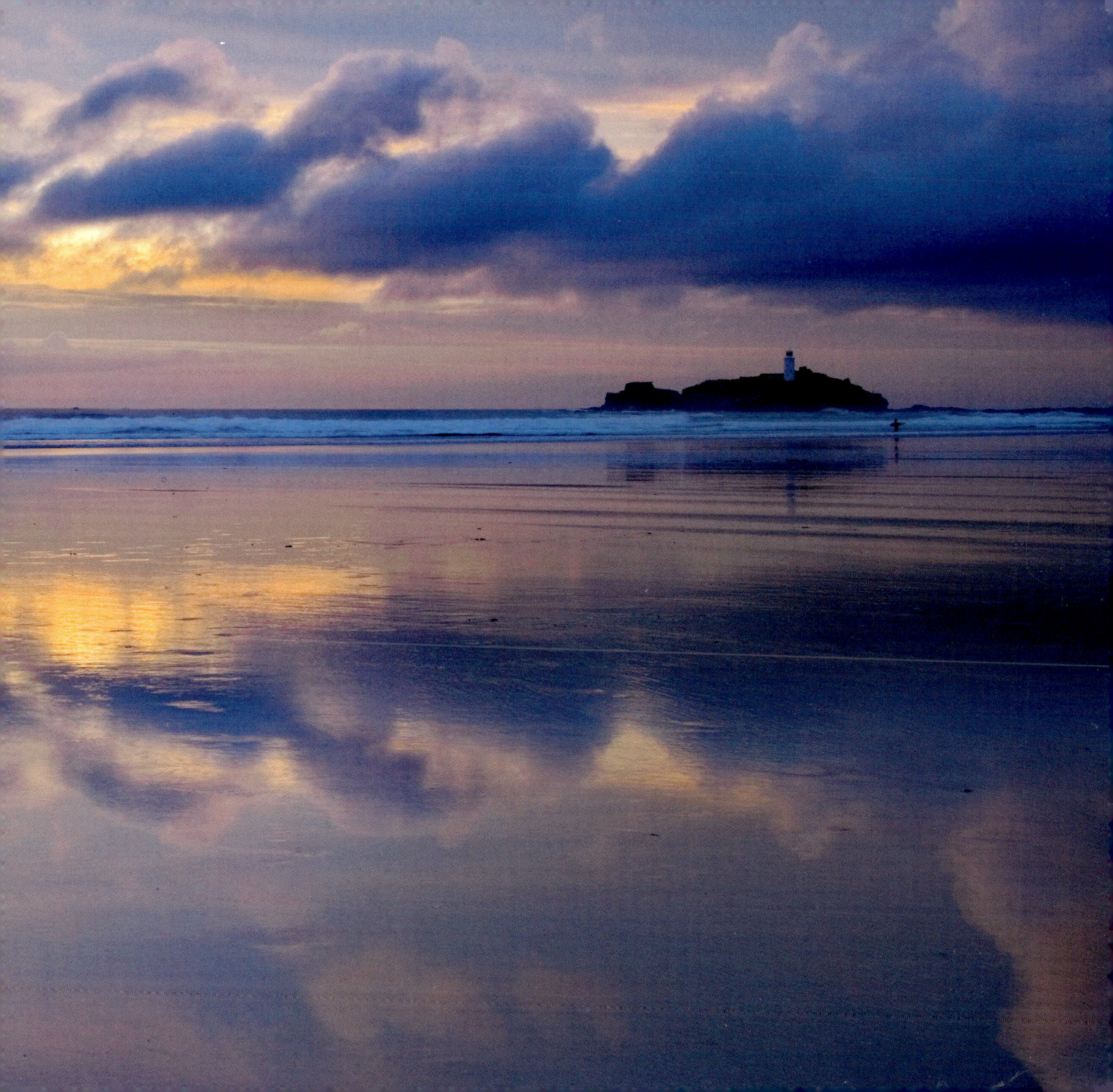

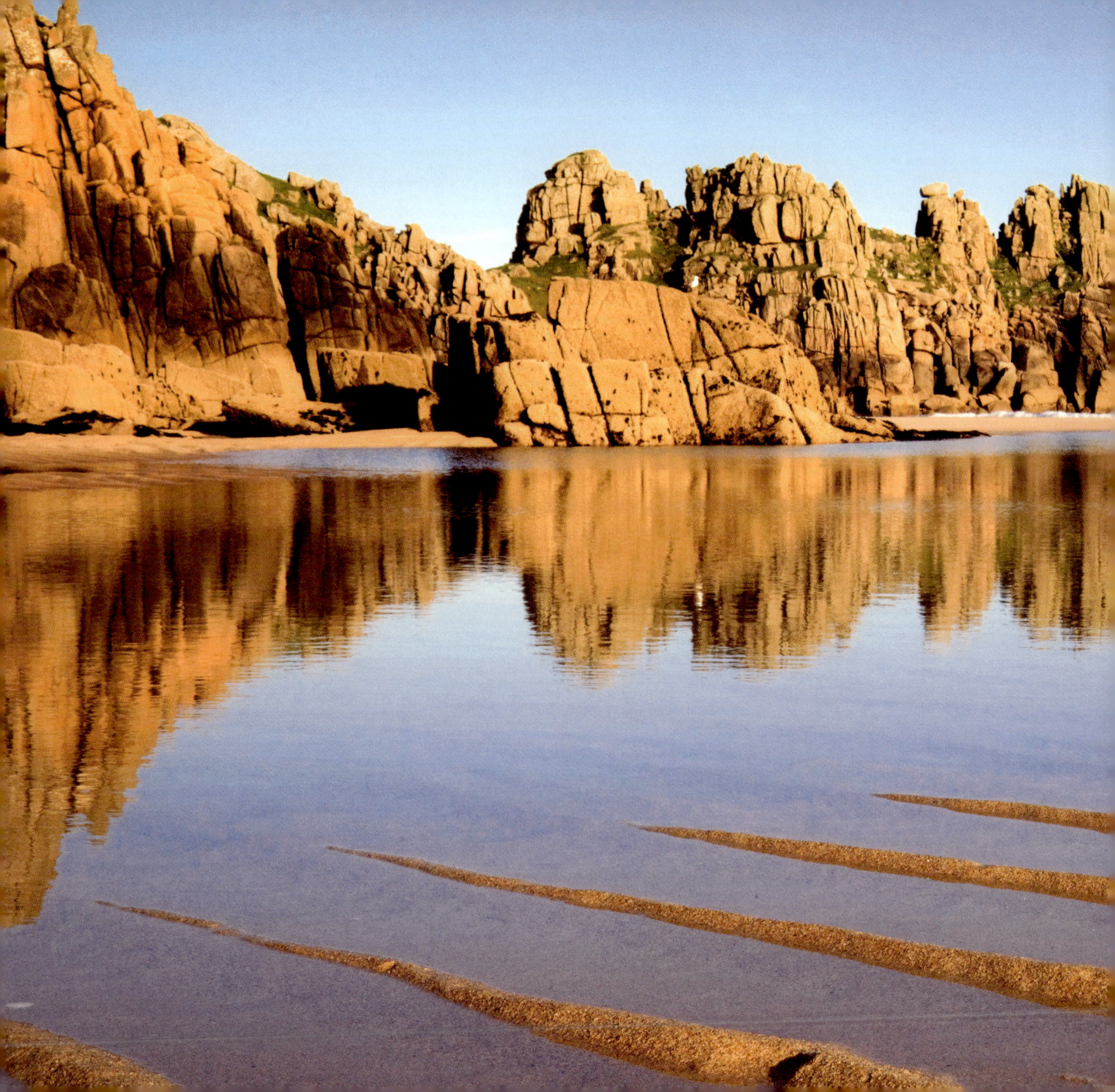

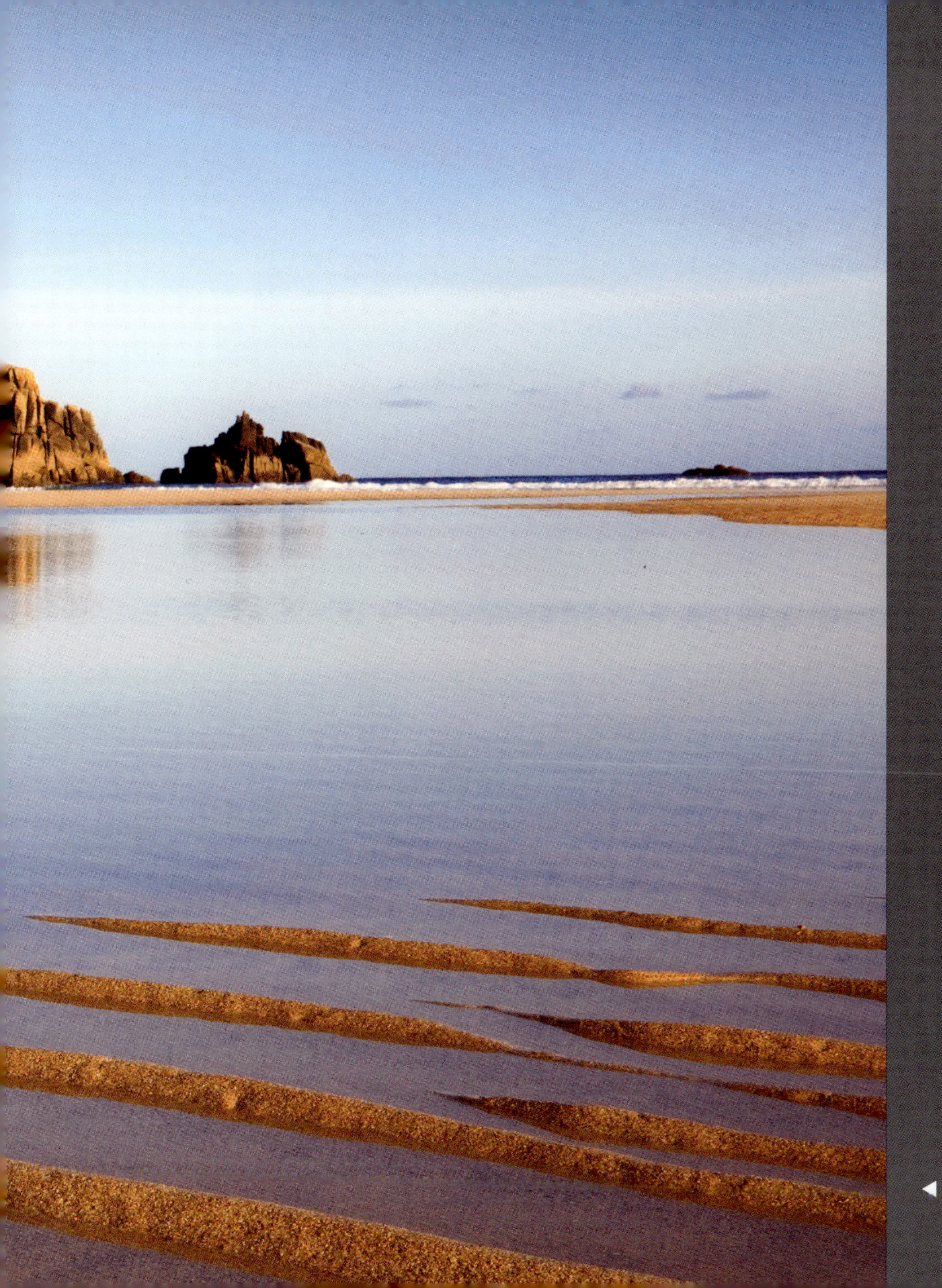

◄ Logan Rock

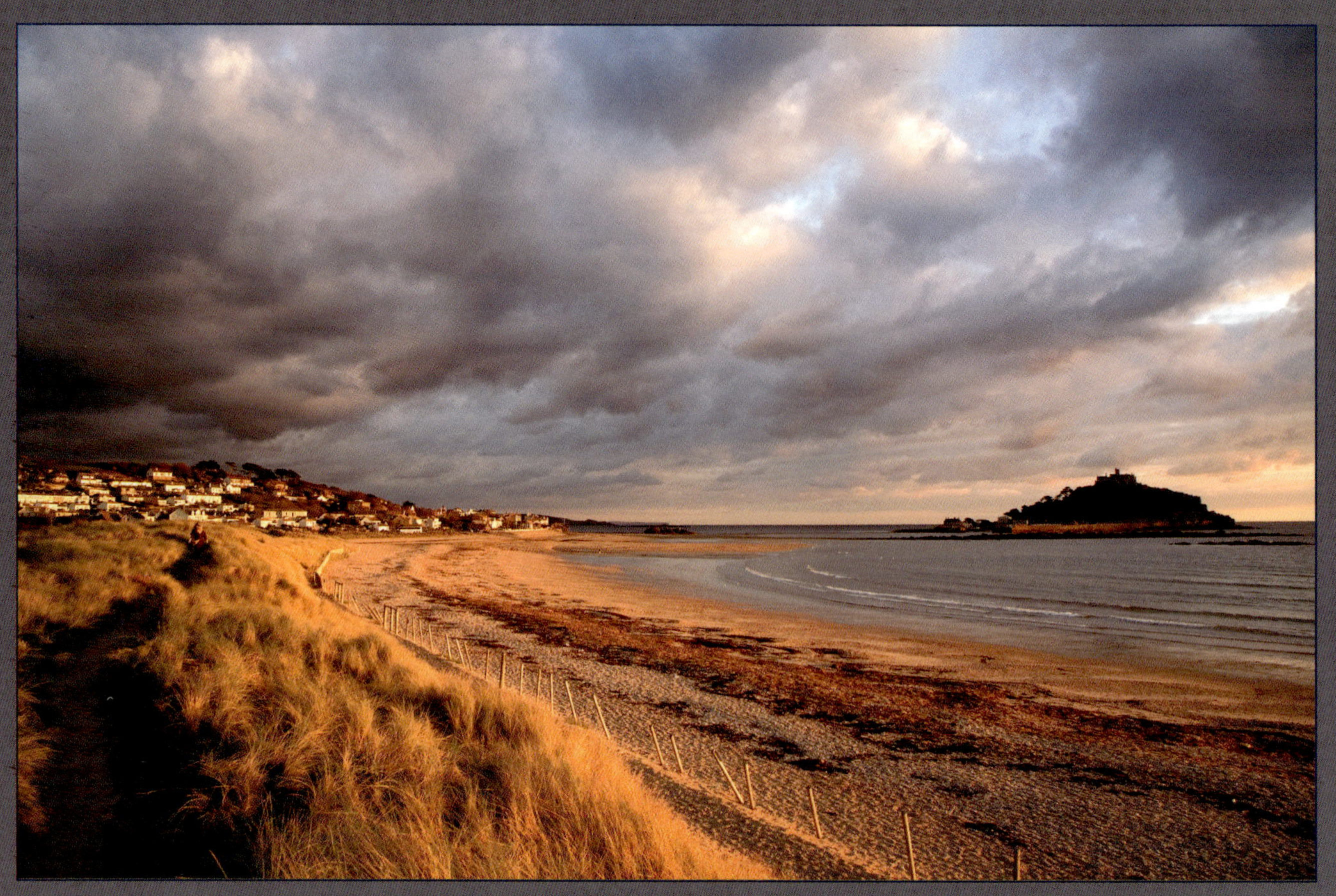

▲ *St Michael's Mount and Marazion*

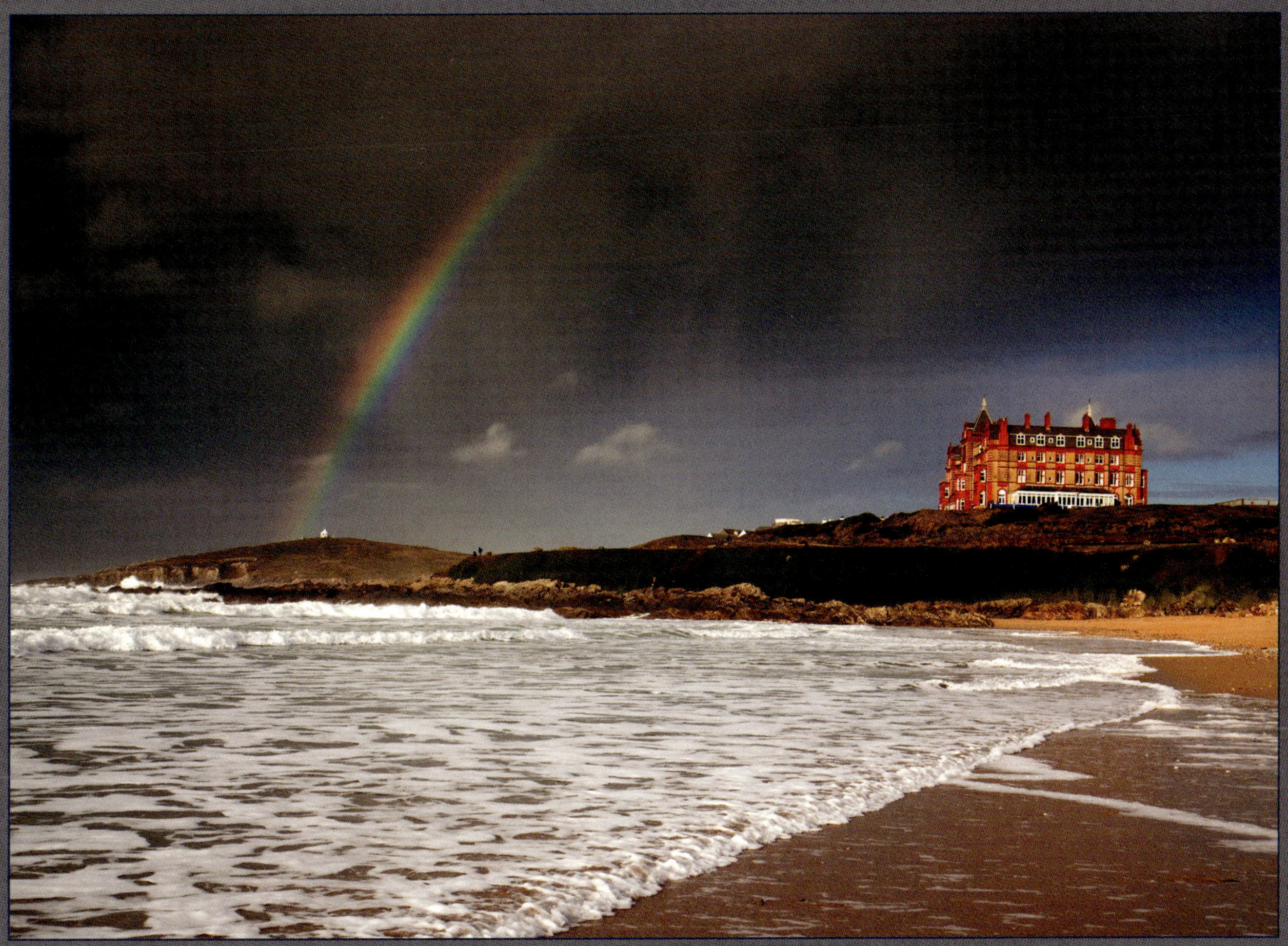

▲ *Fistral Beach*

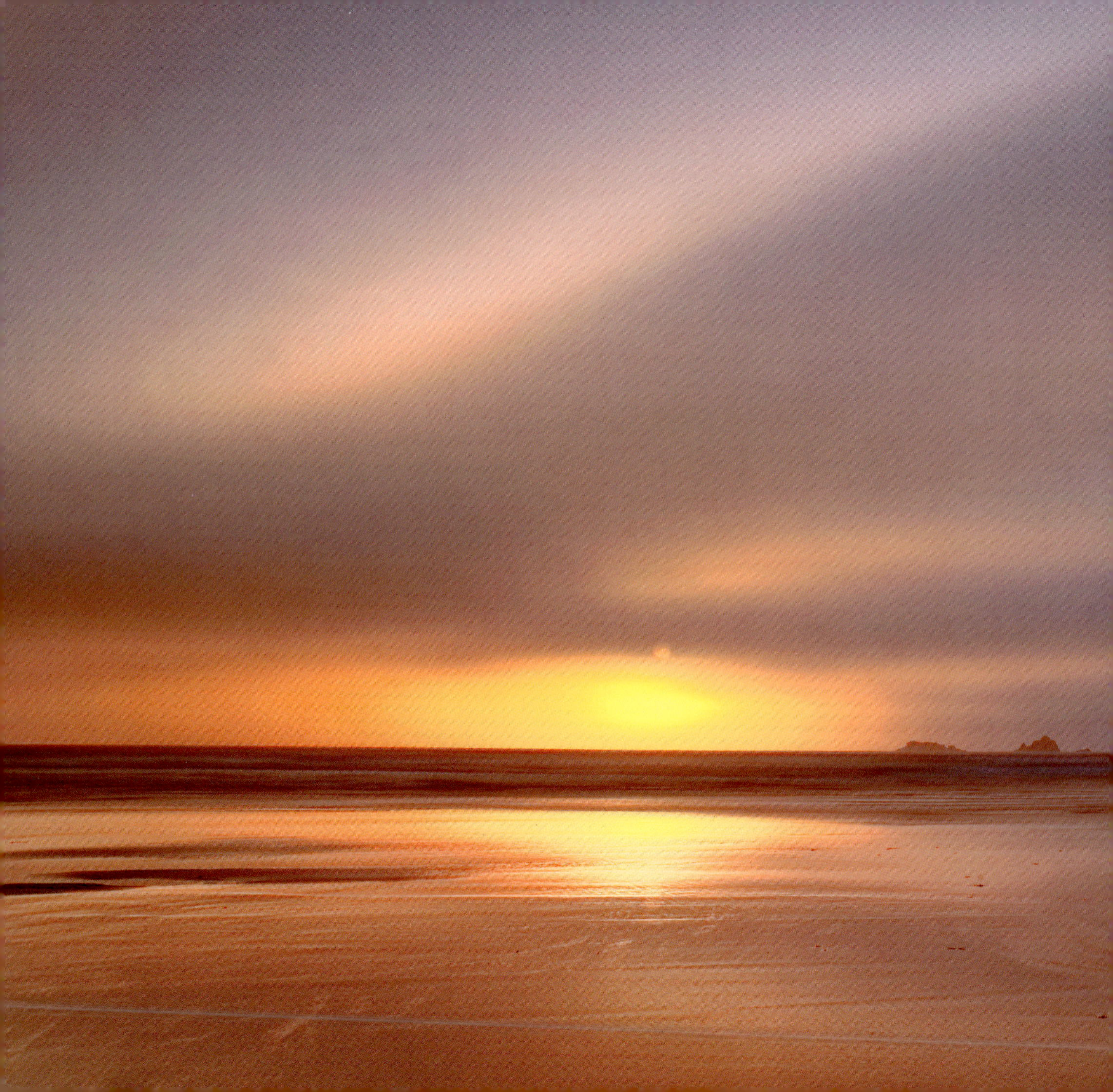

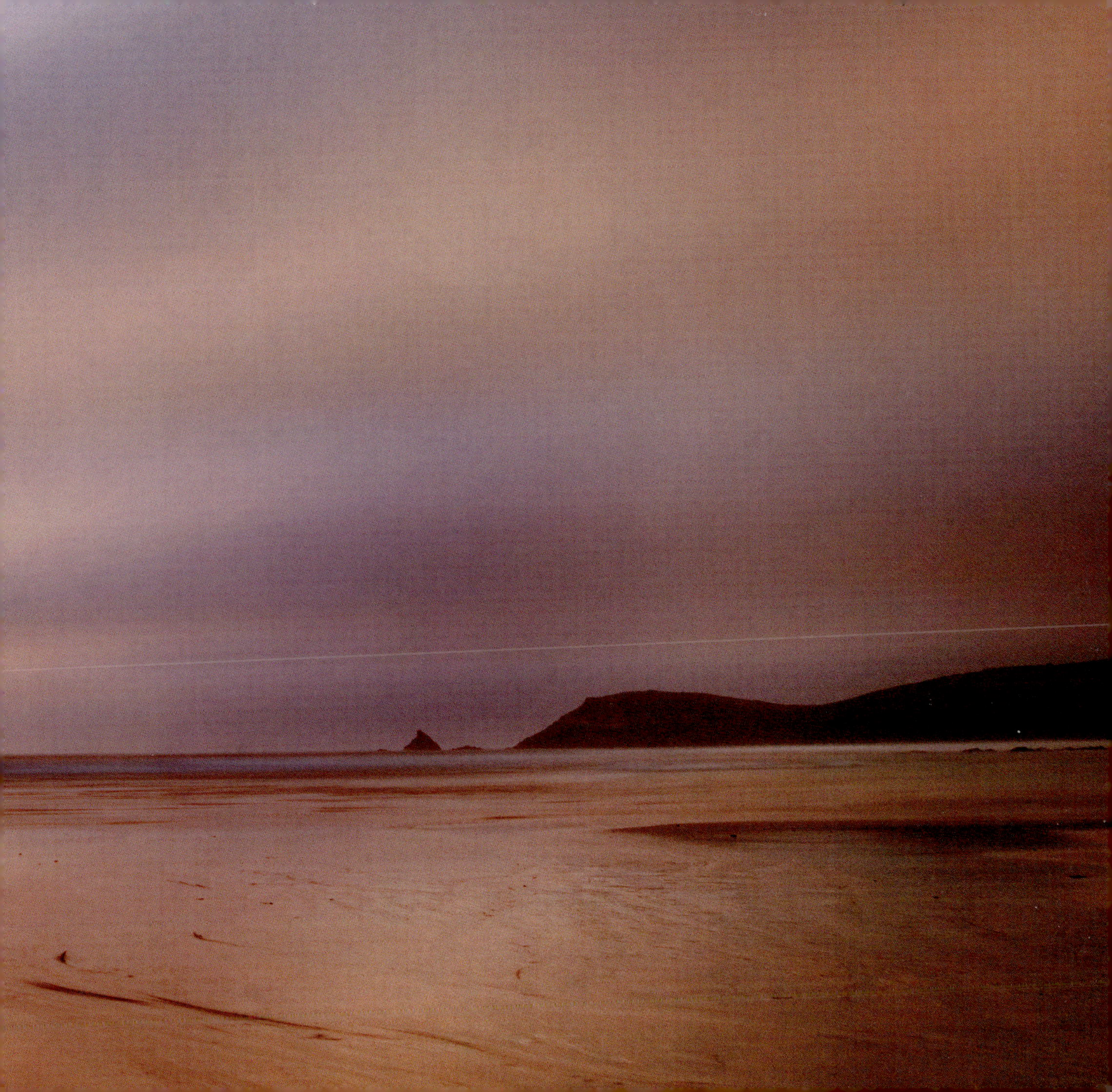

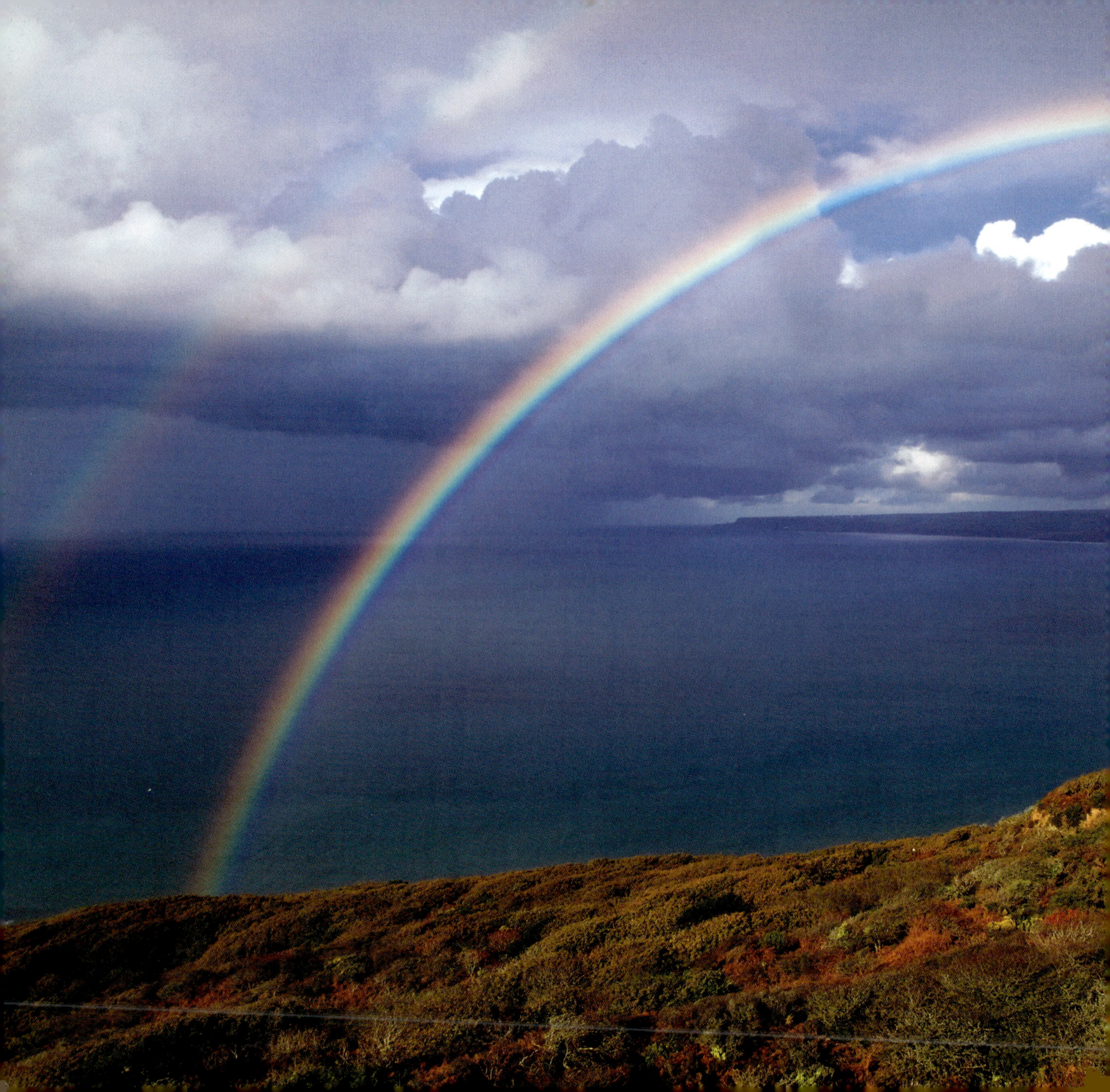

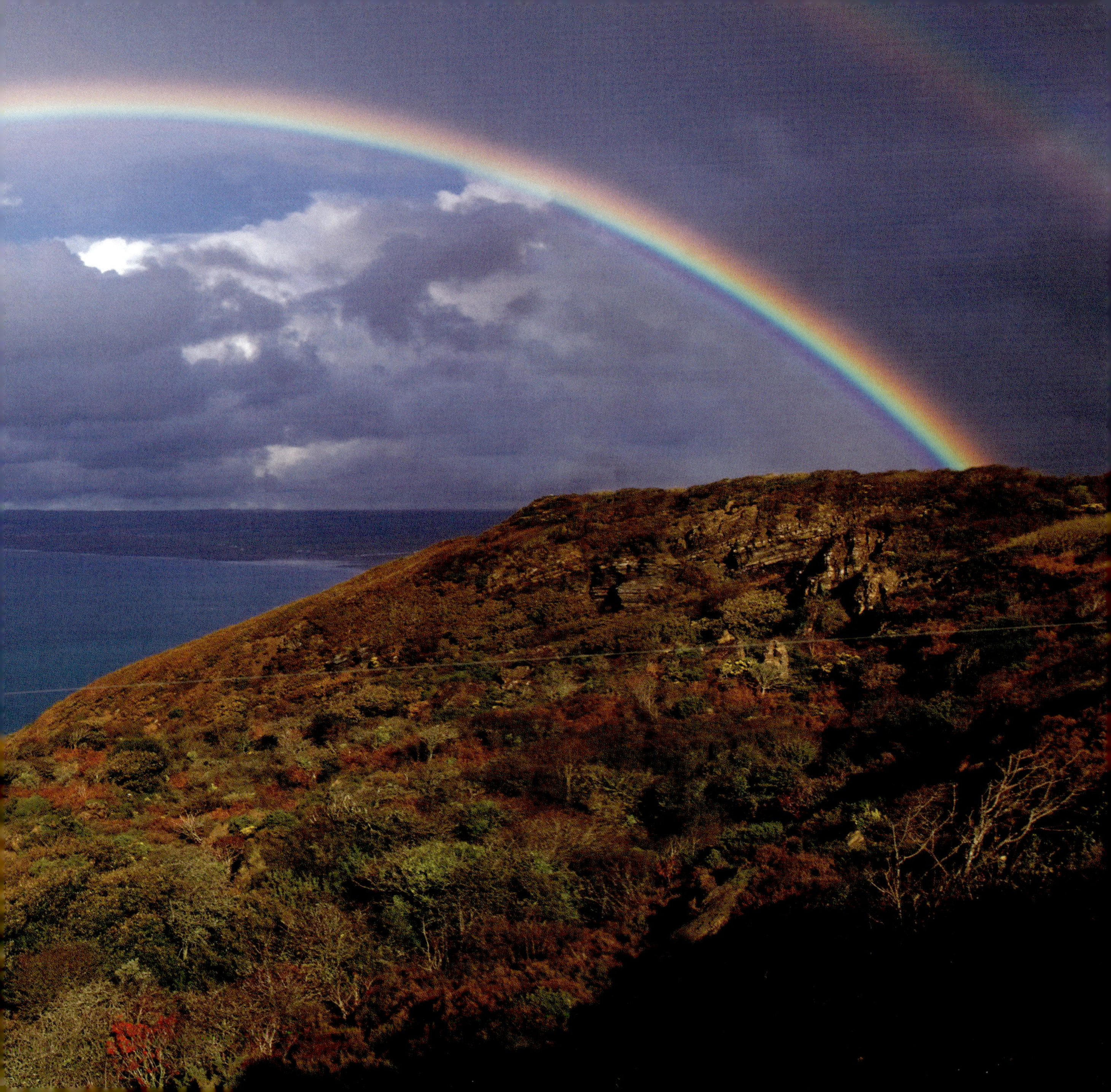

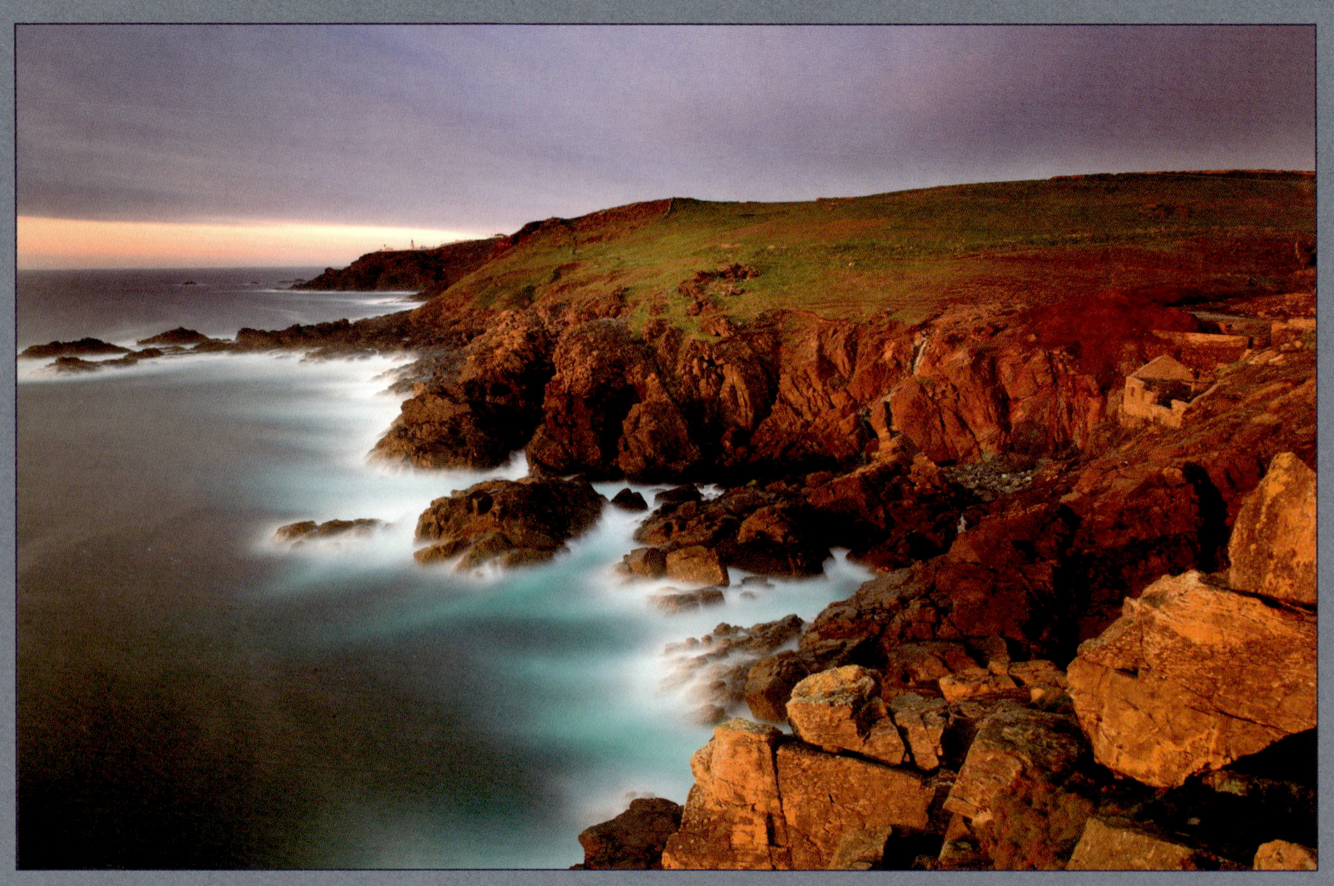

▲ Trewellard Zawn

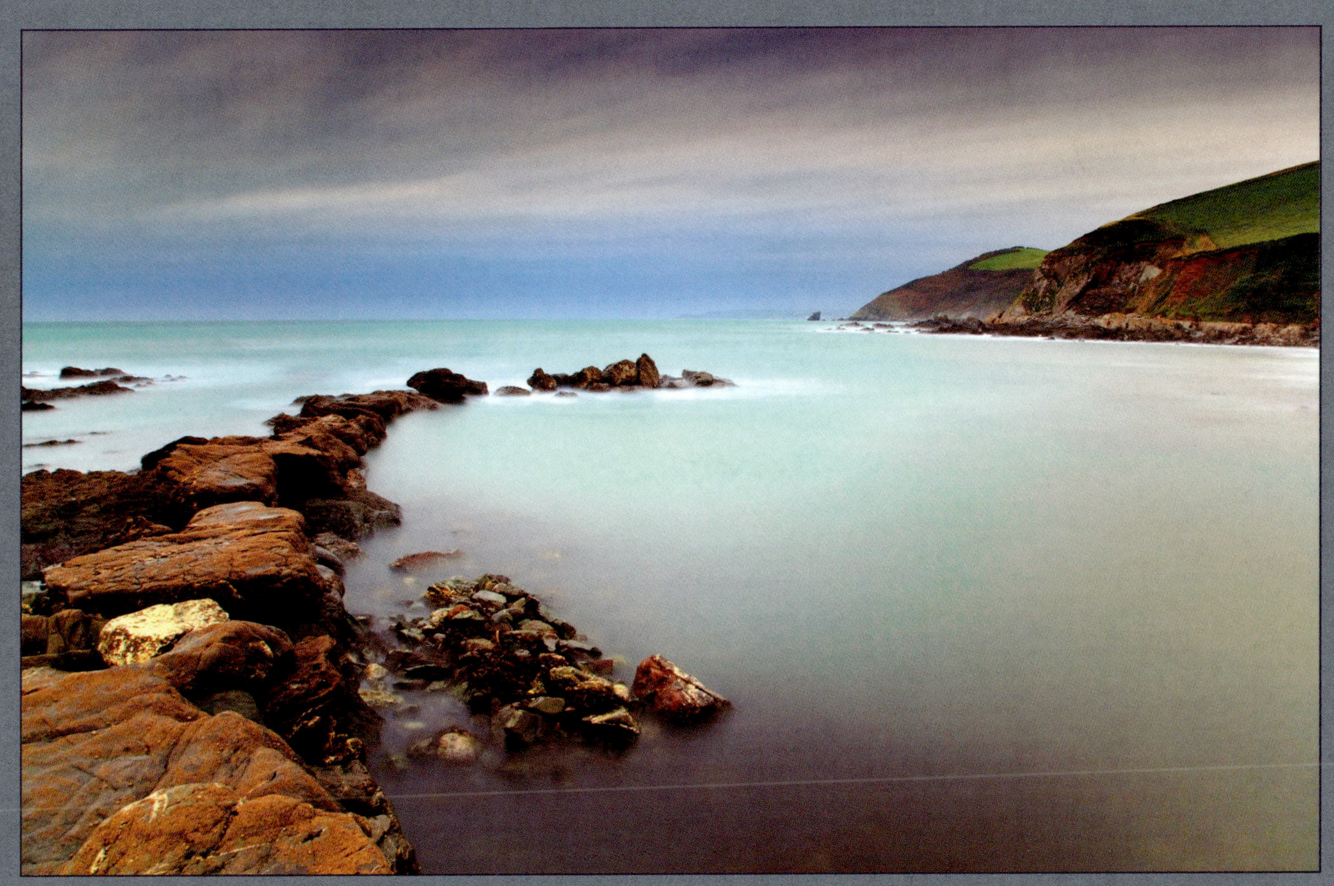

Duckpool ▶

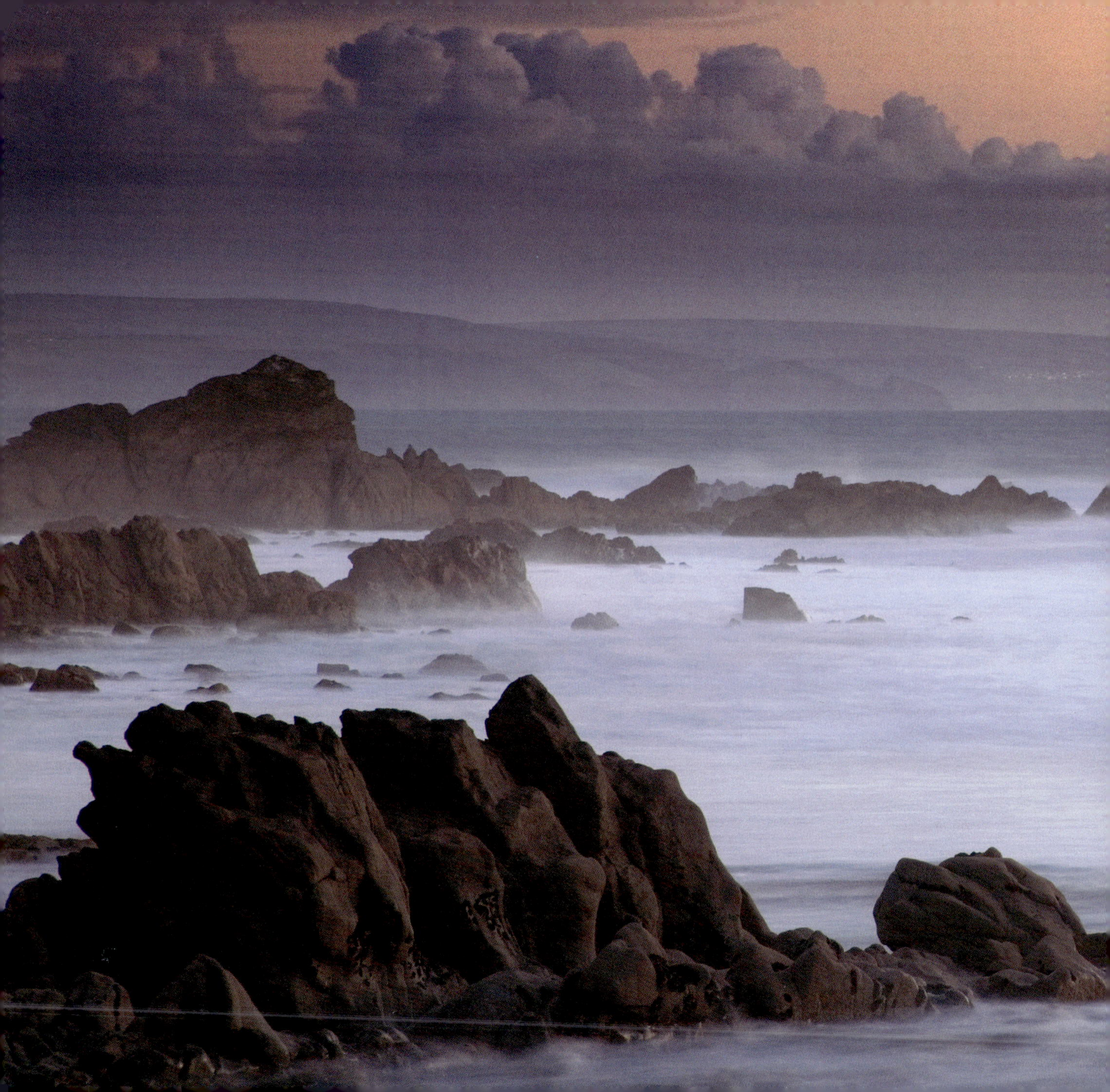

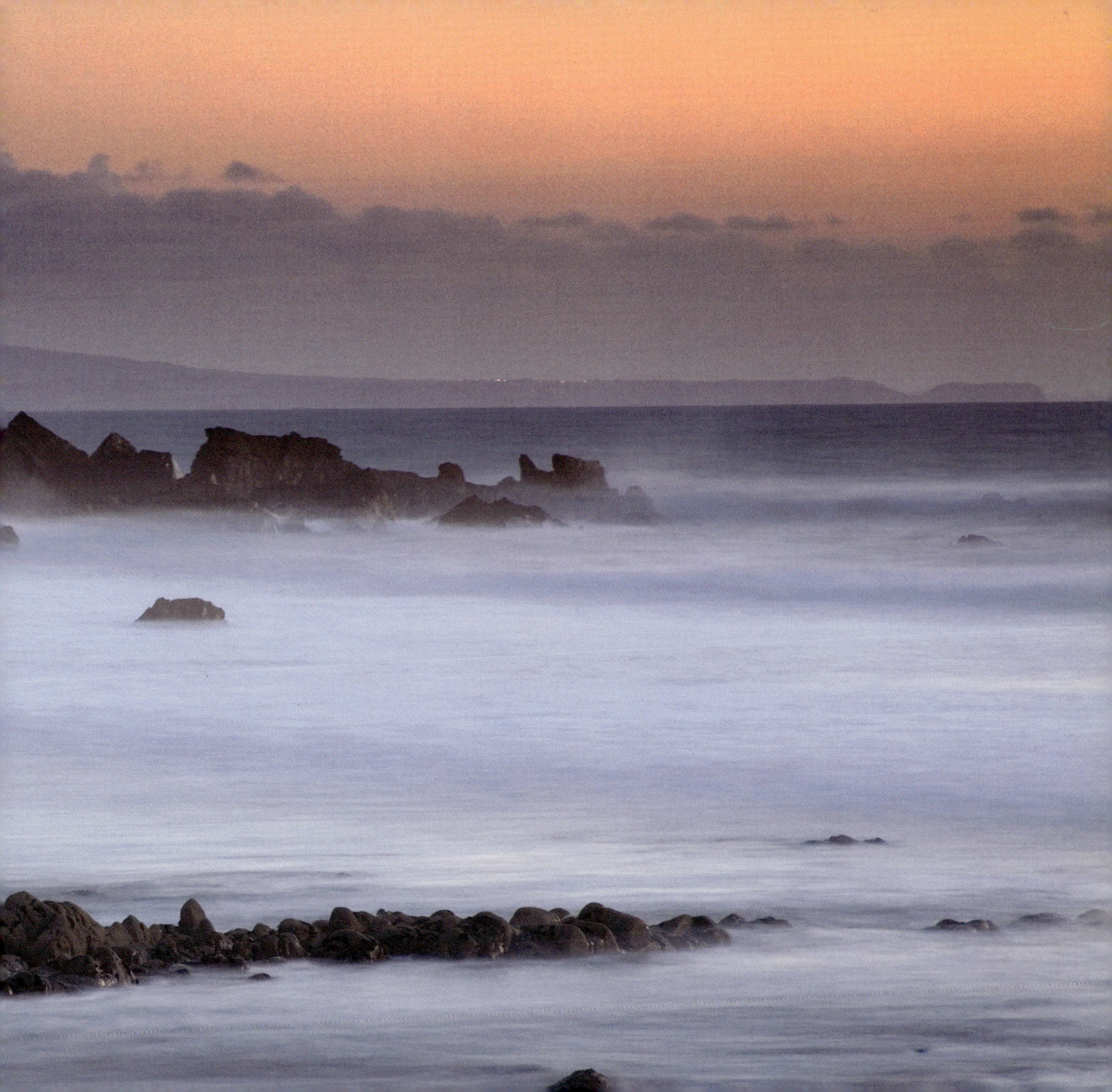

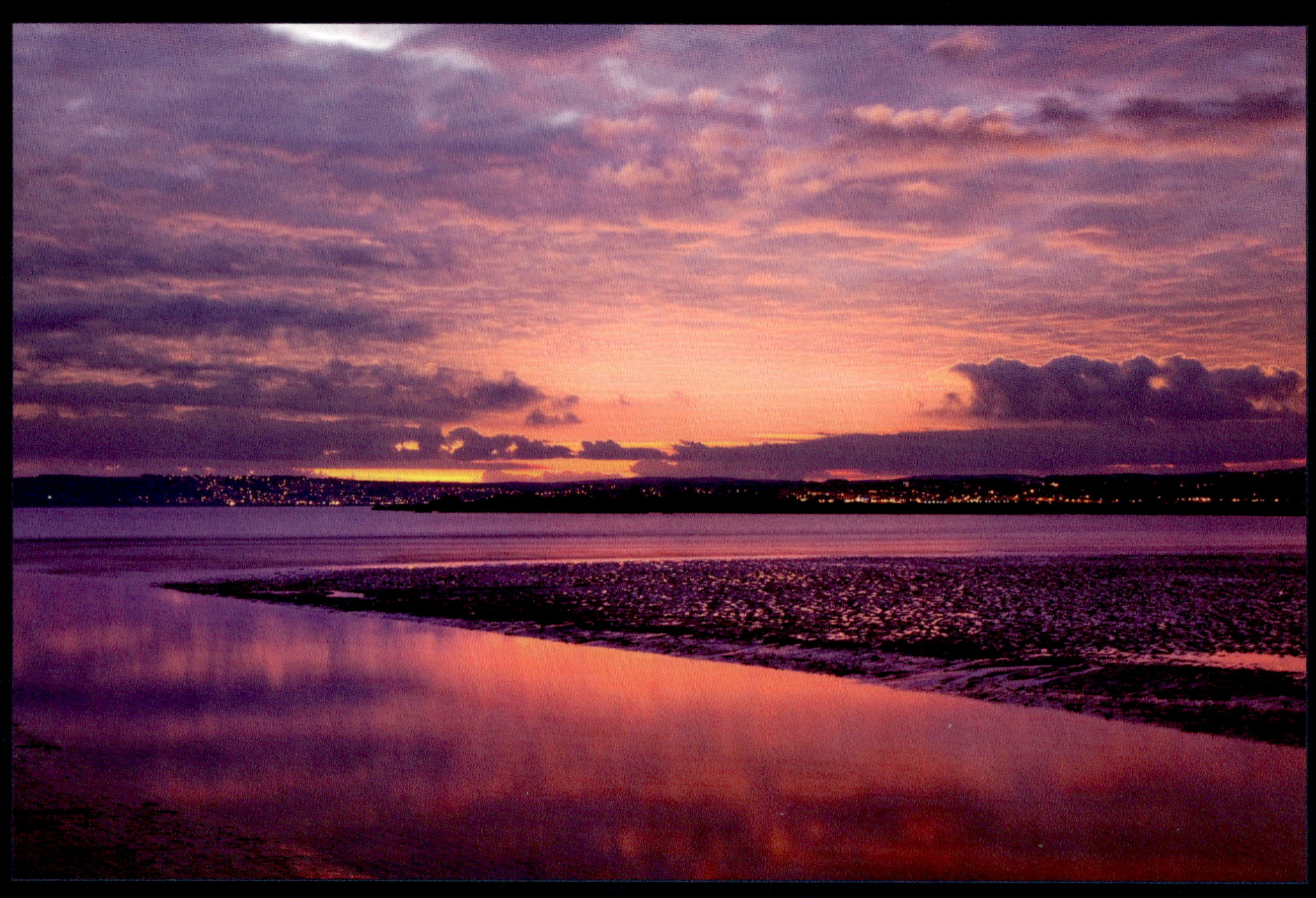

▲ Mount's Bay

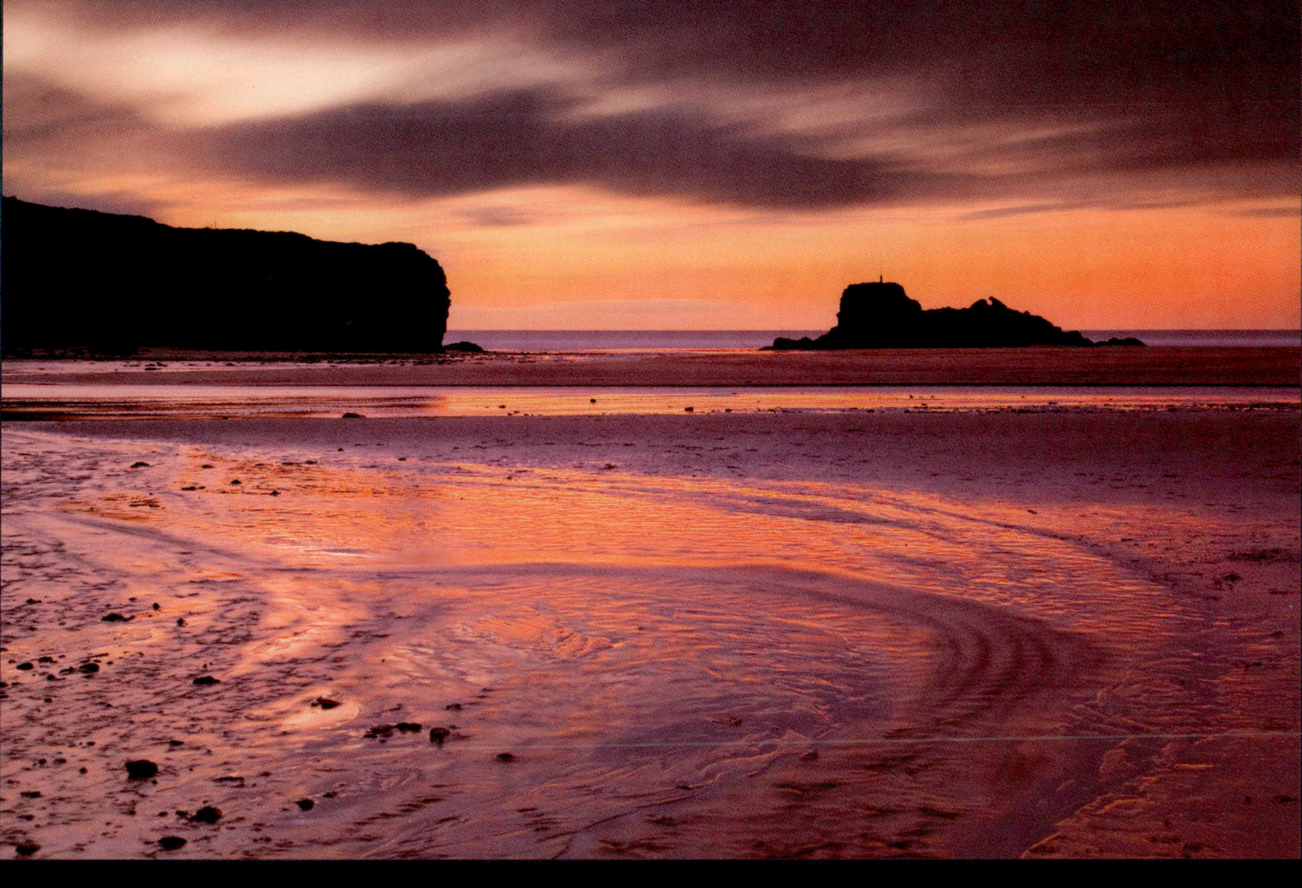

▲ *Perranporth Beach and Chapel Rock*

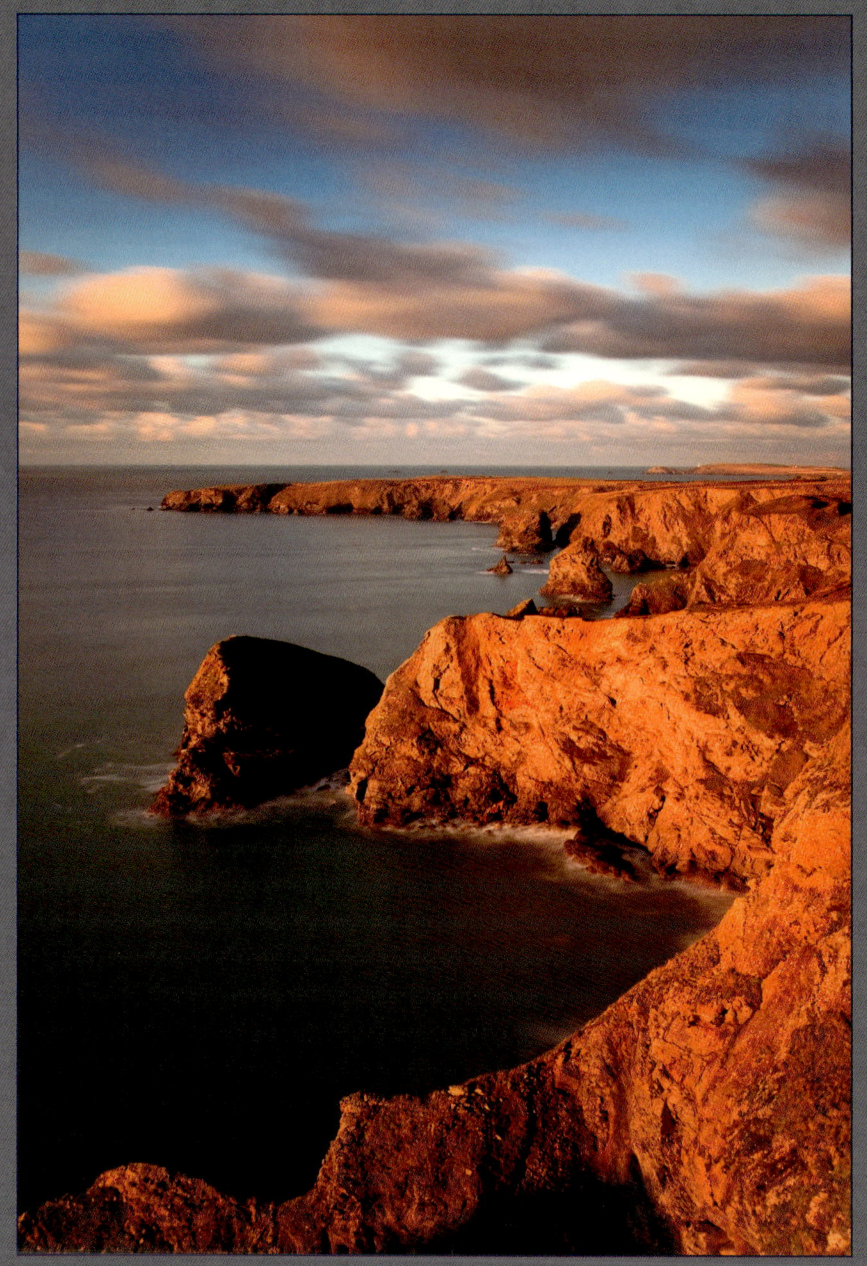

◀ Bedruthan Steps

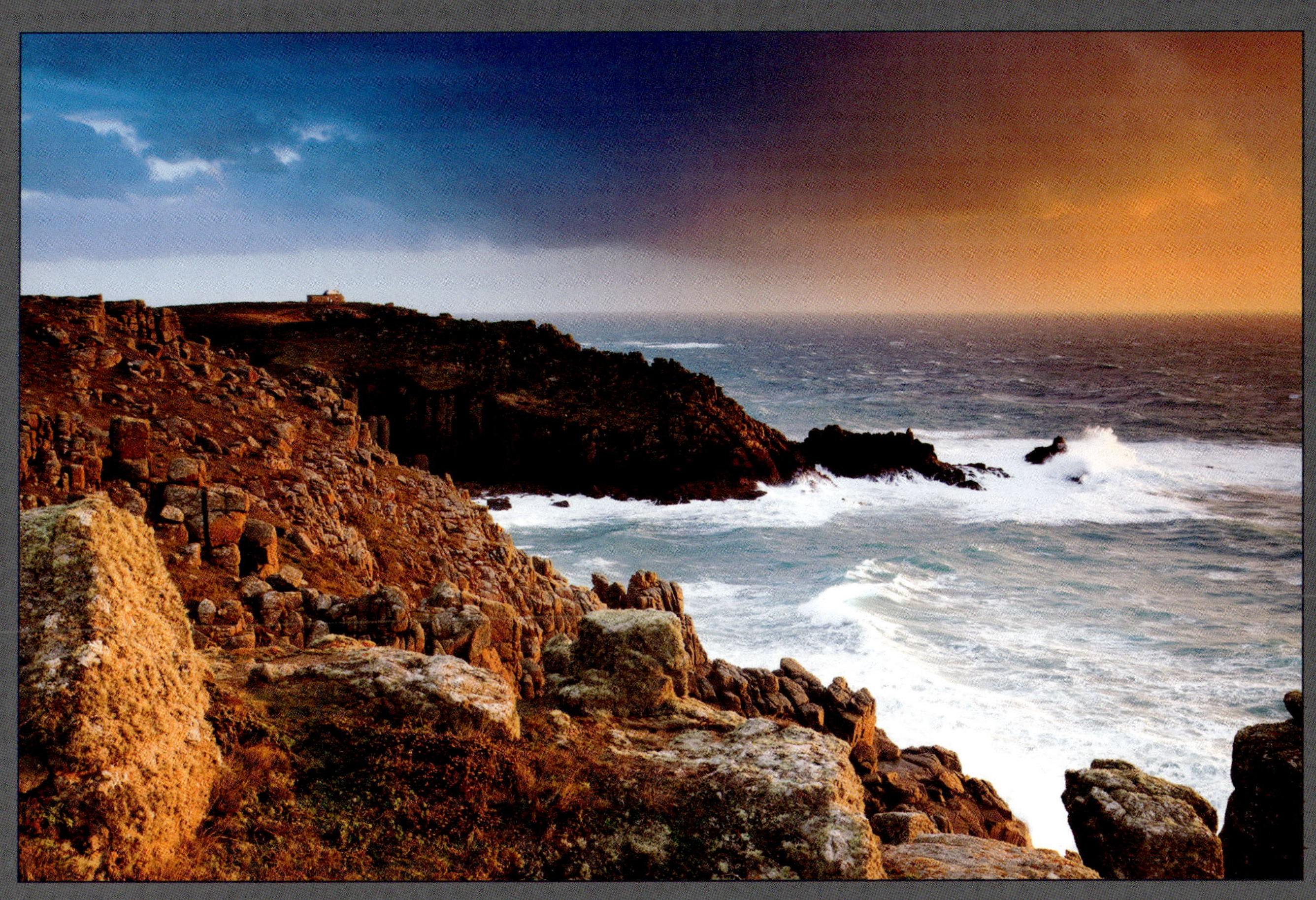

▲ Gwennap Head

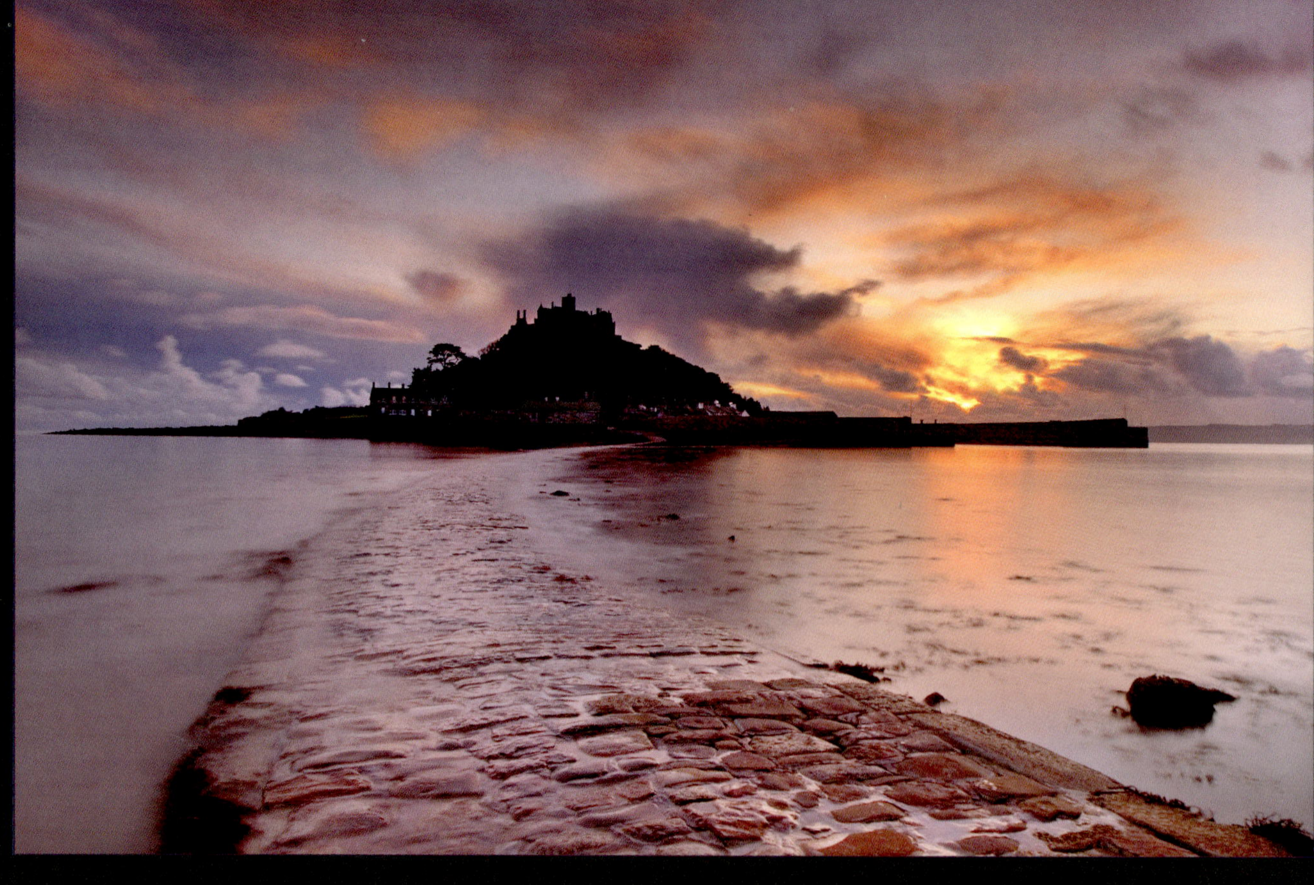

▲ *St Michael's Mount and causeway*

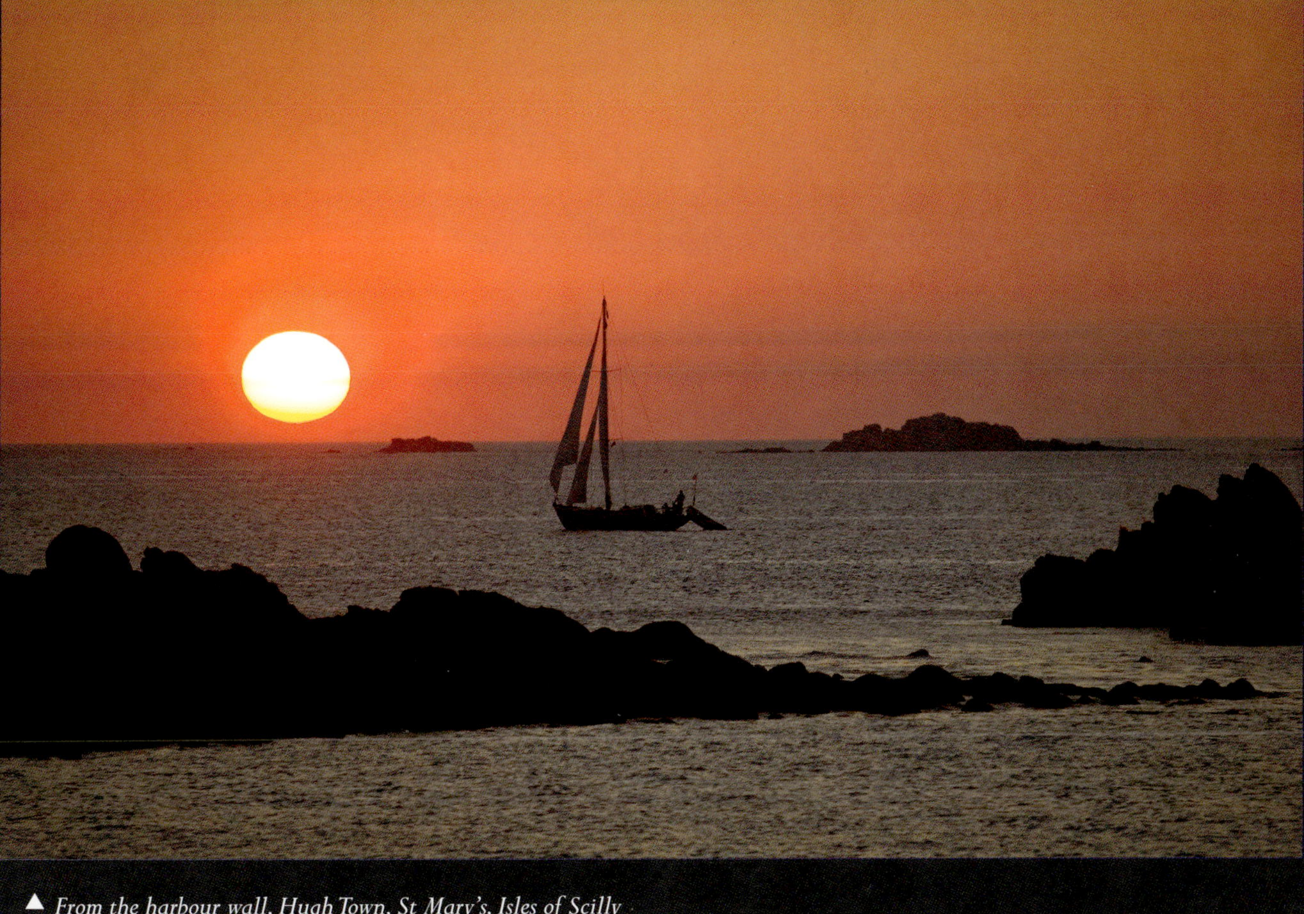

▲ *From the harbour wall, Hugh Town, St Mary's, Isles of Scilly*

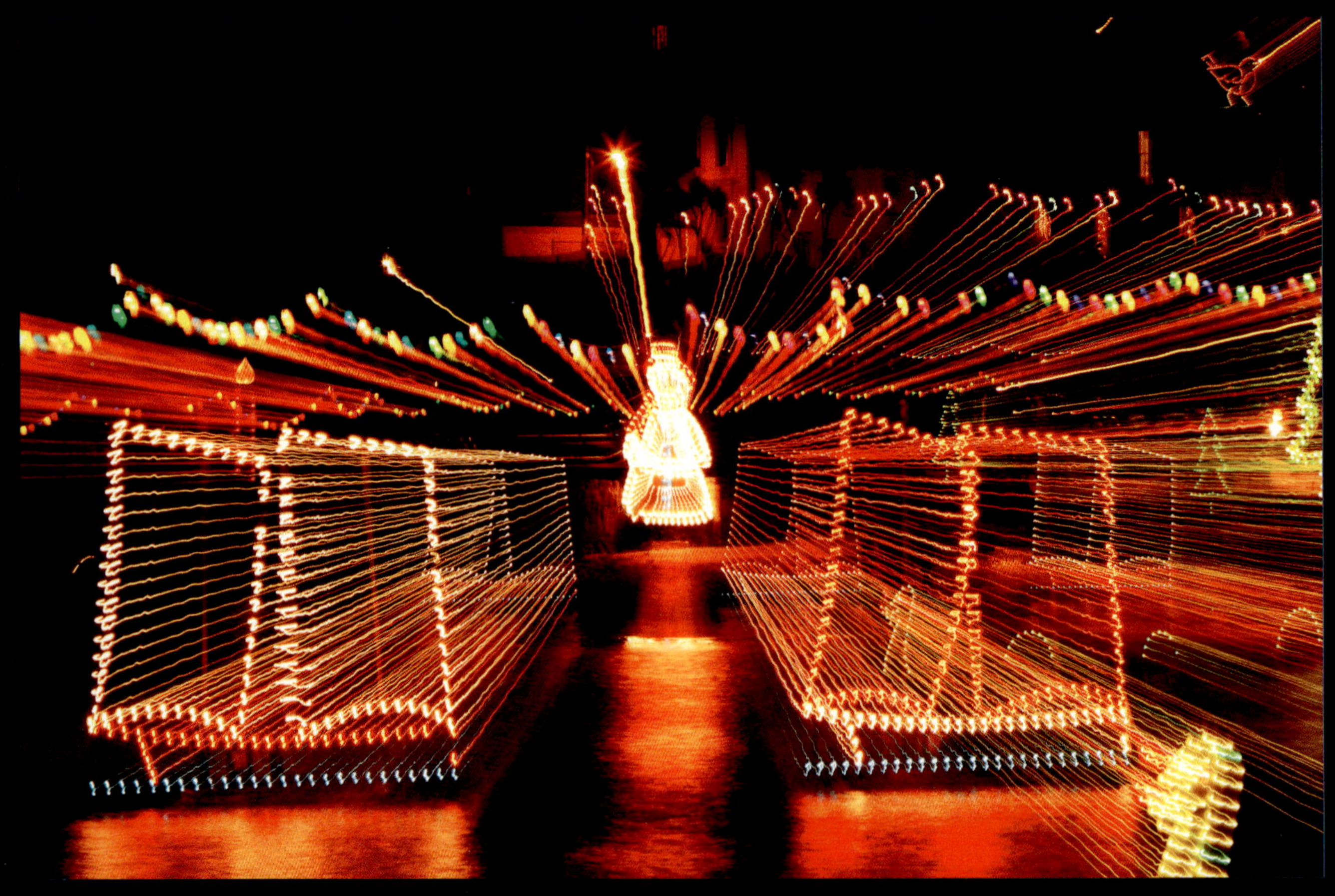

▲ Mousehole Christmas lights

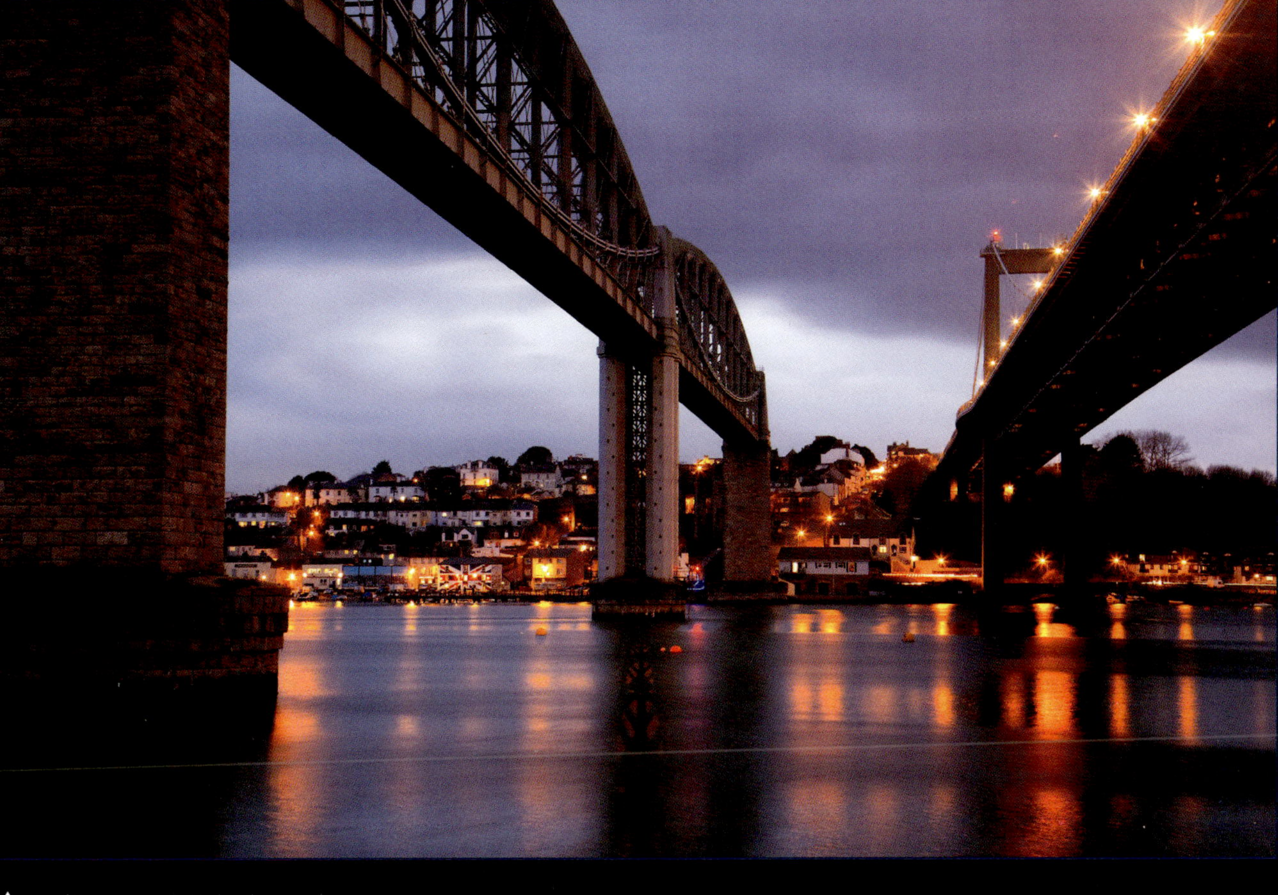

Looking towards Saltash

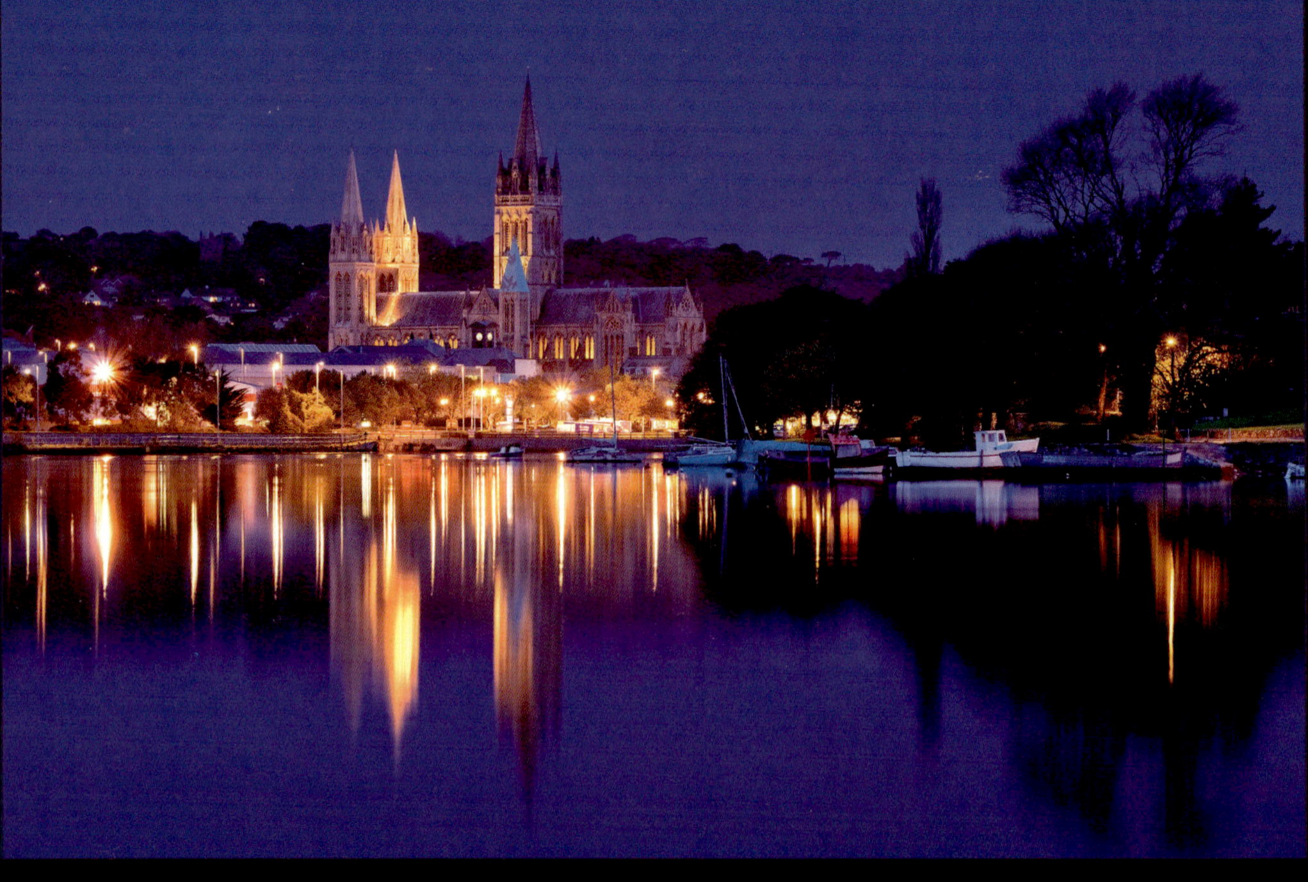

▲ *Truro Cathedral*

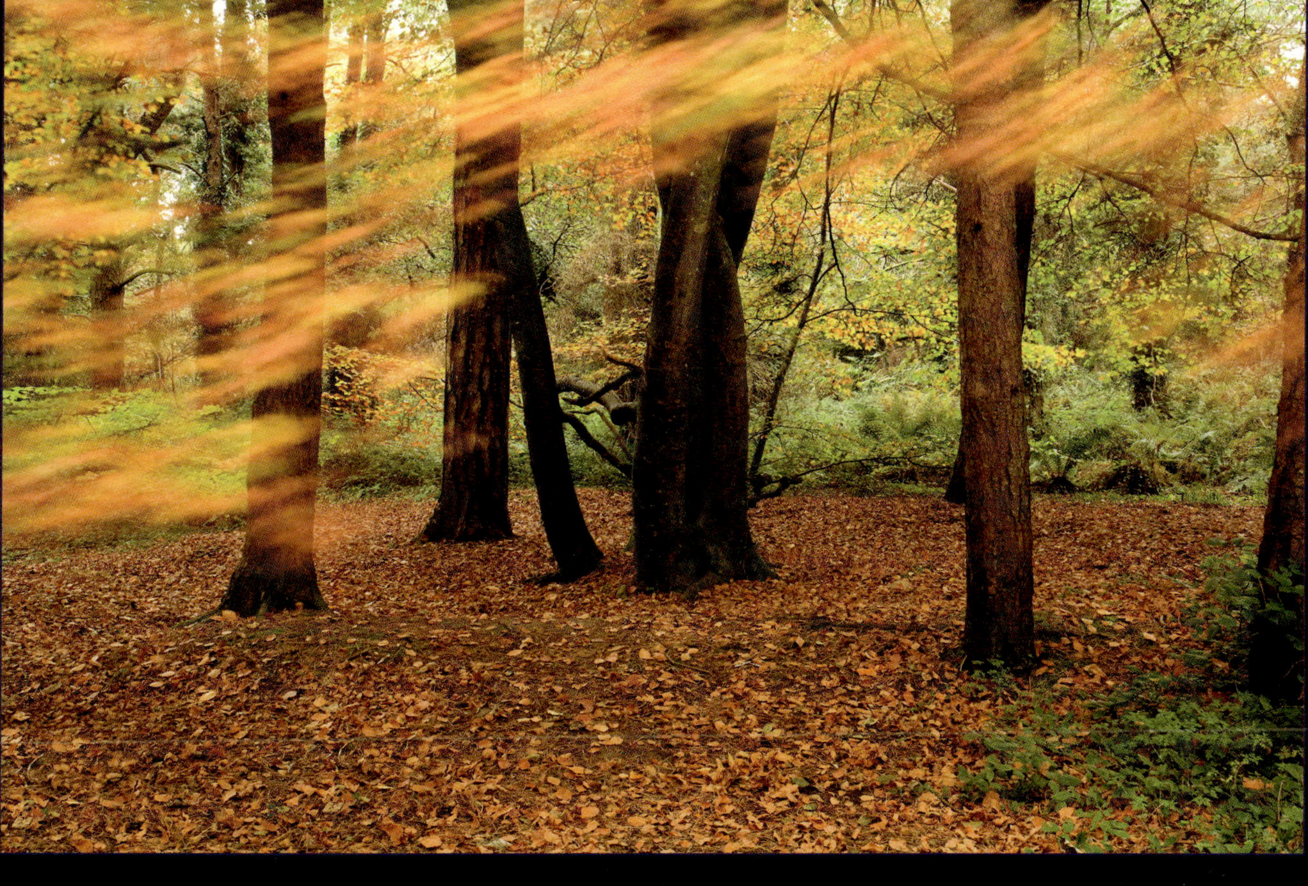

▲ *Godolphin Woods*

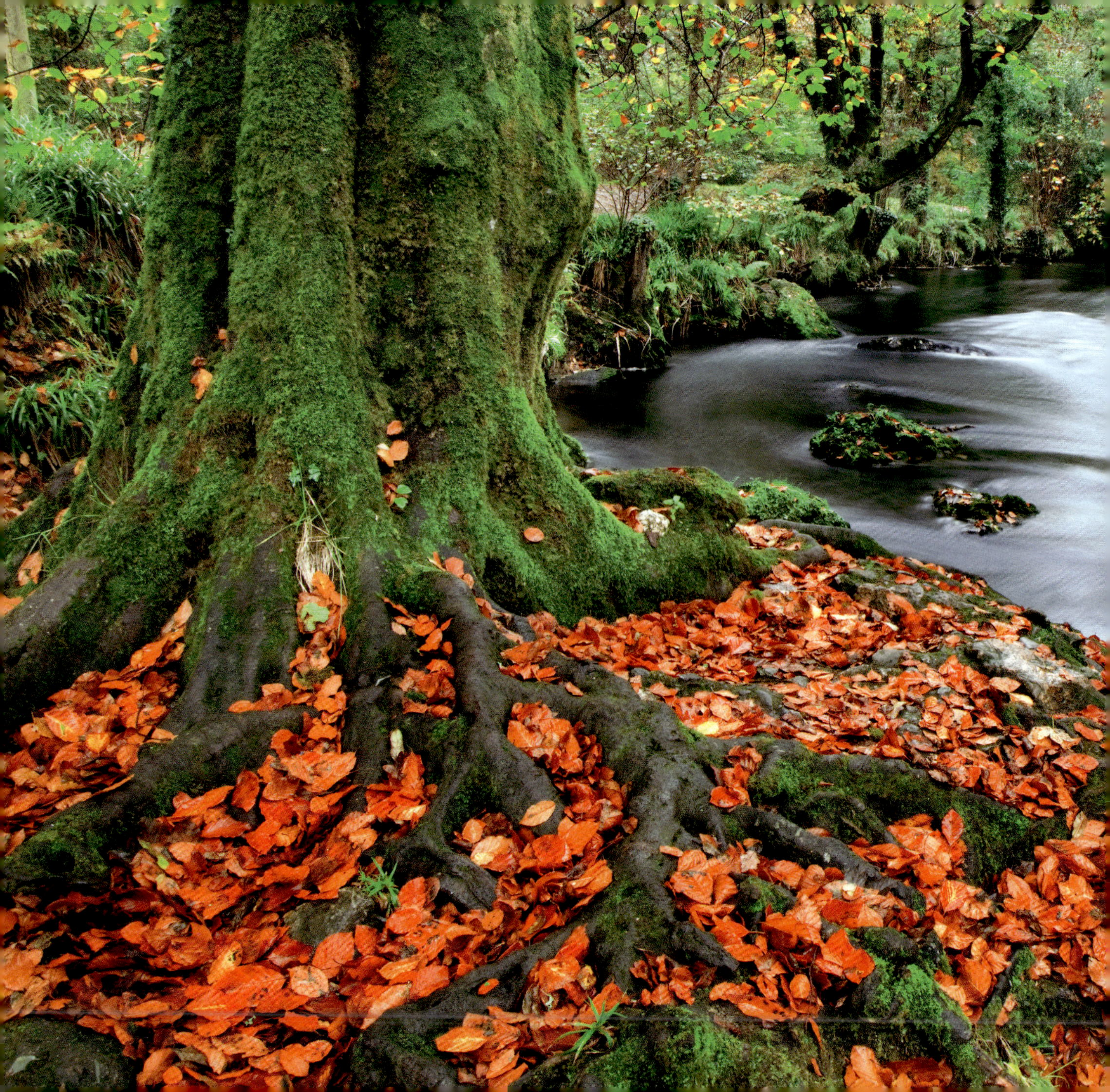

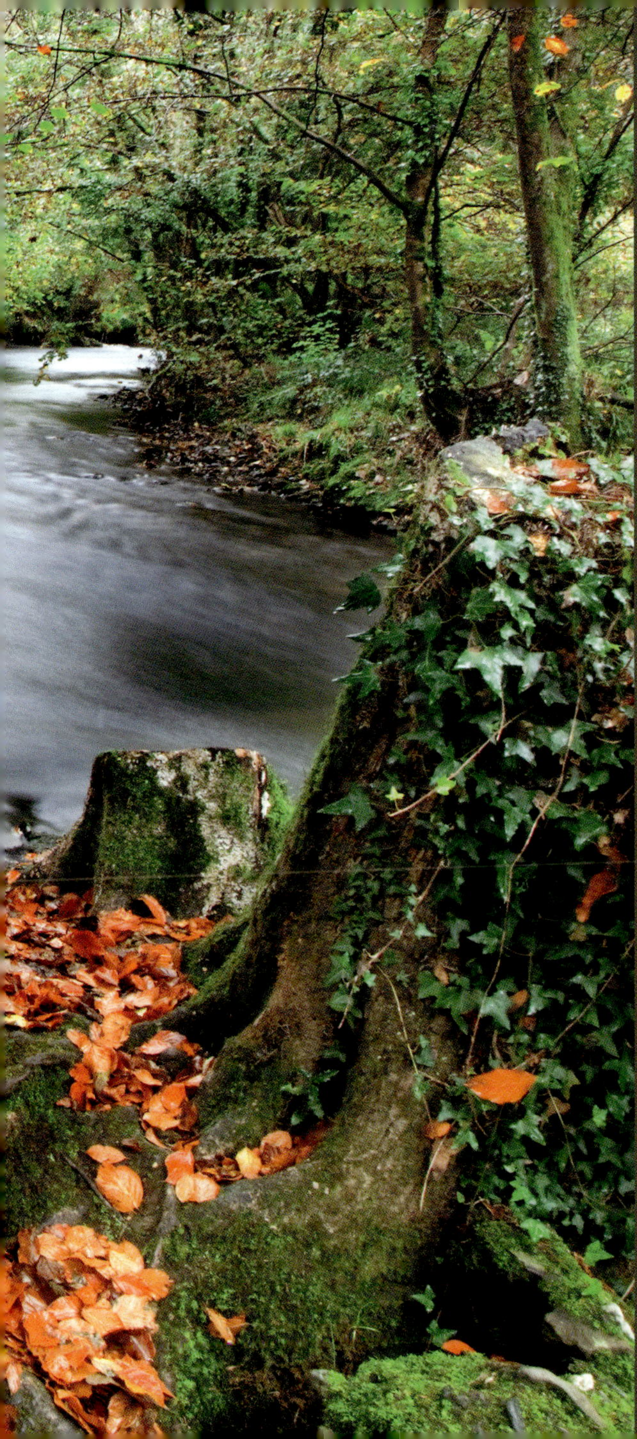

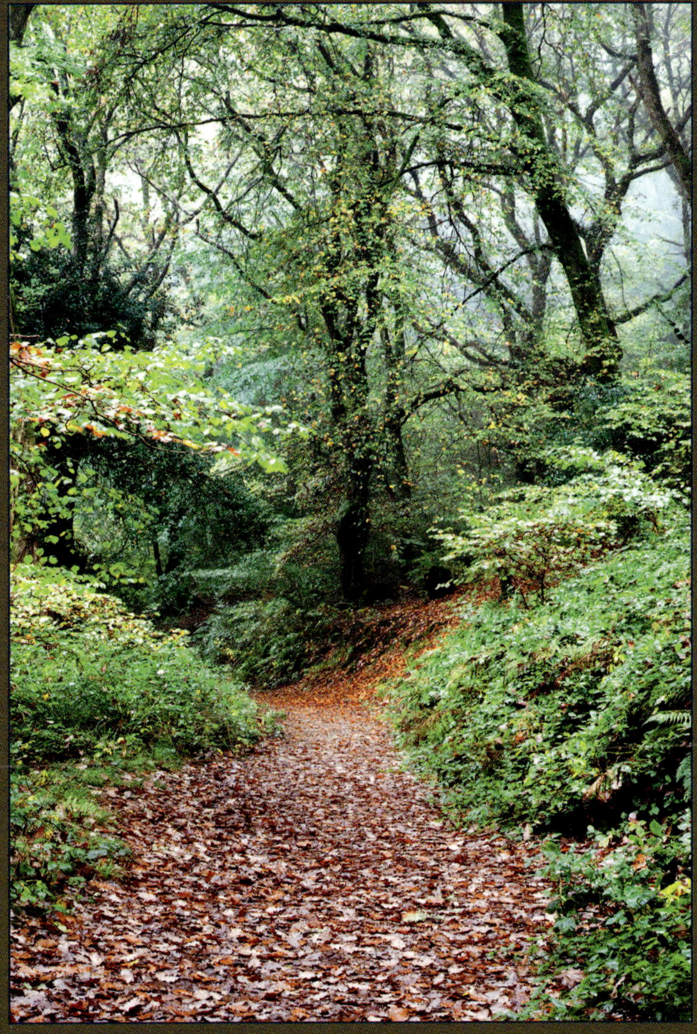

▲ *Kilminorth Woods*
◀ *The River Lynher*

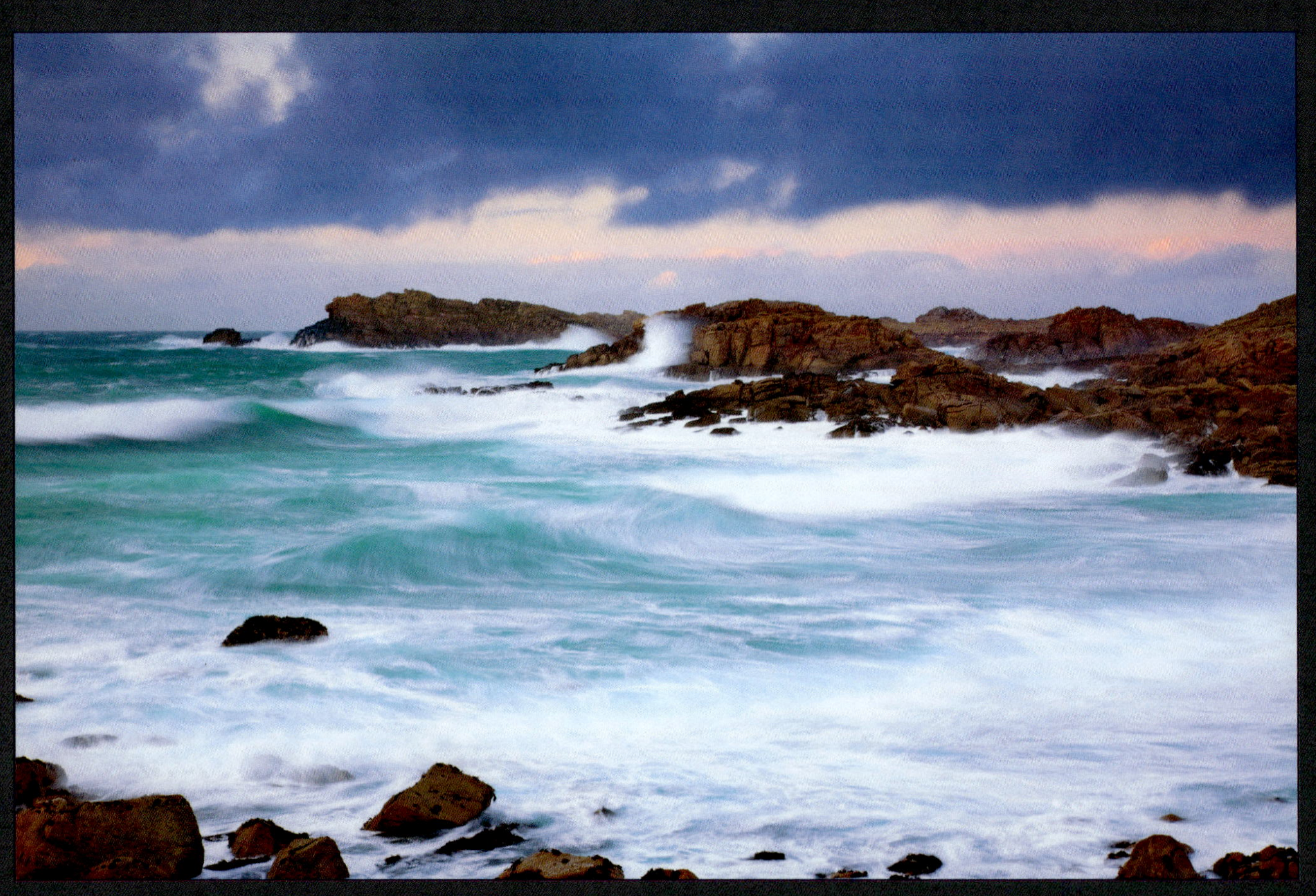

▲ *Hell Bay, Bryher, Isles of Scilly*

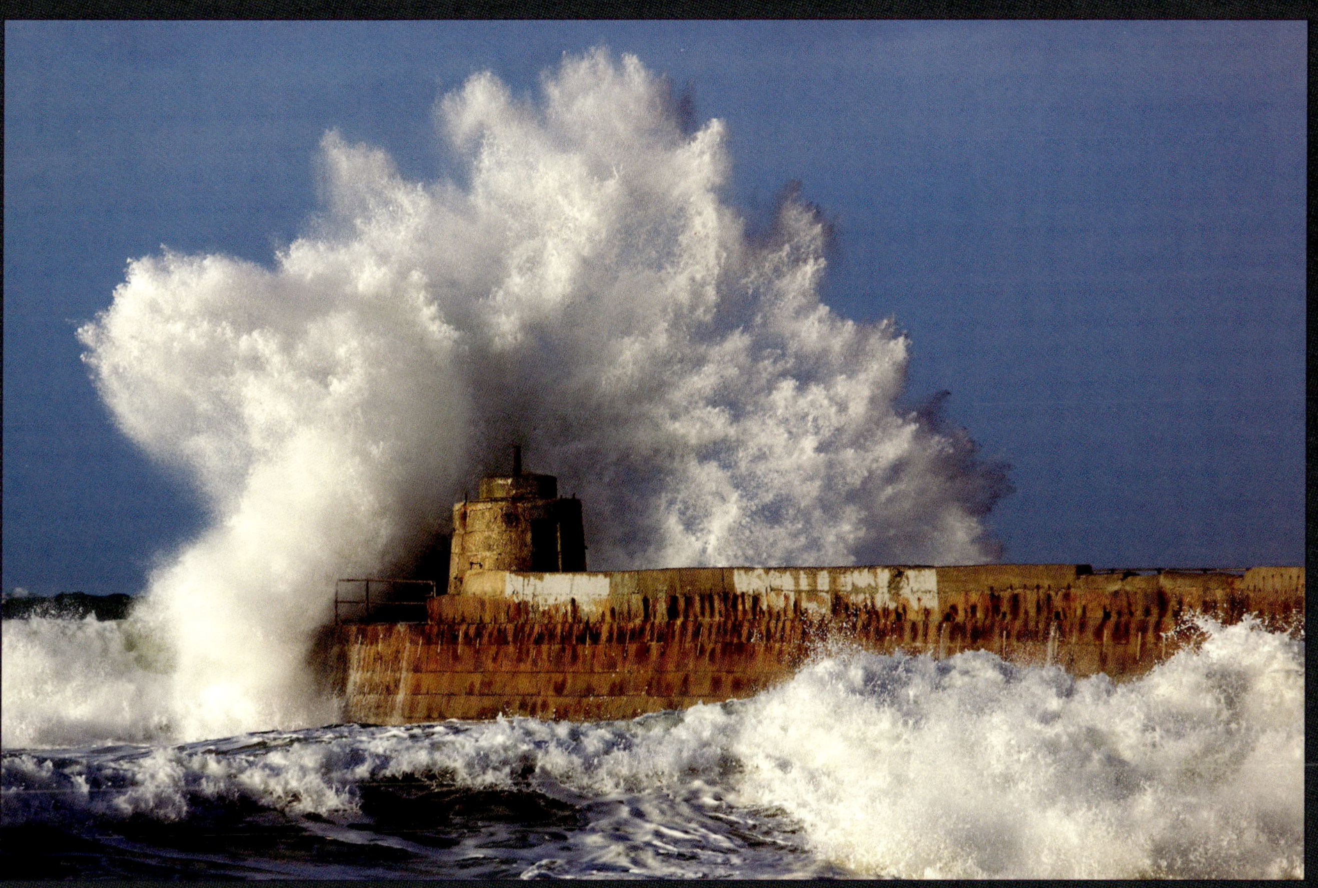

▲ *Harbour wall, Portreath*

Rinsey Head ▶

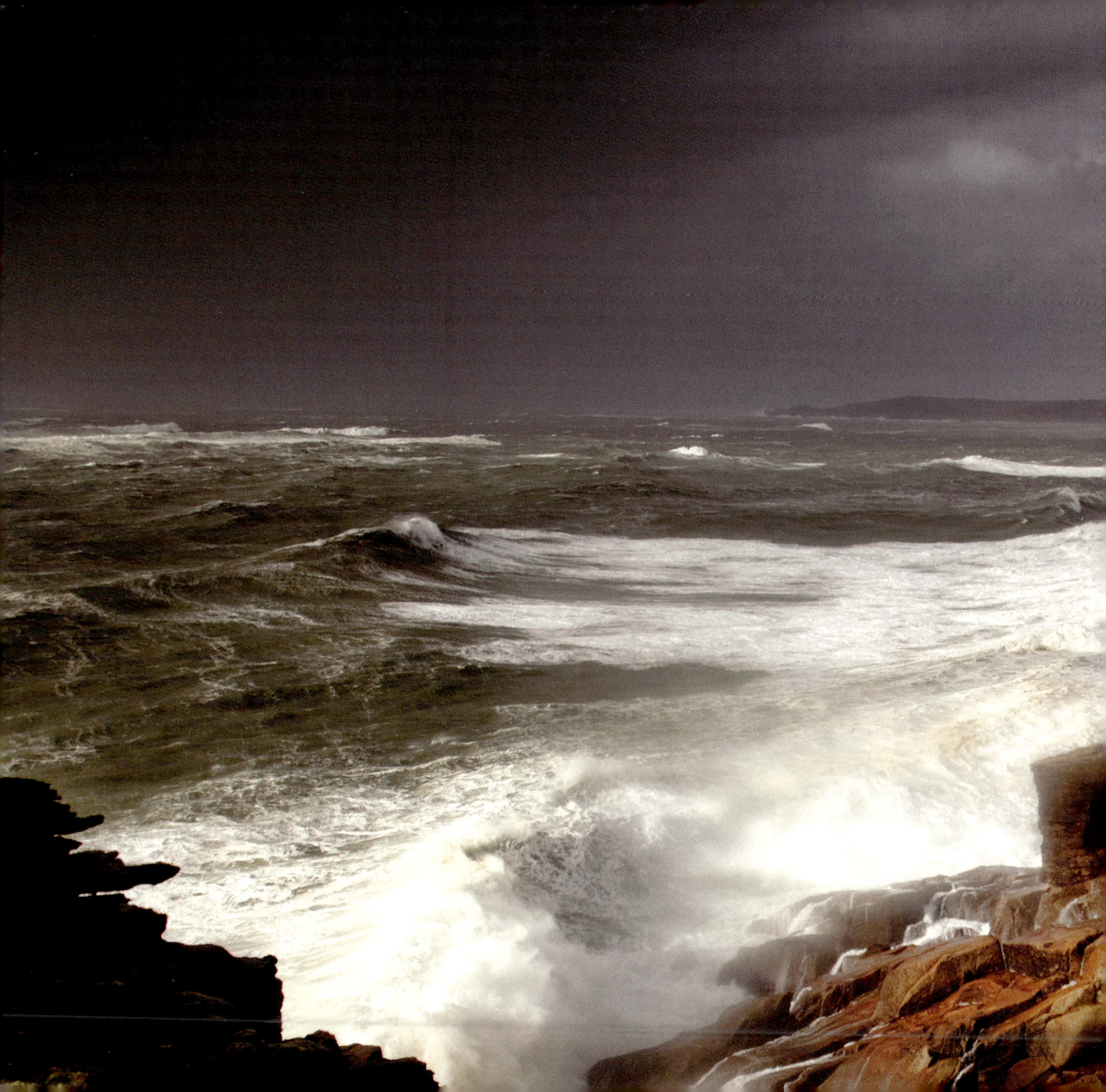

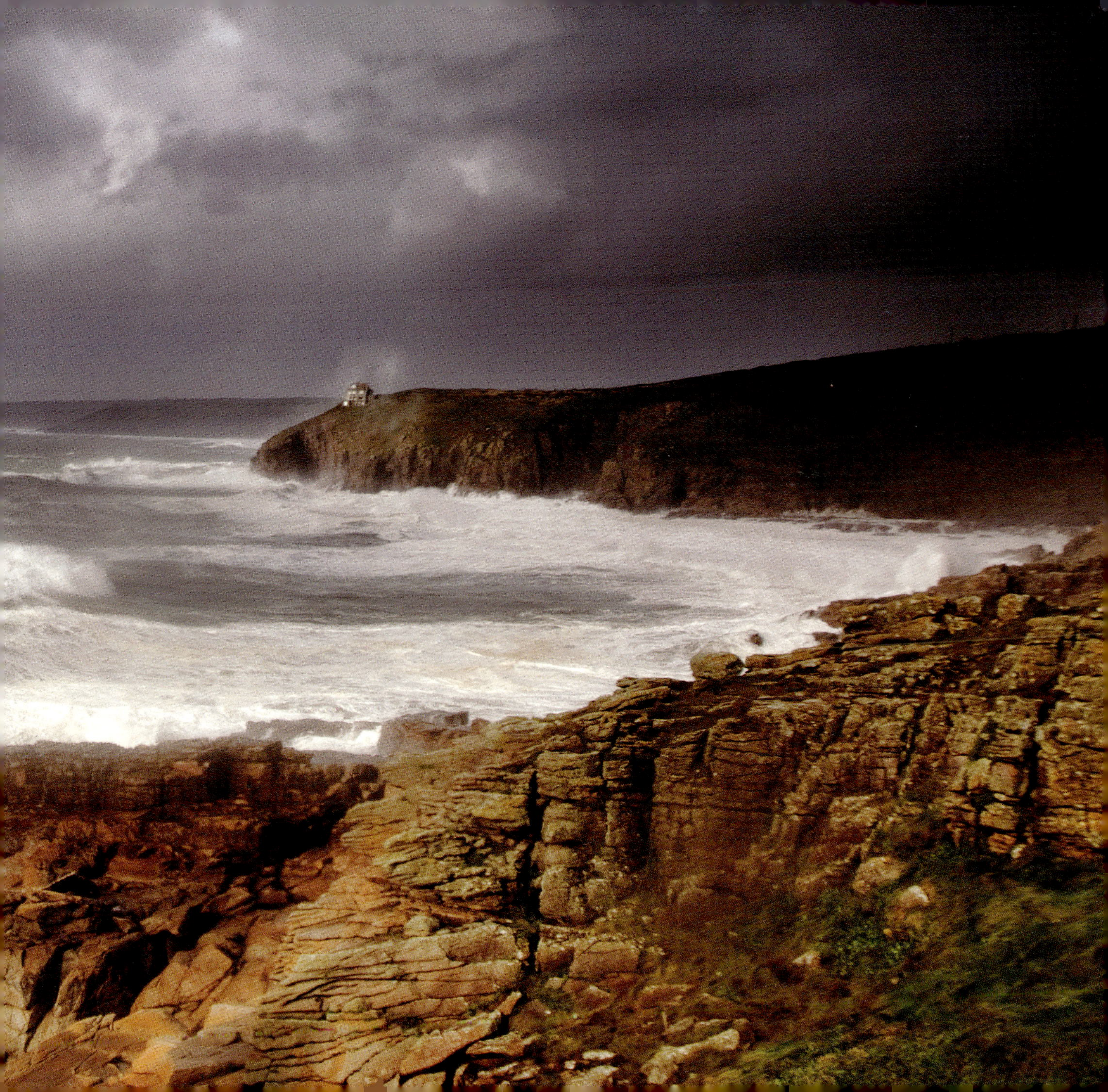

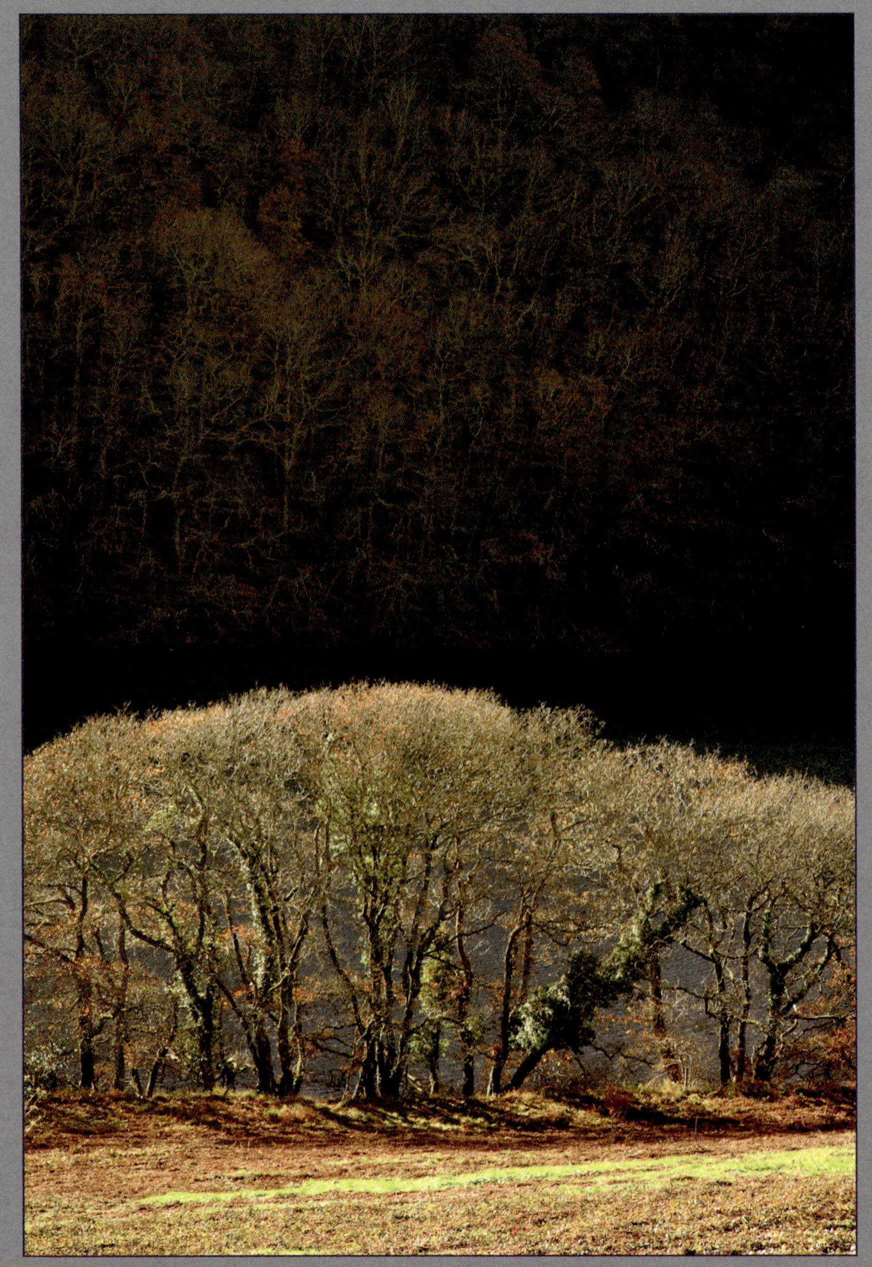

◀ Kilminorth Woods

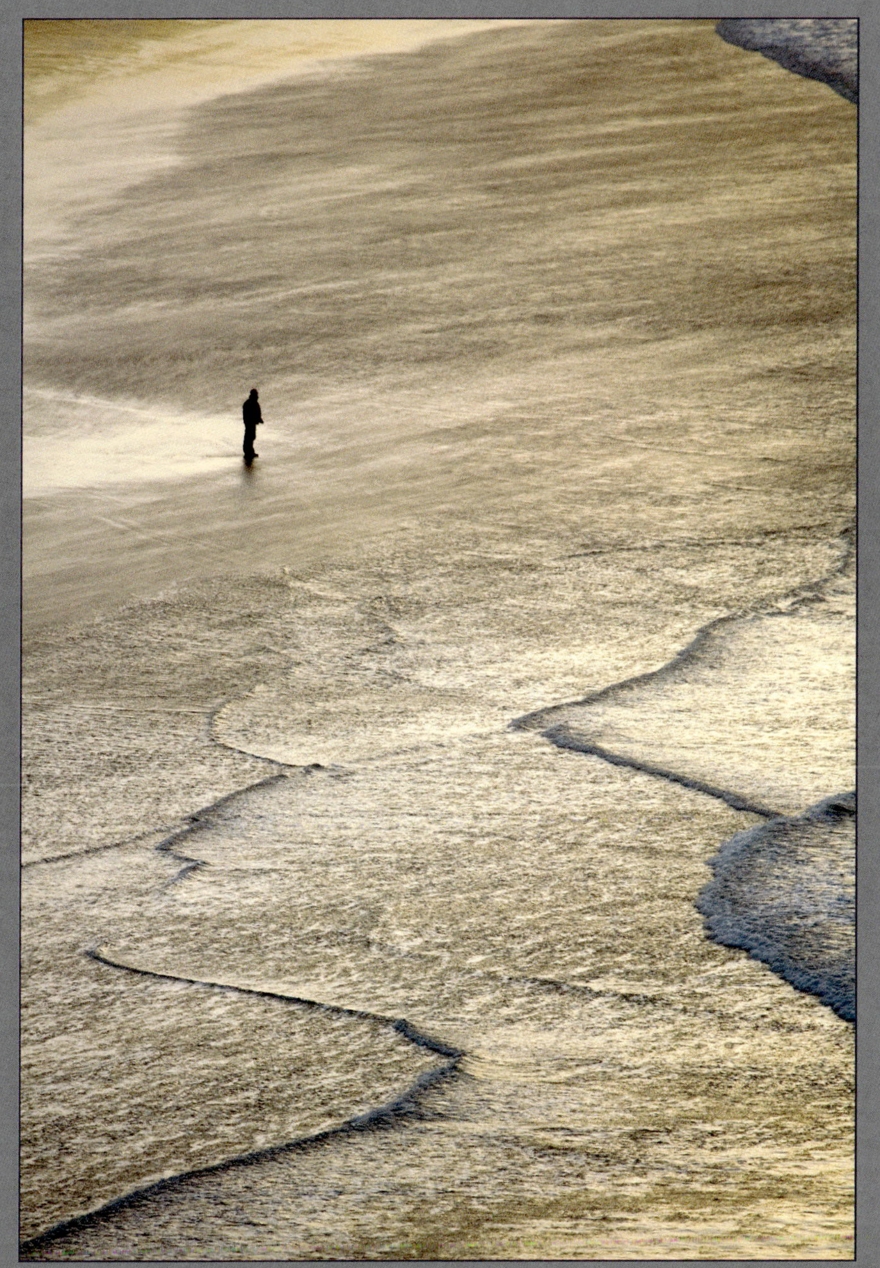

Crantock Beach ▶

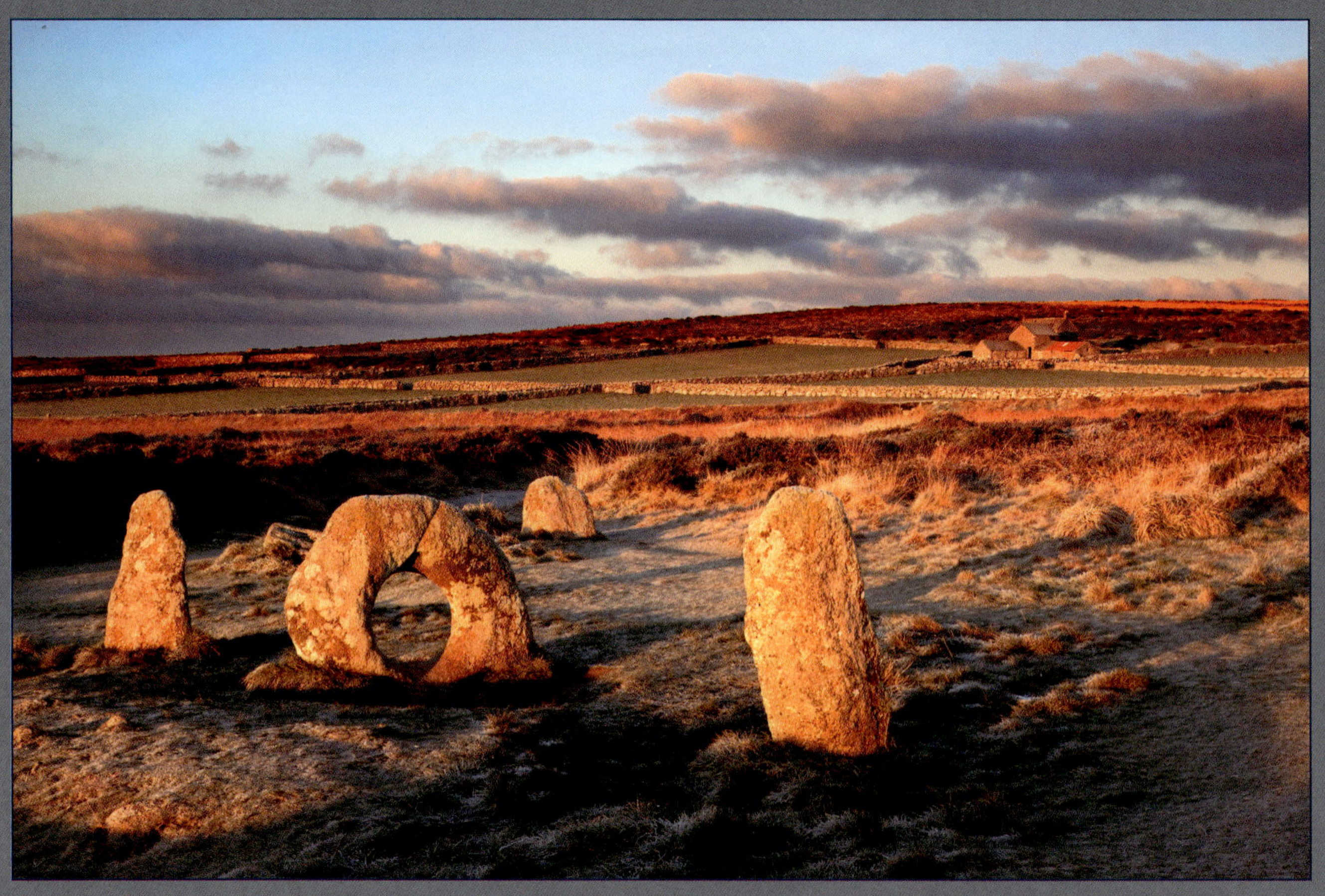

Men-an-tol

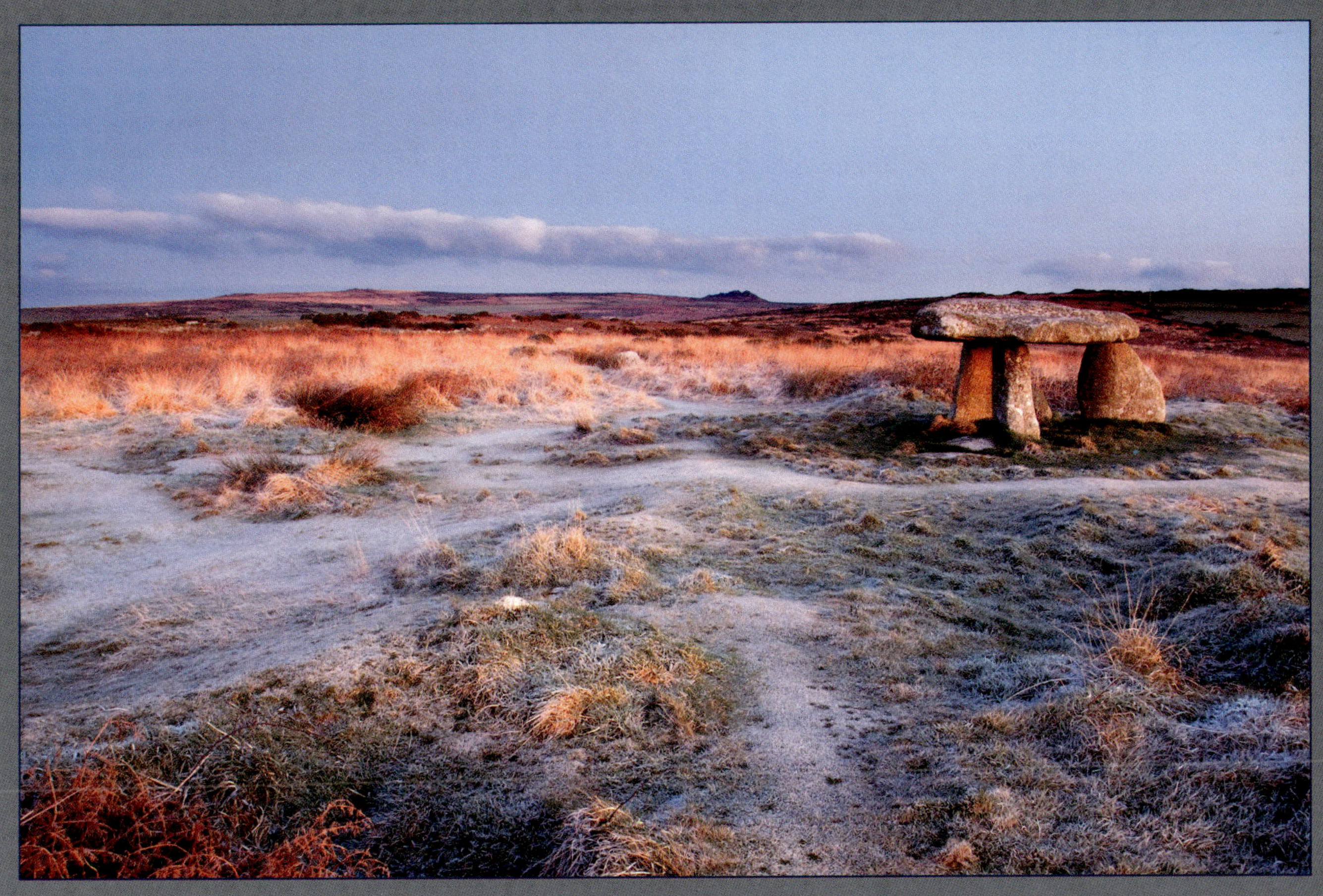

Lanyon Quoit

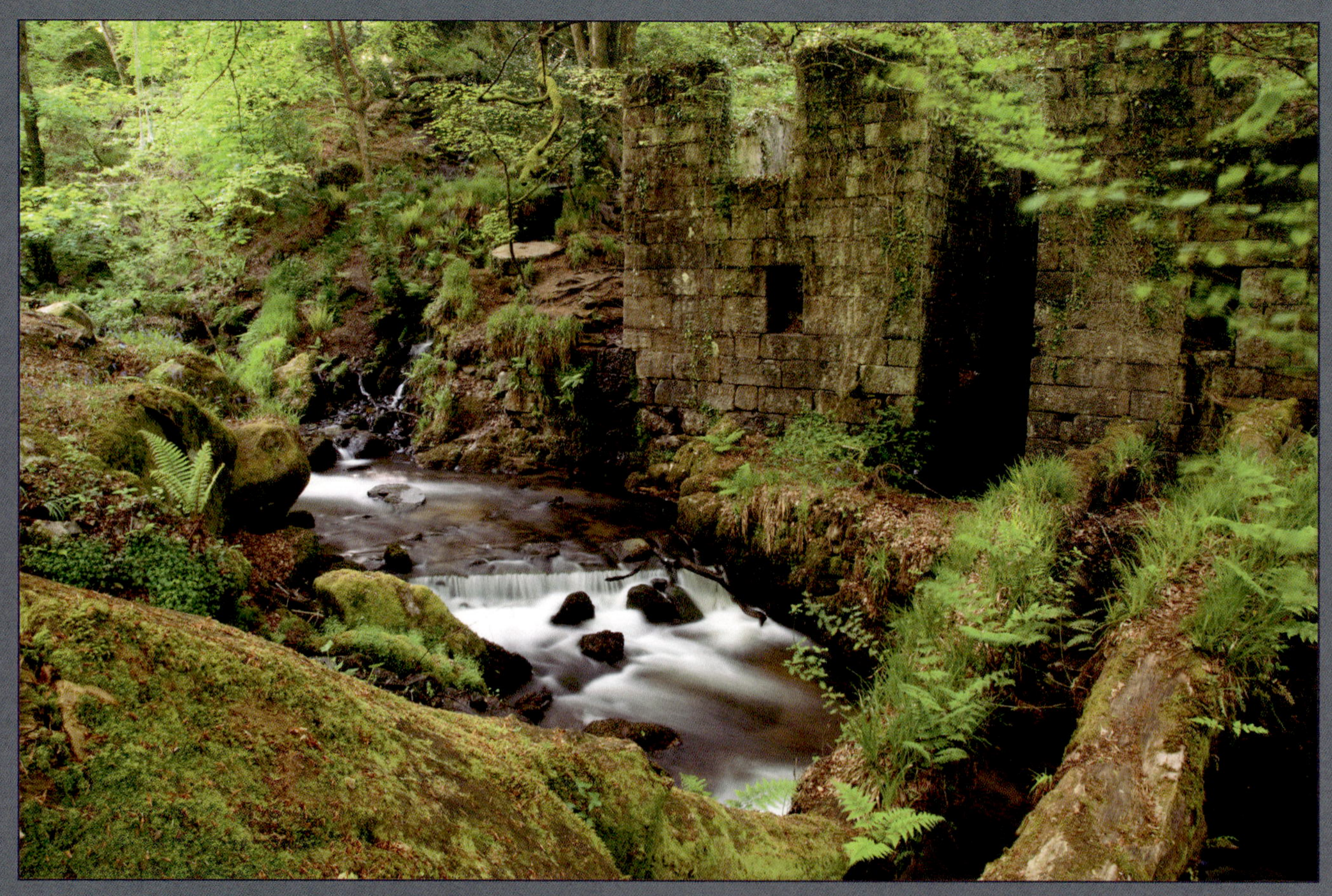

▲ *Gunpowder factory ruins, Kennall Vale*

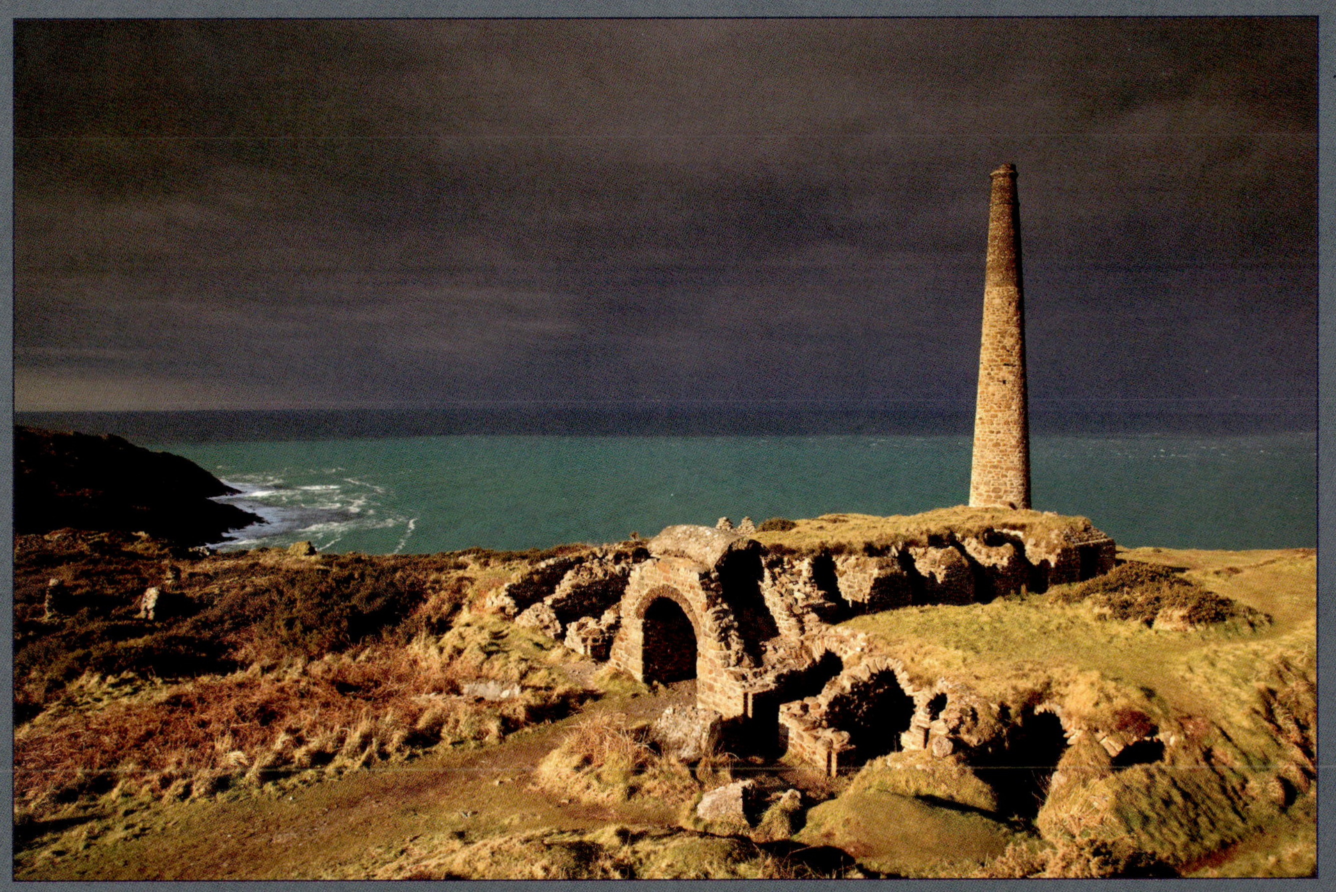

Brunton calciner, Botallack

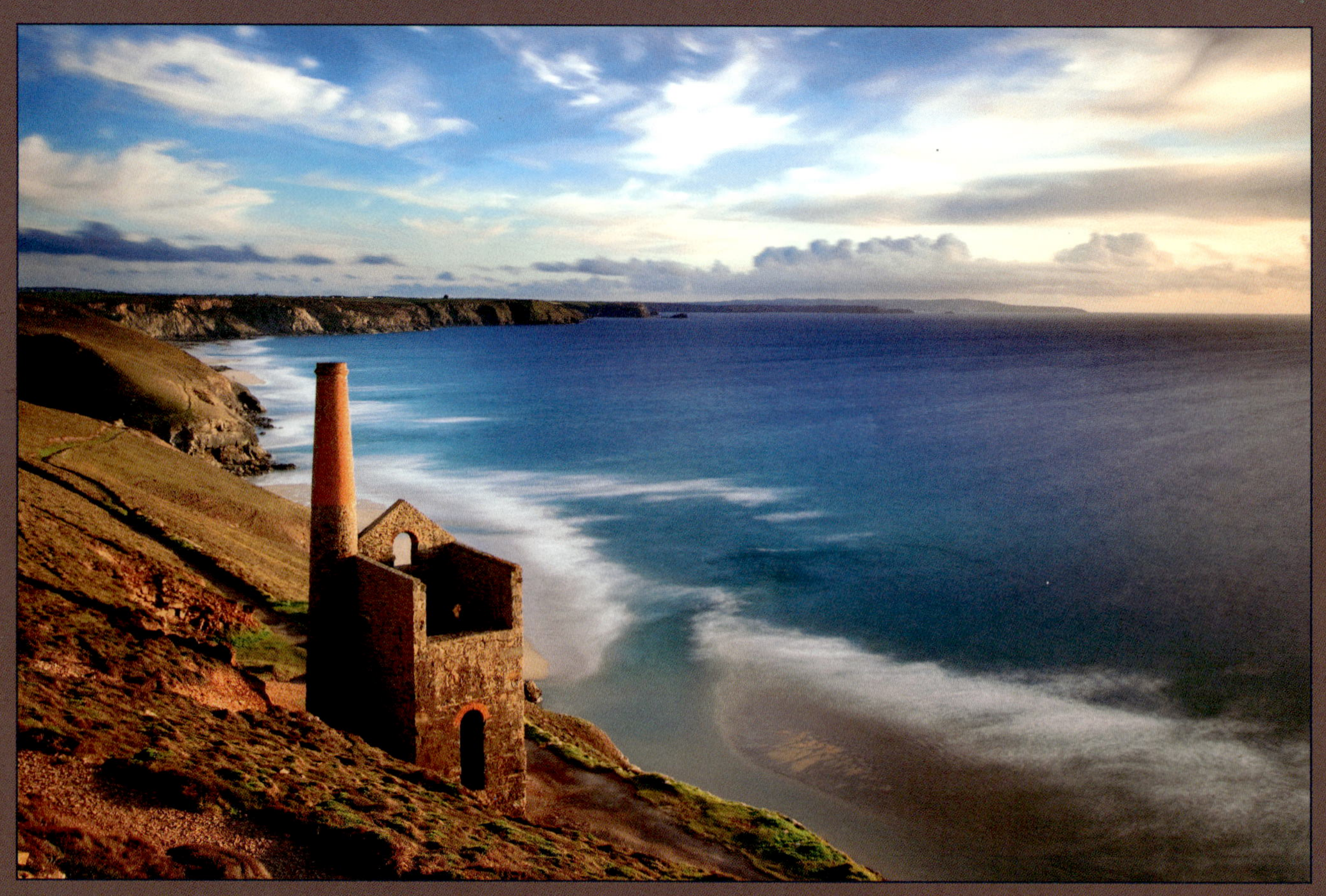

▲ Wheal Coates, St Agnes

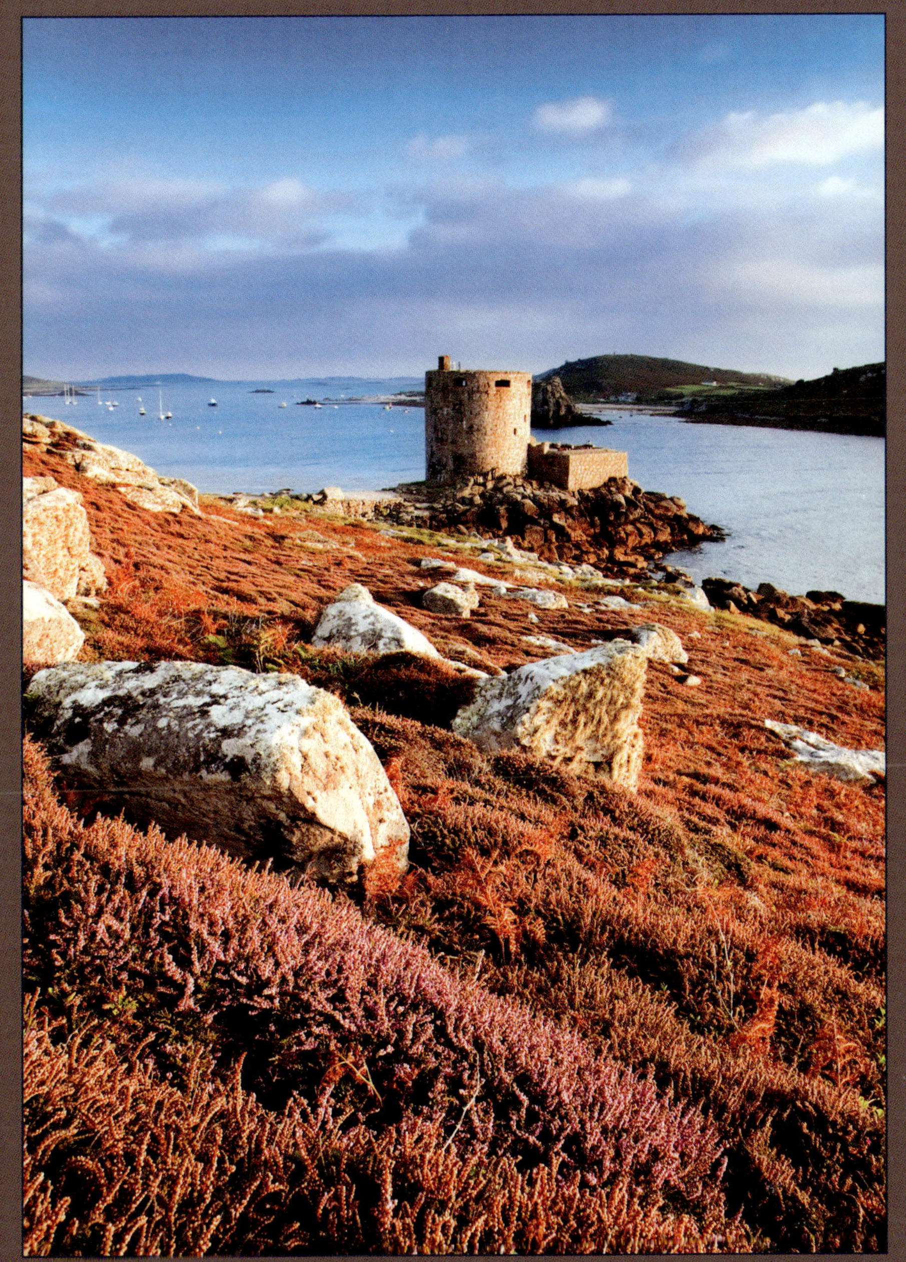

Cromwell's Castle,
Tresco, Isles of Scilly ▶

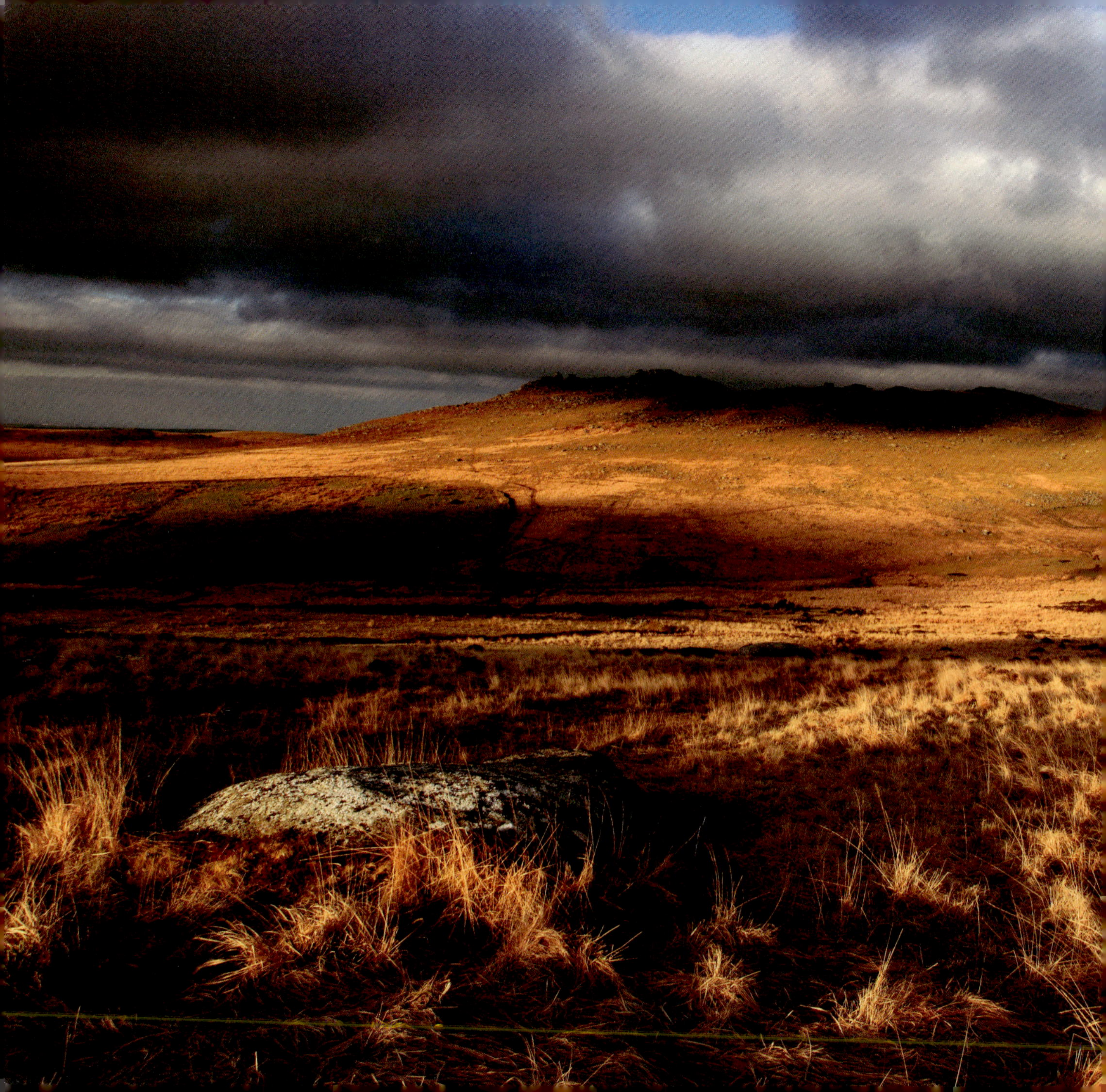

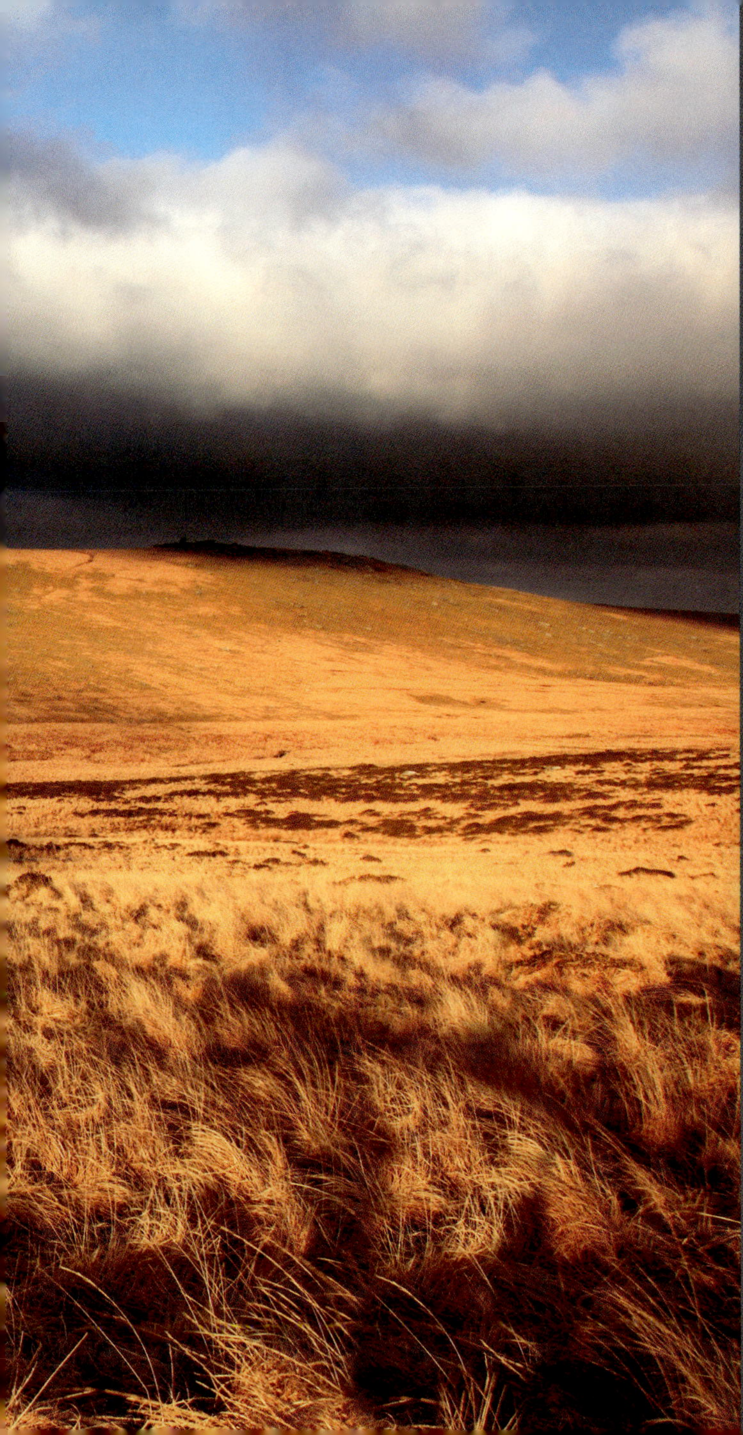

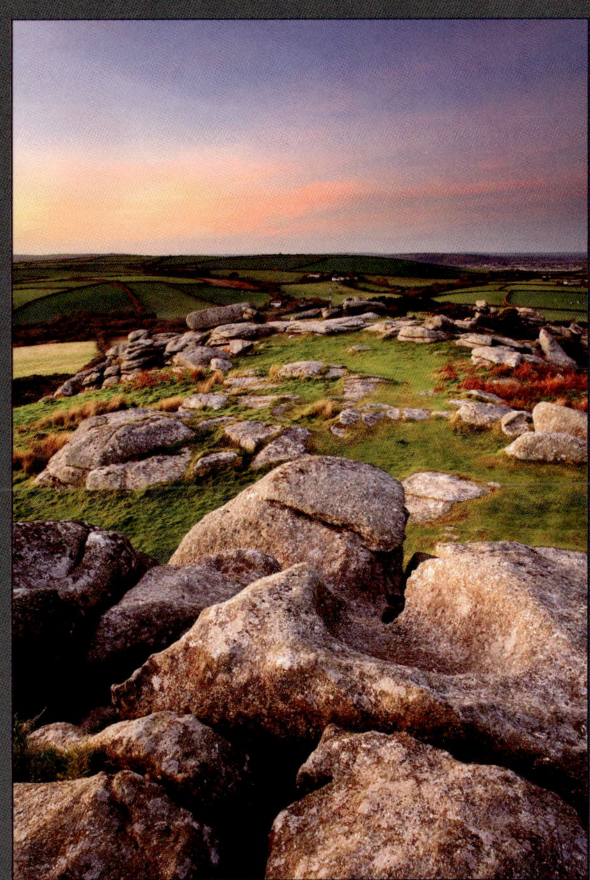

▲ Helman Tor
◄ Roughtor

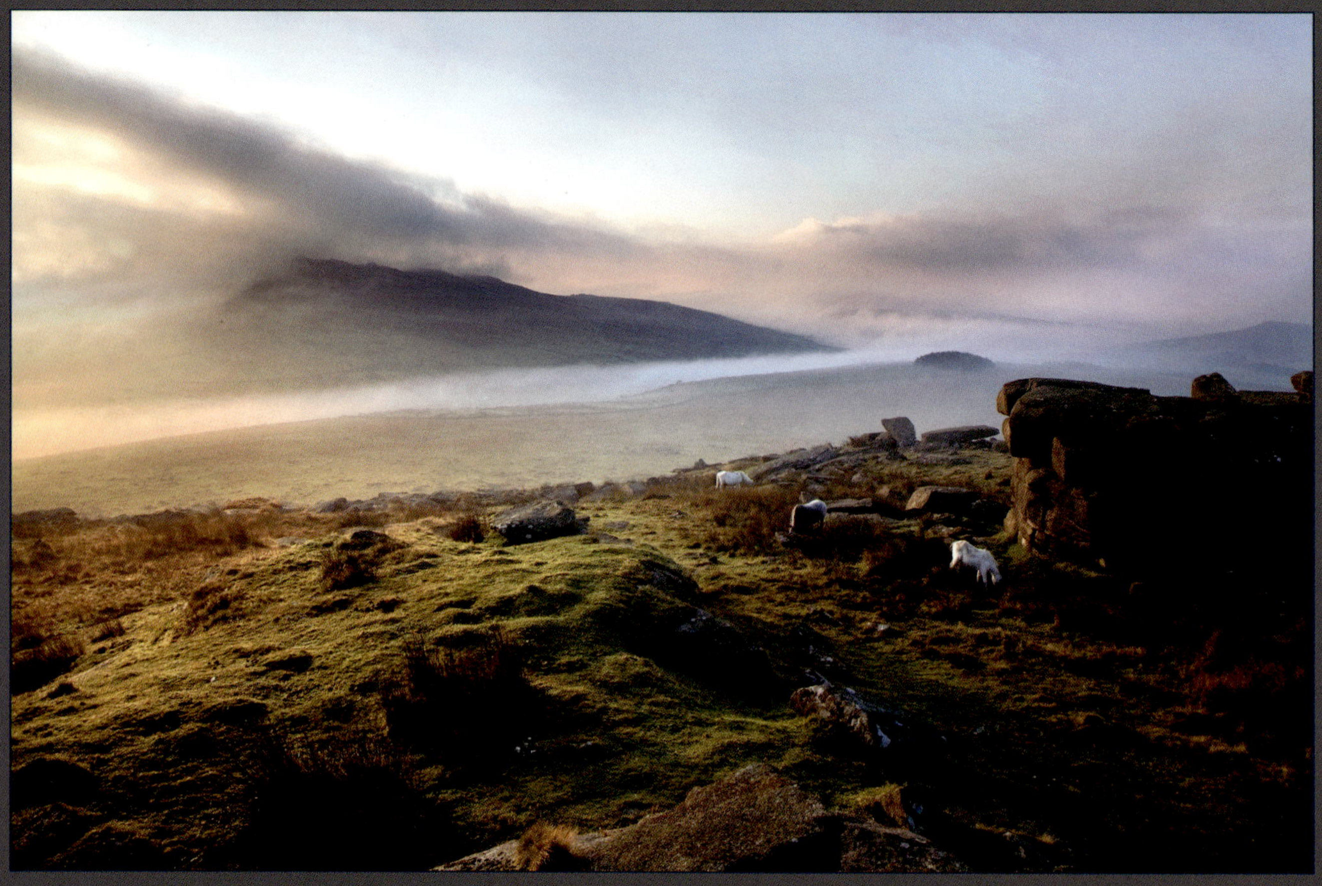

Brown Willy from Roughtor

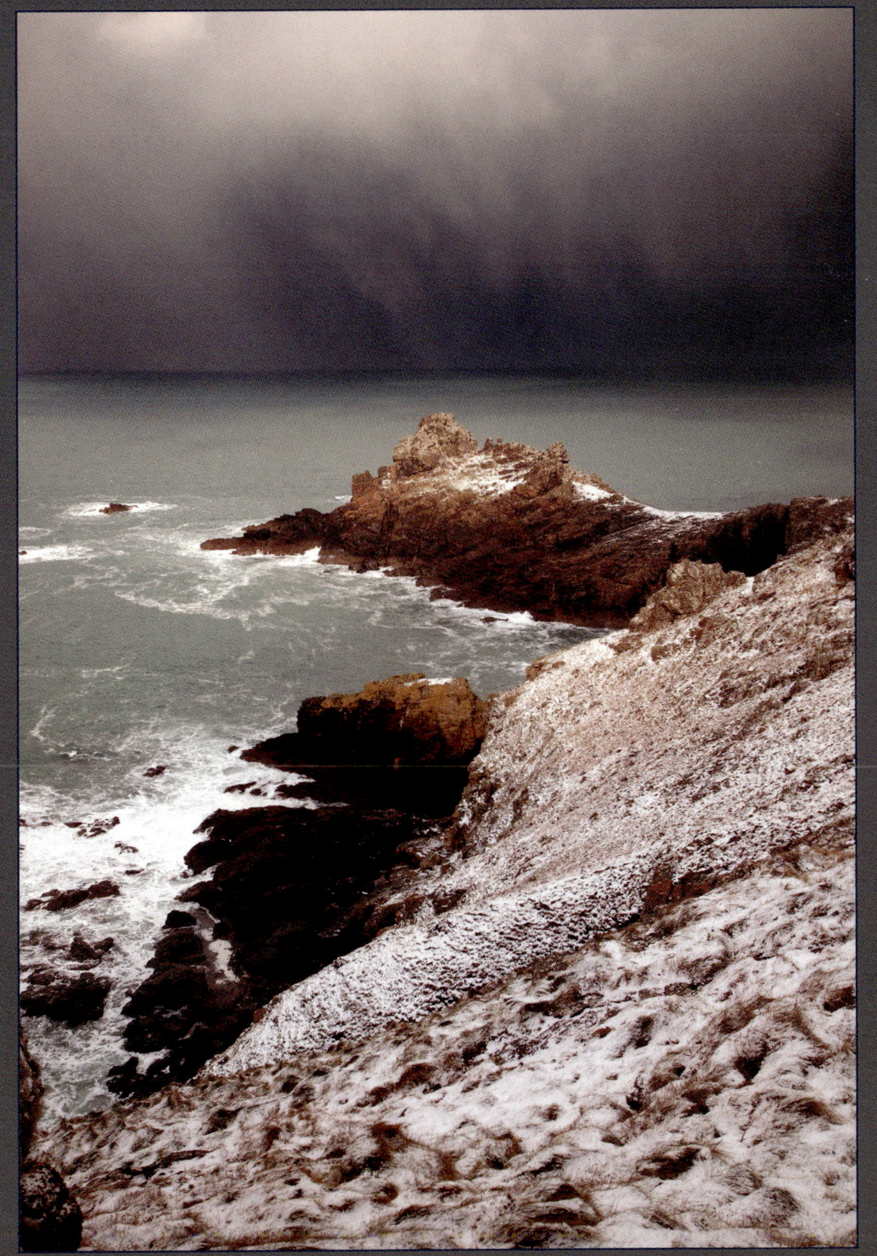

Gurnard's Head ▶

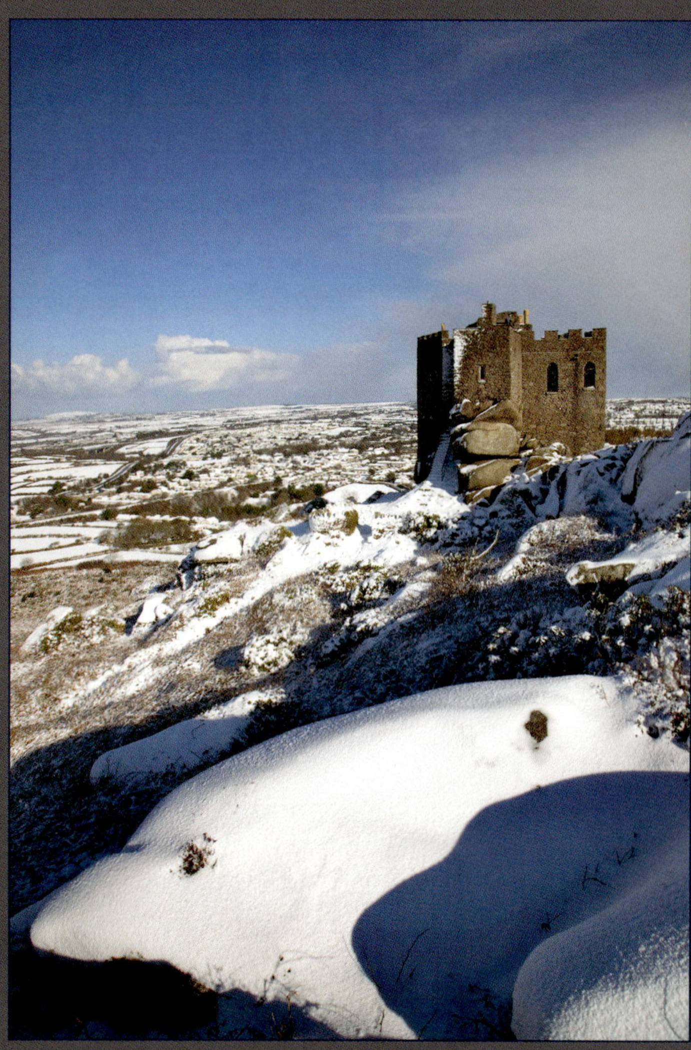

▲ Carn Brea Castle
The Crowns engine houses, Botallack ▶

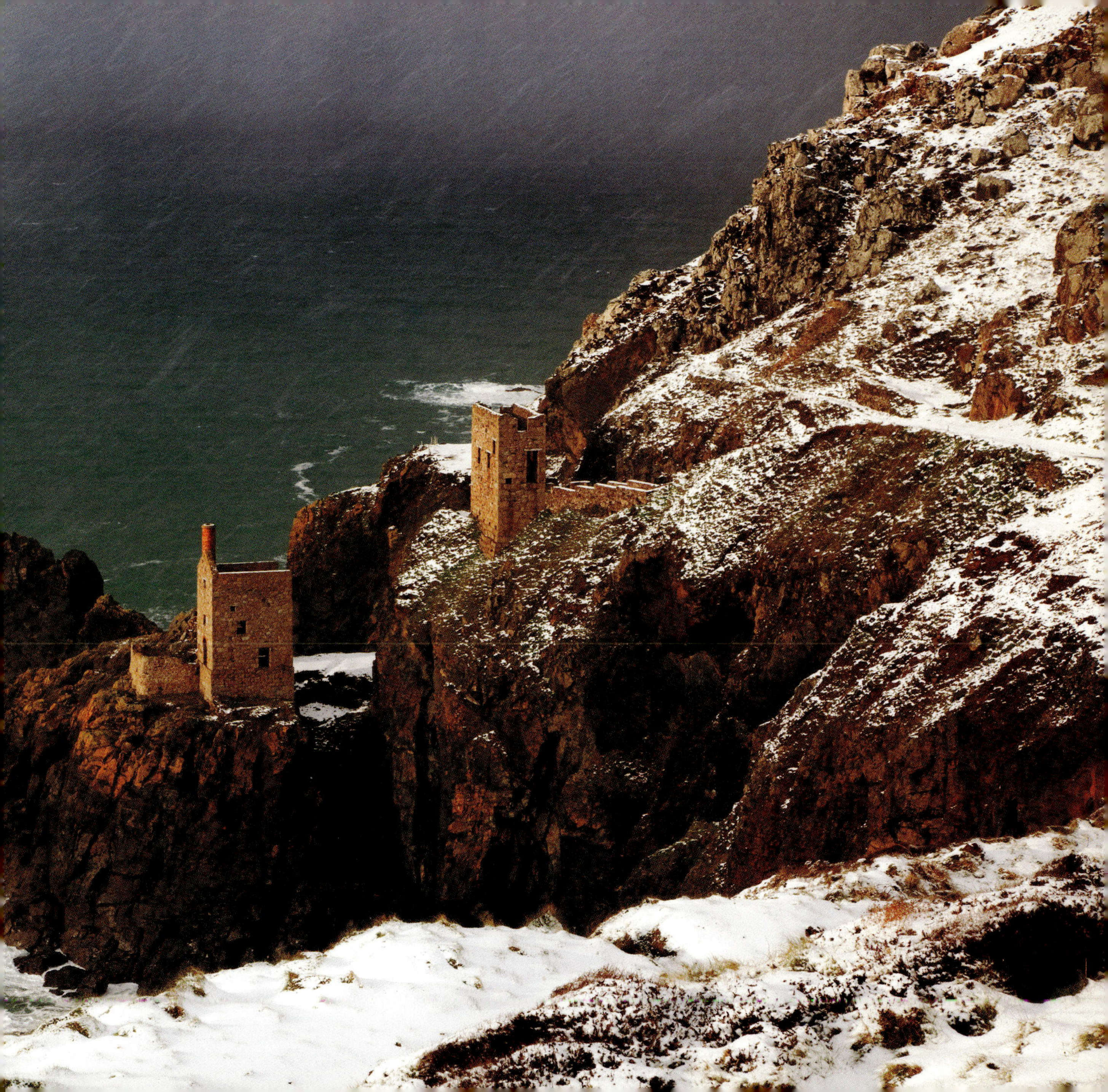

NOTES ON THE PHOTOGRAPHS

For each photograph in this book, I start by telling why I took it: the inspiration behind the image and my thoughts about it.

I give the location of the point from which each photo was taken; an approximate grid reference (where appropriate and possible) and, for selected images, further information where I think it serves a purpose. Often the time of day and time of year are critical, because of the angle of sunlight, and sometimes the state of the tide is also important.

All of my photographs are taken in RAW and processed in Photoshop. Standard processing includes adjustments to colour temperature, contrast (levels and curves), saturation and colour. In some instances I apply a neutral-density graduated filter in Photoshop RAW processing, or selectively darken areas of the frame in Photoshop to better balance the contrast and light within an image (this often applies to skies), though I don't use High Dynamic Range (HDR) software.

For each image, I list some technical information: aperture; shutter speed; exposure compensation; ISO; focal length; camera used; any filters; use of a tripod, where approriate.

The equipment I use currently for the majority of my landscape photography includes: Canon EOS 5D Mark II camera with 24–105 mm lens (previously I used the EOS 5D); B+W 10-stop neutral-density filter; Manfrotto tripod and Kirk ball head. I have used a variety of other equipment in capturing the images for this book over the last four years, including the Canon 15 mm Fisheye lens; Canon 100–400 mm lens, and an 800 mm lens.

Title page: *The Lookout, Cape Cornwall.* This is not the best focal point in the world, but the heather here was fantastic.

Taken in late August after sunset. The sky has been darkened in this image. SW 350 318. F18; 2 sec; exp -1; ISO 100; 24 mm; Canon EOS 5D; tripod.

Page 3: *Oyster fishing, Carrick Roads.* When photographing into the sun, the subject of the photograph becomes silhouetted, so to succeed with this sort of image you need the subject to have a strong outline. Here I thought the oyster fishing boats provided exactly that – and very Cornish too!

Taken in the Carrick Roads, between Falmouth and The Roseland, from a sailing boat. F11; 1/800th sec; exp -1; ISO 125; 35 mm; Canon EOS 5D Mark II.

Page 5: *Looe Island.* Since I am a trustee of Cornwall Wildlife Trust, I was lucky enough to be able to camp on Looe Island for a night one August. This was the view from near my tent. Watching the huge ball of the moon rise above the horizon was a magical experience – one which no photograph could ever capture fully, but this is a good reminder for me of that moment.

Taken at about 9 p.m. in late August from Looe Island, just after sunset as the full moon was rising over Rame Head. SX 260 514. F7.1; 20 sec; exp -1/3rd; ISO 200; 40 mm; Canon EOS 5D; tripod.

SPRING

Page 6: *Crocuses, churchyard, St Teath.* My challenge here was to show the whole of the church while making the crocuses dominate the picture. My solution was to get the camera down on the ground. Fortunately, there is a bank which makes this easier than it might otherwise have been.

There is a great showing of crocuses in the churchyard at St Teath. This was taken in mid-February. SX 064 806. F13; 1/100th sec; exp -1/3rd; ISO 125; 24 mm; Canon EOS 5D Mark II.

Pages 6–7: *Bluebells, St Loy.* This is a beautiful place when the bluebells are in flower, but it is a difficult place to photograph as it is a bit 'messy'. Here I used the footpaths to create a sensible composition, while the fallen trees and various foliage add atmosphere.

At St Loy, near Lamorna, there is a wooded valley with bluebells flowering in early May. This was taken on a cloudy day, and I have cooled the colour temperature to bring out the blues. SW 420 234. F20; 1 sec; exp -1/3rd; ISO 100; 24 mm; Canon EOS 5D Mark II; tripod.

Page 8, left: *Thrift, Holywell.* I love thrift, and am always looking for massed ranks of this beautiful flower on our coast. I used a wide-angle lens and tipped the camera forwards to fill the frame as much as possible with the flowers. I like the effect of the slow shutter speed on the clouds, as their movement helps draw the eye into the picture.

Taken from Penhale Point, looking into Holywell Bay, with thrift in the foreground; mid-May in the early evening. SW 757 592. F22; 2 min; exp 0; ISO 100; 24 mm; Canon EOS 5D Mark II; 10-stop neutral-density filter; tripod.

Page 8, right: *Thrift at Godrevy.* I like the dappled effect of the lighting on the thrift in the foreground: that is the reward for getting up early!

Taken in mid-May early in the morning; the low angle of the sun creates a pattern of light and shade on the thrift flowers. SW 582 427. F18; 1/60th sec; exp 0; ISO 100; 35 mm; Canon EOS 5D Mark II; tripod.

FARMING

Page 9: *Viper's bugloss, Boscregan Farm.* These fields can be a carpet of colour, so I take no credit for this photograph -- all credit goes to the farmer and the National Trust for managing the fields to encourage this 'arable weed'. Access from lay-by at Nanjulian; farm owned by National Trust, access allowed around field edges. Viper's bugloss is in flower around mid- to late June, sometimes into July.

Taken mid-afternoon. SW 359 297. F11; 1/320th sec; exp -2/3rd; ISO 100; 38 mm; Canon EOS 5D.

Pages 10–11: *Daffodils by moonlight, Gulval.* Daffodils are very much a Cornish phenomenon, and I love the way their rows create strong patterns to lead the eye into a photograph.

Fields around Gulval, early morning, with Penzance and Newlyn in the distance. Taken in March. F11; 1/8th sec; exp -1/3rd; ISO 100; 50 mm; Canon EOS 5D Mark II; tripod.

Pages 12–13: *Daffodils, Leedstown.* I was attracted by the diago-nal patterns of the rows of daffodils, and the fact that the whole landscape is made up of these bright yellow flowers.

Fields near Leedstown; April. F10; 1/200th sec; exp -1/3rd; ISO 100; 65 mm; Canon EOS 5D Mark II; tripod.

Pages 14–15: *Silhouettes, Siblyback reservoir.* Being a keen bird-watcher, I felt this scene summed up a lot about Bodmin Moor in winter. There are still some quite large roosts of starlings in trees around the moor, and when the sun goes down they can be seen sweeping in from every direction.

Cattle, about to be surrounded by starlings flying to roost. Taken at Siblyback reservoir, Bodmin Moor. SX 235 716. F6.3; 1/100th sec; exp -2/3rd; ISO 200; 105 mm; Canon EOS 5D.

Pages 16–17: *Grazing, Lanhydrock.* For me, this picture was about the shapes of the trees emerging from the mist. The sheep gave added interest.

Sheep grazing at Lanhydrock. Taken from public footpath, early morning in winter, with mist clearing. SX 094 636. F8; 1/250th sec; exp -2/3rd; ISO 100; 105 mm; Canon EOS 5D.

GARDENS

Pages 18–19: *Bonython Estate Gardens.* Reflections always add interest to a photograph. Here I tried to use the different textures of the grasses to create a pleasing composition.

Taken early morning with special permission at Bonython Manor on the Lizard. For general access details, visit www.bonythonmanor.co.uk. F10; 1/13th sec; exp -2/3rd; ISO 100; 70 mm; Dynax 7D; tripod.

Page 19: *Gaia, Abbey Garden, Tresco.* There are not many gardens where a plain blue sky lends itself to a decent photograph, but in the subtropical gardens of Tresco it seems somehow appropriate.

The sculpture of Gaia at Tresco Abbey Garden, Isles of Scilly. For access details, visit: www.tresco.co.uk. F10; 1/200th sec; exp -2/3rd; ISO 125; 24 mm; Canon EOS 5D.

Pages 20–21: *Trebah Garden.* I work very closely with Trebah

Garden, providing images for their calendar among other ventures. Continually striving for new images is a challenge. I particularly liked the early autumnal lighting on the side of the valley when I took this picture.

Photo showing the last of the hydrangeas at Trebah Garden, near Falmouth. Taken early morning, with special permission; September. For general access details, visit: www.trebah-garden. co.uk F11; 30 sec; exp -1; ISO 200; 99 mm; Canon EOS 5D Mark II; 10-stop neutral-density filter; tripod.

Page 21: *Cotehele house and terraced garden.* The combination of flowerbeds and the house at Cotehele are irresistible; here I waited for the pattern in the sky to change so that it complimented the shape of the house, filling in what would otherwise have been a large area of blue.

Taken early morning in July at Cotehele House with special permission. For access details, visit: www.nationaltrust.org.uk. F13; 1/125th sec; exp 0; ISO 100; 15 mm; Canon 5D Mark II; tripod.

Page 22, left: *View from Mount Edgcumbe to Plymouth.* My aim here was to create an unusual juxtaposition of flowers and the distant cityscape. Using a telephoto lens has helped to give the impression that the two are much closer together than they actually are.

View from Mount Edgcumbe garden, near Kingsand, showing rhododendrons, with Plymouth in the distance; March/April. F22; 1/20th sec; exp -2/3rd; ISO 100; 180 mm; Dynax 7D; tripod.

Page 22, right: *Boathouse, Trevarno Gardens.* The Italianate Victorian boathouse at Trevarno is one of the most photographed spots in Cornwall. The shallow, sheltered lake almost guarantees good reflections, and here I wanted to include the colourful azaleas to frame the view of the boathouse.

Taken on a cloudy, calm day, at Trevarno Gardens near Helston; April/May. For access details, visit: www.trevarno. co.uk. F5.6; 1/160th sec; exp 0; ISO 100; 35 mm; Dynax 7D; tripod.

BEACHES

Page 23: *Gwithian.* Here I was taken by the shape of the pool around the foreground rocks and the great sky. A wide-angle lens has helped to give a good sense of depth to the photo.

Taken from Strap Rocks, Gwithian, looking towards Godrevy Lighthouse at low tide. SW 577 415. F16; 1/100th sec; exp -1/3rd; ISO 100; 24 mm; Canon EOS 5D Mark II.

Pages 24–5: *Porth Kidney.* It is the ripples that make this photograph. Lots of foreground shapes and textures are emphasized by the low angle of sun.

Taken during the morning on a winter's day, looking towards St Ives from Porth Kidney. SW 547 383. F13; 1/125th sec; exp 0; ISO 100; 32 mm; Canon EOS 5D.

Page 25: *St Ives.* The low sunlight in winter helps to reveal the depth of the ripples on the beach, and I love the way these ripples give a sense of depth to the image, leading the eye towards the buildings of St Ives.

This is the beach in the harbour area in St Ives. The photo was taken early on a winter's day at low tide. SW 519 407. F16; 1/100th; exp -1/3rd; ISO 100; 24 mm; Canon EOS 5D.

Page 26, left: *Gugh Bar.* The white sand and blue sky of Scilly are simply beautiful. It is difficult not to be inspired by this sort of scenery, and it is relatively straightforward to photograph it!

The view of Gugh across the tidal bar from St Agnes, Isles of Scilly. SV 886 084. F11; 1/250th sec; exp -1/3rd; ISO 100; 32 mm; Canon EOS 5D.

Page 26, right: *Constantine Bay.* It had been dull and cloudy, when suddenly the sky cleared from the west. For just a few moments there were some attractive clouds in the sky, but they didn't last long. Here I thought the path down to the beach made a quite appealing foreground.

Looking towards Trevose Head from the dunes at Constantine Bay. SW 859 747. F22; 25 sec; exp 0; ISO 100; 24 mm; Canon EOS 5D Mark II; 10-stop neutral-density filter; tripod.

Page 27, left: Sennen. I couldn't resist the horseshoe-shaped rock on the beach, so had to use it as a foreground to this image. The setting sun added a lovely warmth to the scene, and Cape Cornwall was the obvious focal point in the distance.

Taken on the beach at Sennen Cove looking towards Cape Cornwall around sunset. SW 355 264. F18; 1 min 15 sec; exp 0; ISO 100; 47 mm; Canon EOS 5D Mark II; 10-stop neutral-density filter; tripod.

Page 27, right: From Freathy Cliff to Rame Head. I was lucky that the most colourful part of the sky appeared above Rame Head. The rocks give a nice crisp foreground; their layered form provides an attractive feature as well as revealing their sedimentary origin.

A view of Rame Head from the beach at Freathy Cliff, taken at sunset on a low tide. SX 395 520. F18; 3 min 30 sec; exp 0; ISO 200; 75 mm; Canon EOS 5D Mark II; 10-stop neutral-density filter; tripod.

COAST

Page 28: Land's End. Arches and stacks help to make the Cornish coastline interesting and varied. Here the late-evening light cast a lovely warmth on the cliffs, yet the sea reveals the strength of the wind!

A view of Land's End from Pordenack Point before sunset in winter. SW 345 243. F11; 1/160th sec; exp -1/3rd; ISO 160; 24 mm; Canon EOS 5D Mark II; tripod.

Page 29, left: The Strangles. Geologically, this is a wonderful part of Cornwall's coastline. I love the fact that we can see a sea stack, an arch and a collapsed cliff; the beach cusps created by the breaking waves have produced a great pattern to lead the eye into the picture.

Looking down to The Strangles Bay in the evening in summer. SX 133 953. F22; 25 sec; exp -1/3rd; ISO 100; 50 mm; Canon EOS 5D Mark II; 10-stop neutral-density filter; tripod.

Page 29, right: Cape Cornwall. I am always looking for colourful flowers around the coast – here they are heather. A windy day created a good swell, and passing clouds constantly changed the light on the landscape.

Taken from a small headland just south of Cape Cornwall, near Carn Gloose, in summer with heather in flower. SW 353 313. F16; 1/125th sec; exp -2/3rd; ISO 100; 24 mm; Canon EOS 5D Mark II; tripod.

HARBOURS

Page 30, top: Gorran Haven. This is a difficult harbour to photograph as a very wide-angle lens is required. The 15 mm lens has distorted the foreground, making it quite rounded, which I think works well compositionally.

The harbour at Gorran Haven. Taken in the afternoon in February. SX 014 416. F7.1; 1/320th sec; exp -1/3rd; ISO 100; 15 mm; Canon EOS 5D Mark II.

Page 30, bottom: Mullion Cove. The lovely evening light created an attractive warmth on the harbour and buildings. I liked the way the low sun reflected off the windows to cast a reflected light on the water.

Taken early evening at high tide. SW 666 178. F10; 25sec; exp 0; ISO 100; 47 mm; Canon EOS 5D Mark II; tripod; 10-stop neutral-density filter.

Page 31, left: Charlestown. I find Charlestown a difficult place to photograph. There is a lot of interest there, but also a lot of clutter, so a successful photograph is as much about what you leave out as what you put in; but that is quite restricting. Here I think I managed a pleasing if not sensational image!

Taken mid-morning. SX 039 514. F11; 1/200th sec; exp -2/3rd; ISO 100; 32 mm; Canon EOS 5D Mark II.

Page 31, right: Polperro. It is very difficult to take different photos of some of our more popular places. Here I used a telephoto lens to pick out the most attractive details at Polperro, and the opening in the harbour wall acts as a welcome to the observer's eye.

Taken from the east side of the harbour, looking back in through the harbour entrance. SX 211 509. F13; 1 ¼ min; exp 0; ISO 100; 105 mm; Canon EOS 5D Mark II; 10-stop neutral-density filter; tripod.

Page 32: *Mevagissey*. I was lucky to be here for a very colourful sunset, though to expose correctly for the setting sun I have had to use the computer to bring out detail in the buildings and boats. Colour alone was the driving force behind this image.

Taken at sunset in February from the east side of the central harbour. SX 016 447. F9; 1/15th sec; exp -1 1/3 rd; ISO 100; 67 mm; Canon EOS 5D Mark II; tripod.

LIGHTHOUSES

Page 33: *Tater-du*. I was attracted by the colour and patterns in the sky, and was fortunate that we sailed past Tater-du at just the right moment to give my image a focal point.

Taken from the *Scillonian* in mid-October, returning from a day trip to the Isles of Scilly. This is the only time of year that sunset shots can be taken from the *Scillonian*, because of the times of sailing. Tater-du is on the coast of West Penwith, between Lamorna and Penberth. F5.6; 1/160th sec; exp -1; ISO 320; 400 mm; Canon EOS 5D.

Pages 34–5: *Bishop Rock*. I was attracted by the fact that the sunlight was shining on the lighthouse but not on the rest of the islands. I also liked the rows of rocks in the sea.

If you find the grid reference on a map, you will see that this photo was taken from the island of Gugh, St Agnes, Isles of Scilly. This is approximately five miles from Bishop Rock Lighthouse, hence the 800 mm lens! It was taken at about 6 a.m. in May, with the sunlight catching the lighthouse but not the rocks, giving a nice recession of detail. SV 887 087. F6.3; 1/250th sec; exp 0; ISO 100; 800 mm; Canon EOS 5D; tripod.

Page 36: *Trevose Head*. It was the shapes of the clouds that attracted me here. I used the rock to fill in the space bottom left.

I had intended to take some shots of Trevose at sunset, but the cloud came in and spoiled it, so this was taken mid-afternoon with a 10-stop neutral-density filter to add a little atmosphere. SW 848 762. F14; 20 sec; exp 0; ISO 100; 24 mm; Canon EOS 5D Mark II; 10-stop neutral-density filter; tripod.

Page 37: *Godrevy*. I have been photographing Godrevy for many years, and on this occasion was pleased to find a new angle (for me!). I had never managed to include the beach before; the challenge was to separate the island from the land, which I just managed to achieve by climbing on a rock.

Taken at sunset with the tide fairly high in March; the sky has been darkened to bring out the detail. SW 581 429. F22; 1/2 sec; exp 0; ISO 100; 47 mm; Canon EOS 5D Mark II; tripod.

GEOLOGY

Pages 38–9: *China clay pit, Wheal Martyn*. Taken from the China Clay Museum near St Austell. The vehicles are huge and that gives some idea of the scale of what you are looking at. For access details, visit: www.wheal-martyn.com. F11; 1/60th sec; exp -1/3rd; ISO 200; 80 mm; Canon EOS 5D.

Page 39: *Boulders, Porth Nanven*. From a different age: these rounded granite boulders are very much a part of Cornwall's history, and make great subjects for photography.
I love the shapes of the rocks and the fact that we can see the crystals of feldspar in them. Once again, I like the contrast of sharp and blurred created by the moving water.

Boulders on the beach at Porth Nanven, Cot Valley. Taken after sunset to allow a slow shutter speed to blur the water. SW 354 309. F20; 4 sec; exp 0; ISO 100; 370 mm; Canon EOS 5D Mark II; tripod.

Pages 40–41: *Colourful shales, Finnygook Beach*. At the south-eastern end of the county, granite is replaced by shale and slate. In places these strata have alternating colours, and I was particularly drawn to this spot as three strong colours came together to create a pleasing composition.

Vibrantly coloured shales on the beach at Finnygook Beach,

near Portwrinkle. Taken after sunset to enhance the colours. SX 359 538. F22; 8 sec; exp 0; ISO 100; 67 mm; Canon EOS 5D Mark II; 10-stop neutral-density filter; tripod.

SUMMER

Page 42: *Crackington Haven*. I am always looking for colourful flowers on the coast, and usually try to show them in the context of their surroundings. I deliberately included the patch of grass to give a little texture to the foreground.

Heather and western gorse in flower on Cambeak, near Crackington Haven. Taken in mid-afternoon in August; the slope here is so steep that it goes into shade at around 3–4 p.m. in August. SX 133 967. F22; 1/40th sec; exp -1/3rd; ISO 125; 32 mm; Canon EOS 5D Mark II; tripod.

Page 43: *Tintagel*. Here I was attracted by the combination of heather, lovely coloured sea and a summery sky.

A view of Tintagel Island with heather in flower. Taken at around midday. SX 052 887. F16; 1/100th sec; exp -2/3; ISO 100; 24 mm; Canon EOS 5D.

Pages 44–5: *Poppy field, West Pentire*. The combination of red and yellow makes a striking foreground. I would have preferred to find a field leading down to the sea in full flower, but this rarely happens so I settled for a moody sky to complete the picture.

Poppies and corn marigolds in flower at the National Trust fields, West Pentire. Taken early morning in late June. SW 775 606. F4.5; 1/800th sec; exp -2/3rd; ISO 100; 24 mm; Canon EOS 5D.

Page 46: *Porthminster Beach, St Ives*. Not my cup of tea, but this is how many people remember Cornwall. In this photo, I wanted to minimize the amount of bare sand to give maximum impact.

This is summer in St Ives! I used a 400 mm lens deliberately here, to fill the frame and compress the image. SW 520 403. F10; 1/400th sec; exp -2/3; ISO 100; 400 mm; Canon EOS 5D.

Page 47: *St Martin's, Isles of Scilly*. Here I was trying to capture the spirit of St Martin's by using the boat as the focal point, but with a wide-angle lens to show the surrounding landscape and attractive sky.

This is typical of St Martin's on the Isles of Scilly: big, empty beaches, a lovely sky, and boats left lying around. SV 920 159. F16; 1/200th sec; exp -/3rd; ISO 100; 24 mm; Canon EOS 5D.

ISLANDS

Page 48: *Gull Rock from Trebarwith Strand*. Many people prefer to take this shot at sunset, but I thought I would try early morning. The sunlight wasn't shining on the foreground rocks but was lighting the island and the breaking wave. I love the finger of rock that points out to the island.

Taken from Trebarwith Strand, early morning in October, with the tide approximately half-way out. SX 048 864. F13; 15 sec; exp 0; ISO 100; 32 mm; Canon EOS 5D Mark II; 10-stop neutral-density filter; tripod.

Page 49: *The Carters from Holywell Bay*. This shot is all about impact. It was a great sky, and here I have emphasized its colour by underexposing the scene, thus silhouetting the rocks. I also used a long exposure to blur the sea, making it somewhat abstract. I increased the saturation of the shot in the processing stage.

The Carters are islands situated off Holywell Bay; this shot was taken after sunset. SW 763 594. F8; 2 min; exp 0; ISO 200; 50 mm; Canon EOS 5D Mark II; 10-stop neutral-density filter; tripod.

Page 50: *The Mouls, near Polzeath*. The distant, very dark cloud was the motivation behind this photograph. I used the rocks in the foreground to lead the eye towards The Mouls.

A classic Cornish view of The Mouls and The Rumps headland, near Polzeath, on this occasion with a storm brewing. SW 936 807. F13; 1/200th sec; exp -1; ISO 100; 24 mm; Canon EOS 5D.

Page 51: *Round Island, from St Martin's, Isles of Scilly*. I loved the combination of distant islands and tropical parasols; the light was good and the distant clouds were quite impressive.

Taken from the road beside the St Martin's Hotel, Isles of Scilly, looking out to Round Island with its lighthouse. Taken mid-morning in May. SV 914 162. F11; 1/160th sec; exp -1/3rd; ISO 100; 55 mm; Canon EOS 7D.

MIST

Page 52, left: *From Trencrom to Carn Brea.* This was a magical morning, with mist covering the entire lowland area between Hayle and Camborne, which in my experience is quite a rare occurrence. The difficulty is to find a focal point, so I used a telephoto lens and picked out Carn Brea in the distance.

A view over Hayle to Carn Brea from Trencrom Hill, near St Ives. Taken early morning in March. SW 517 363. F10; 1/15th sec; exp 0; ISO 160; 190 mm; Canon EOS 5D; tripod.

Page 52, right: *Roundwood Quay, near Trelissick.* This was a truly magical moment, and I am not sure it is really possible to portray the full atmosphere of the occasion in a photograph. The mist was quite dense and only started to clear as the sun broke over the woodland. Photographically, I struggled to find an interesting foreground but found the curving ripples an attractive feature.

Taken at about 6 a.m. in April, looking across the river from Roundwood Fort, near Trelissick, at a high tide. SW 838 404. F7.1; 1/160th sec; exp 0; ISO 100; 50 mm; Canon EOS 5D Mark II.

Page 53: *Fowey from Polruan.* Having seen a weather forecast for mist, I set off very early in the morning for Polruan. I was a bit disappointed to find the mist was less extensive in the valley of the River Fowey than I had hoped; but there was a bit of mist clinging to the slopes around the town of Fowey which, combined with the early-morning sunlight, made a pleasing image.

Taken from the viewpoint in Polruan overlooking the mouth of the mouth of the River Fowey at about 6.30 a.m. in April. SX 125 507. F18; 30 sec; exp -1/3rd; ISO 100; 95 mm; Canon EOS 5D Mark II; 10-stop neutral-density filter; tripod.

Page 54: *Cotehele Quay.* I was hoping for a little more mist than this, but it still adds atmosphere to the image. I did worry about the reeds at first, but I think they add a pleasing splash of colour and texture.

Taken early morning in December on a high tide from Cotehele Quay. SX424 682. F8; 1/3rd sec; exp -2/3rd; ISO 100; 97 mm; Canon EOS 5D Mark II; tripod.

REFLECTIONS

Page 55: *Loe Pool.* A short while after sunset, I often find the best colour in the sky is in the east, away from the setting sun. Often the difficulty with sunset shots is that the foreground is very dark relative to the sky, but if you can use reflections you can reduce the impact of this problem.

Looking over Loe Pool from near the sluice on Loe Bar, near Porthleven. Taken after sunset in October, the warm glow in the east being reflected by the water on a calm day and a long exposure. SW 642 243. F22; 5 sec; exp 0; ISO 100; 60 mm; Canon EOS 5D Mark II; 10-stop neutral-density filter; tripod.

Pages 56–7: *St Gothian Sands and Godrevy.* The patterns in the sky at sunset were stunning: not only was there good colour and form, but the clouds led perfectly towards the lighthouse.

Taken from near Gillick Rock on the beach adjacent to St Gothian Sands Nature Reserve (between Gwithian and Godrevy). Here the beach is wet, and offers good reflections of Godrevy Lighthouse. Taken just after sunset in July. SW 579 419. F13; 1/5th sec; exp -1/3rd; ISO 100; 35 mm; Canon EOS 5D Mark II.

Pages 58–9: *Logan Rock.* I took up a very low angle for this photograph, to emphasize the ripples in the foreground and to keep my shadow out of the picture! The warm effect of the sun at this time of day really helped to light up the granite of Logan Rock headland.

Taken from Pednvounder Beach, accessed down a narrow path from the Coast Path between Porthcurno and Logan Rock, at low tide in the evening. SW 394 224. F18; 1/80th sec; exp -1/3rd; ISO 125; 47 mm; Canon EOS 5D Mark II; tripod.

SKIES

Page 60: *St Michael's Mount and Marazion*. The marbled pattern of the clouds in the sky at this moment was just fantastic. Fortunately, the sun broke on to the foreground for a few short moments and I was able to get a photograph. It never did light up the Mount.

Taken late in the day in November when the sun emerged briefly to light up the foreground, revealing a wonderful pattern in the clouds. SW 513 311. F9; 1/25th sec; exp -1/3rd; ISO 100; 24 mm; Canon EOS 5D.

Page 61: *Fistral Beach*. I felt a little odd paddling in the sea during a storm in December, but I think it was worth it. The good thing about rainbows is that there must be a combination of sun and heavy rain, which can be great for photos, but you have to be in a suitable place.

Taken from Fistral Beach looking to Towan Head; the white breaking waves create a little underexposure which helps to saturate the colour in the rainbow and darken the sky. SW 790 620. F10; 1/400th sec; exp -2/3rd; ISO 125; 40 mm; Canon EOS 5D Mark II.

Pages 62–3: *Constantine Bay*. This shot is all about the sky. It had been an unusual day, with low cloud coming and going, but the sun had just enough power to break through when it was low over the horizon. I wanted to include a bit of land, but it is the shape of the edge of the cloud that is most important to the image.

Taken from the beach at Constantine, looking towards Trevose Head, at low tide after sunset in April. SW 857 747. F14; 30 sec; exp -1/3rd; ISO 100; 24 mm; Canon EOS 5D Mark II; 10-stop neutral-density filter; tripod.

Pages 64–5: *Dizzard Point*. At Dizzard Point there is stunted oak wood growing on the coastal area. In the autumn there is a lovely range of hues coming from the woodland, and when the rainbow broke what else could a photographer do?

This was taken mid-afternoon in October, when a wonderful double rainbow formed. I took two shots and stitched them together to take in the full rainbow; a little under-exposure has helped to capture the colour in the rainbow. SX 165 988. F11; 1/250th sec; exp -1; ISO 100; 24 mm; Canon EOS 5D Mark II.

TIME AND TIDE

Page 66: *Trewellard Zawn*. I love the sumptuous colours of the rocks in the foreground and the shallower parts of the sea. They seem to be really brought out during long exposures with the 10-stop neutral-density filter.

A view looking north across Trewellard Zawn near Geevor Mine, towards Pendeen Watch. Taken in May, as the final rays of sunshine hit the cliffs, giving a golden glow. SW 372 349. F8; 5 min; exp 0; ISO 100; 24 mm; Canon EOS 5D Mark II; 10-stop neutral-density filter; tripod.

Page 67: *Portwrinkle*. Here I was trying to emphasize the shape of the old jetty, which leads the eye into the scene.

The remains of a small harbour wall stretch out into the sea. Taken at mid-tide, at sunset in October. SX 354 538. F11; 1 min; exp 0; ISO 200; 24 mm; Canon EOS 5D Mark II; 10-stop neutral-density filter; tripod.

Pages 68–9: *Duckpool*. The crashing waves, at the mouth of the Coombe Valley in North Cornwall, provide the misty atmosphere, and the characteristic slates and shales provide the shapes. I like the subtle hues in this photo.

Taken a long time after sunset, when there was just a hint of colour left in the sky. SS 200 115. F13; 5 sec; exp -1/3rd; ISO 100; 135 mm; Canon EOS 5D; tripod.

SUNSET

Page 70: *Mount's Bay*. I couldn't resist including this, a photograph of very little! In the distance are Penzance and Newlyn, but the sunset is everything.

A view of Mount's Bay after sunset, from the beach near Marazion; low tide. Taken in October. SW 514 307. F10; 10 sec; exp -1/3rd; ISO 100; 45 mm; Canon EOS 5D Mark II; tripod.

Page 71: *Perranporth Beach and Chapel Rock.* The bright light led to a little underexposure, deepening the colour saturation of the image and silhouetting the rock. As well as trying to show a great sunset, I aimed to use the S-shaped stream to lead in to the photo.

Taken from Perranporth Beach, looking into the setting sun past Chapel Rock at low tide in March. SW 757 547. F8; 2 min; exp 0; ISO 200; 50 mm; Canon EOS 5D Mark II; 10-stop neutral-density filter; tripod.

Page 72: *Bedruthan Steps.* I loved the warm tones of the setting sun on the cliffs at Bedruthan, and the shapes of the cliffs lead the eye nicely into the picture as far as the distant lighthouse of Trevose Head.

A view of Bedruthan Steps with Park Head and Trevose Head in the distance. Taken at sunset in December. SW 846 687. F8; 20 sec; exp -1/3rd; ISO 100; 32 mm; Canon EOS 5D Mark II; 10-stop neutral-density filter; tripod.

Page 73: *Gwennap Head.* This is the edge of Cornwall, where the Atlantic meets granite. Strong wind, a surging sea and a great burst of light just before sunset. Interesting how the sun has lit half of the sky and the other half is shaded by the large cloud.

Taken from Tol-pedn-Penwith looking towards Gwennap Head, just before sunset in December. SW 365 216. F9; 1/40th sec; exp -2/3rd; ISO 200; 35 mm; Canon EOS 5D Mark II; tripod.

Page 74: *St Michael's Mount and causeway.* To get the sun setting behind the Mount, with the causeway in the foreground, you have to visit around the shortest day of the year, and that is what I did here. If you want the tide to be lapping across the causeway at the same time, then the choice of dates is further restricted. To get all of this right along with a decent sky means it can be many years before a successful photo is taken!

A classic view of St Michael's Mount with the causeway at sunset, taken on a mid-tide at the end of December. SW 517 304. F9; 30 sec; exp 0; ISO 100; 24 mm; Canon EOS 5D Mark II; 10-stop neutral-density filter; tripod.

Page 75: *From the harbour wall, Hugh Town, St Mary's, Isles of Scilly.* I wish I had caught the yacht a couple of seconds earlier, as I find it just a little too central in the frame; however, it is good that it is between the two distant rocks. This works because the yacht is such a distinctive shape in silhouette; the rocks give a good recession of detail, and the sun is a huge, colourful shape.

Taken from the harbour wall in Hugh Town, St Mary's, Isles of Scilly, at sunset in September. SV 902 107. F5.6; 1/250th sec; exp +2/3rd; ISO 200; Canon EOS 5D.

DARKNESS FALLS

Page 76: *Mousehole Christmas lights.* Many photographers visit Mousehole Christmas lights, and the key is to try to get something a little different. Here I used a special effect by performing a 'zoom-burst', which is achieved by zooming the lens in or out during the exposure, so a tripod is essential. This helps to fill the frame with colour, rather than leaving large black gaps, but I can quite accept that it won't be everybody's cup of tea!

Taken during December. SW 470 263. F14; 5 sec; exp -2/3rd sec; ISO 400; 105 mm; Canon EOS 5D Mark II; tripod.

Page 77: *Looking towards Saltash.* You might notice that this is the only photo in the book that was taken from outside the county — looking back to Saltash underneath the Tamar bridges from 'the other side'. I liked the strong sense of perspective created by the bridges leading the eye into the frame. I tried to use the Union Jack on the pub as a focal point, but it was only after I took the shot that I spotted the lovely light passing through the pattern on the railway bridge supports.

Taken at around 6 p.m. in December. SX 437 587. F8; 15 sec; exp 0; ISO 100; 47 mm; Canon EOS 5D Mark II; 10-stop neutral-density filter; tripod.

Page 78: *Truro Cathedral.* The best 'night-time' shots are actually taken just after dusk while there is still some colour left in the sky, and this is a case in point. The reflections at high tide can be sensational. I am pleased that I have almost managed to hide Tesco's behind the trees.

Taken from Boscawen Park, Truro, 6.20 p.m., early November on a high tide. SW 834 437. F13; 25 sec; exp 0; ISO 100; 180 mm; Canon EOS 5D Mark II; 10-stop neutral-density filter; tripod.

AUTUMN

Page 79: *Godolphin Woods.* Here I was trying to give a sense of colour and the movement of the trees on a typical windy autumnal day. I also like the contrast between the solid, motionless tree trunks and the branches and leaves waving in the wind.

On a very dark, windy day I used a long shutter speed to blur the movement in the branches of the trees. SW 603 323. F20; 13 sec; exp -2/3rd; ISO 100; 47 mm; Canon EOS 5D; white balance set to cloud; tripod.

Pages 80–81: *The River Lynher.* I was most captivated by the roots of the tree, which have been exposed by people walking and the effects of the river in flood. I thought the beech leaves scattered around the roots helped to emphasize their shape, as well as giving a rich colour to this autumnal image.

A dull, overcast day in autumn, in woods near Newbridge, Cadsonbury, on the River Lynher. SX 347 678. F22; 8 sec; exp 0; ISO 100; 24 mm; Canon EOS 5D Mark II; tripod.

Page 81: *Kilminorth Woods.* It had been raining very heavily as I wandered around Kilminorth Woods, but it was very calm and quite warm. The rain eventually ceased, but the air was humid and misty. I was trying to capture this mist through the trees.

Taken on a dull, wet day in autumn. SX 240 543. F14; 6 sec; exp -1/3rd; ISO 100; 60 mm; Canon EOS 5D Mark II; tripod.

STORMS

Page 82: *Hell Bay, Bryher, Isles of Scilly.* Just before taking this photo, I turned around to find that my wife, Sarah, had been blown over by the wind. Of course, I helped her up before taking the picture, but that demonstrates just how wild Hell Bay can get. The challenge for me was keeping my camera still enough, even on a tripod, so I hid behind rocks. This somewhat limited my scope for composition!

Taken at Hell Bay, Bryher, Isles of Scilly during a storm one March; around sunset. SV 877 157. F22; 1 1/3rd sec; exp 0; ISO 50; 55 mm; Canon EOS 5D; tripod.

Page 83: *Harbour wall, Portreath.* The waves here regularly break over the harbour wall, and this has become an iconic image of Cornwall. Fortunately, this view faces north, so the photo can be taken at any time of day – all you need is a good swell. The telephoto lens has helped focus the eye just on the end of the pier, giving the wave a bit of extra impact.

Taken mid-afternoon in November during a period of strong winds at high tide. SW 654 453. F7.1; 1/640th sec; exp -1/3rd; ISO 100; 300 mm; Canon EOS 5D Mark II; tripod.

Pages 84–5: *Rinsey Head.* This was probably the most dangerous photograph in the book. The storm on this particular day was as fierce as I have ever felt. You can see the spray breaking over the house on the cliff top in the distance. My difficulty was getting a moment when the sun momentarily broke through the cloud at a time when I could dash down to the cliff top to take a picture. Even in this photo, you can see where some spray has got on to my lens while taking the photo. I ended up drenched and cold; but don't tell my wife, she worries!

Rinsey Head, near Praa Sands, seen from Trewavas Head during a storm. Taken in the morning at high tide. SW 596 265. F5.6; 1/800th sec; exp -1/3rd; ISO 200; 24 mm; Canon EOS 5D Mark II.

AGAINST THE LIGHT

Page 86: *Kilminorth Woods.* I loved the way the sunlight lit the foreground trees from behind, but because the hillside of Kilminorth in the background is so steep its trees remained in the shade.

Taken from Trenant Woods, near Looe, looking into Kilminorth Woods over the West Looe River. SX 243 546. F7.1; 1/100th sec; exp -1; ISO 200; 105 mm; Canon EOS 5D Mark II.

Page 87: *Crantock Beach.* This is quite an iconic Cornish scene, and to me speaks volumes of Cornwall in winter when the beaches are almost deserted. The shapes of the waves breaking on the beach are important, and the lone person gives a sense of scale.

Taken from Pentire Point East, Newquay, looking south on to Crantock Beach. SW 784 615. F8; 1/125th sec; exp 0; ISO 125; 400 mm; Canon EOS 5D; tripod.

ANCIENT HISTORY

Page 88: *Men-an-tol*. The warmth of the early-morning sun on the stones and the long shadows created by the low angle of the light made this appealing to me.

An early morning shot of Men-an-tol in the frost during January. SW 427 349. F22; ¼ sec; exp 0; ISO 100; 55 mm; Canon EOS 5D Mark II; tripod.

Page 89: *Lanyon Quoit*. I like the contrast of the warm tones in the grasses and bracken with the coolness of the frosty ground and sky.

Taken early morning, before sunrise, in February during a frost. SW 430 337. F14; 15 sec; exp 0; ISO 100; 24 mm; Canon EOS 5D Mark II; tripod.

HISTORY

Page 90: *Gunpowder factory ruins, Kennall Vale*. Here I was trying to capture the ethereal quality of the ruined gunpowder workings in Kennall Vale. The long exposure has helped achieve this by blurring the leaves on the trees.

The ruins of a gunpowder factory in the wooded valley of the River Kennall near Ponsanooth. This is a Cornwall Wildlife Trust nature reserve; for access details, visit: www.cornwallwildlifetrust.org.uk. SW 750 374. F22; 10 sec; exp -2/3rd; ISO 100; 24 mm; Canon EOS 5D Mark II; tripod.

Page 91: *Brunton calciner, Botallack*. Sometimes light is everything. On this occasion, the sun broke through suddenly and vividly; I simply photographed what I could where I was, and fortunately I was at Botallack where the ruined calciner stands high above the cliffs.

This is a labyrinth of tunnels to remove arsenic from waste fumes, at Botallack near St Just, West Penwith. Taken on a winter morning. SW 363 334. F13; 1/125th sec; exp -2/3rd; ISO 125; 24 mm; Canon EOS 5D Mark II.

Page 92: *Wheal Coates, St Agnes*. Another iconic Cornish viewpoint. On this particular evening, I was taken by the intensity of colour, on both land and sea — the latter, I suspect, because it was very shallow on the sand.

Wheal Coates is situated on St Agnes Beacon. Taken on a summer's evening at a fairly low tide. SW 699 501. F18; 2 min; exp 0; ISO 160; 32 mm; Canon EOS 5D Mark II; 10-stop neutral-density filter; tripod.

Page 93: *Cromwell's Castle, Tresco, Isles of Scilly*. I deliberately set out to capture the castle with heather in the foreground, and found just the one colourful patch in an accessible position, so my composition was a little limited: ideally, I would have placed the castle off-centre with the sea behind it.

Cromwell's Castle is situated on the north-west side of Tresco on the Isles of Scilly. Taken in late summer, in the evening. SV 882 160. F11; 1/30th sec; exp -2/3rd; ISO 125; 24 mm; Canon EOS 5D; tripod.

TORS AND MOORS

Pages 94–5: *Roughtor*. I love the dappled effect of the sunlight, created by the pattern of cloud, on the landscape. It looks bleak — but then it is bleak!

Roughtor seen from the slopes of Brown Willy. Taken during the morning in winter. SX 157 803. F14; 1/80th sec; exp -2/3rd; ISO 125; 24 mm; Canon EOS 5D Mark II.

Page 95: *Helman Tor*. What struck me here were the shapes that have been carved out of the granite by wind and rain over many thousands of years.

A view from the summit of Helman Tor, near Luxulyan. Taken in the evening in November. SX 063 615. F10; 1 1/3rd sec; exp 0; ISO 100; 24 mm; Canon EOS 5D.

Page 96: *Brown Willy from Roughtor.* Here I was trying to capture the combination of mist, cloud and early-morning light. The ponies could have been better positioned, but they didn't seem concerned.

A view of Brown Willy from Roughtor. Taken early morning in September. SX 145 809. F9; 1/160th sec; exp -1; ISO 125; 24 mm; Canon EOS 5D; tripod.

WINTER

Page 97: *Gurnard's Head.* Gurnard's Head is an impressive sight at any time of year, but it is rare to see it with snow falling. This will be a moment that lives with me.

A view of Gurnard's Head from Treen Cliff, mid-afternoon, 2 February 2009, just before a snow storm hit the coast. SW 431 383. F13; 1/100th sec; exp -1/3rd; ISO 100; 35 mm; Canon EOS 5D Mark II; tripod.

Page 98: *Carn Brea Castle.* I walked to the summit of Carn Brea, and found this dolphin-shaped patch of snow on a rock – a rather surreal foreground to this picture.

Carn Brea Castle after heavy snow. Taken early afternoon 3 February 2009. SW 684 408. F13; 1/320th sec; exp -1/3rd; ISO 125; 24 mm; Canon EOS 5D Mark II.

Pages 98–9: *The Crowns engine houses, Botallack.* An iconic location, I was lucky enough to get a little bit of sun on the engine houses just as the next snow storm was approaching.

The Crowns engine houses at Botallack. Taken around 4 p.m. 2 February 2009 during a snow storm. SW 363 334. F11; 1/40th sec; exp -1/3rd; ISO 100; 65 mm; Canon EOS 5D Mark II; tripod.

COVER

This was a very calm evening, and initially I had thought of taking a photo from the causeway; but there was a queue of other photographers all waiting there for the same photo! Instead, I let the colour in the sky decide my position, so this photo was taken from the end of the harbour wall just to the east. Evening,

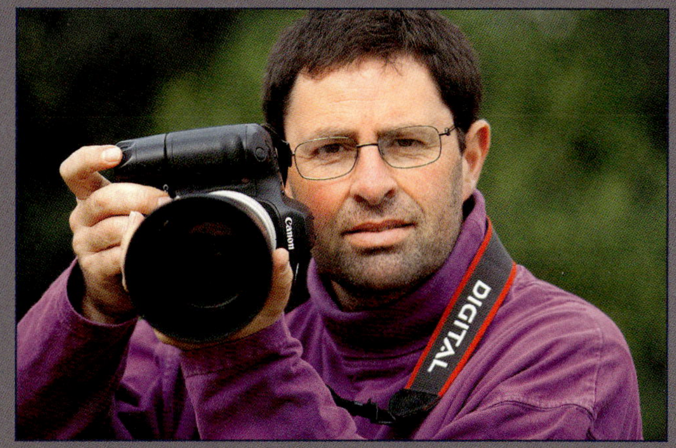

▲ *David Chapman*

1 October 2010. SW 520 305. F8; 30 sec; exp 0; ISO100; 35 mm; Canon EOS 5D Mark II; 10-stop neutral-density filter; tripod.

TAKING LANDSCAPE PHOTOGRAPHS

Composition

Before you take a photo, stop to consider where you are standing. Don't just take the picture as you see it, but try moving left or right, up or down: it's amazing how the composition of a photograph can be dramatically changed by the smallest of moves. Consider these points when composing your image:

- Try to include a focal point where the eye can settle: somewhere off-centre is best.
- Use diagonal lines or S-shapes, such as the coastline, to draw the eye towards the focal point.
- Provide some foreground interest as a counterbalance to the focal point: for example, compose the image with foreground flowers bottom left, and a distant focal point top right.
- Concentrate on getting your horizon level, and usually place it one-third or two-thirds of the way up the frame.
- Keep your composition simple; don't include too many competing elements.
- If the sky is interesting, use it in the image and try to wait for the clouds in the sky to help the composition.
- Overall, try to balance the key points within the image around the frame; don't place them all on top of each other or across the middle of the image.

Light and timing

It is possible to take consistently good photos by mastering compositional techniques, but to take great photos you have to understand that the quality of light can make a huge difference.

- The best light is often around sunset and sunrise.
- Don't stop taking photographs as the sun sets, but use a tripod and continue to take photos for up to an hour afterwards, depending on conditions; this is when long exposures can create atmospheric 'moving water' images.
- Winter offers better lighting conditions than summer, as the sun is lower in the sky and shadows are enhanced.
- Don't go out to take photos only on sunny days; often the light between heavy showers is fantastic, while mists can be ethereal and storms dramatic.
- If you want to take 'night-time' photos, often the best time to take them is at dusk when there is still a little light left in the sky.
- Plan your photographs: some images can only be taken at a certain time of day, on a certain tide, and even at a specific time of year; make a note in your diary and go back when the timing is right.